AF600299

QUIXOTIC MEMORIES

Quixotic Memories

Cervantes and Memory in Early Modern Spain

JULIA DOMÍNGUEZ

UNIVERSITY OF TORONTO PRESS
Toronto Buffalo London

Toronto Buffalo London
utorontopress.com

ISBN 978-1-4875-4392-1 (cloth)
ISBN 978-1-4875-4393-8 (EPUB)
ISBN 978-1-4875-4391-4 (PDF)

Toronto Iberic

Library and Archives Canada Cataloguing in Publication

Title: Quixotic memories : Cervantes and memory in early modern Spain / Julia Domínguez.
Names: Domínguez, Julia, author.
Series: Toronto Iberic ; 73.
Description: Series statement: Toronto Iberic series ; 73 | Includes bibliographical references and index.
Identifiers: Canadiana (print) 20210272430 | Canadiana (ebook) 20210272570 | ISBN 9781487543921 (hardcover) | ISBN 9781487543938 (EPUB) | ISBN 9781487543914 (PDF)
Subjects: LCSH: Cervantes Saavedra, Miguel de, 1547–1616. Don Quixote. | LCSH: Cervantes Saavedra, Miguel de, 1547–1616 – Criticism and interpretation. | LCSH: Memory in literature. | LCSH: Memory – Social aspects – Spain – History.
Classification: LCC PQ6353 .D66 2022 | DDC 863/.3 – dc23

We wish to acknowledge the land on which the University of Toronto Press operates. This land is the traditional territory of the Wendat, the Anishnaabeg, the Haudenosaunee, the Métis, and the Mississaugas of the Credit First Nation.

University of Toronto Press acknowledges the financial support of the Government of Canada, the Canada Council for the Arts, and the Ontario Arts Council, an agency of the Government of Ontario, for its publishing activities.

Canada Council for the Arts Conseil des Arts du Canada

Funded by the Government of Canada | Financé par le gouvernement du Canada | Canada

To Chad,
my light,
for making everything possible.

Contents

Acknowledgments

As I prepared to write this section of my book, I realized that despite all the work (*sudor y lágrimas*) that I, myself, put into this project, it would not have been possible without the support and encouragement of the many people I met during this journey. While I have always been intrigued by human memory, its faulty and yet decisive function for our identity, my formal engagement with the topic started ten years ago when I presented on memory for the first time at the groundbreaking first conference on Cognitive Futures for the Humanities at the University of Bangor in the UK. There I met the incomparable Alan Richardson, which began a series of extraordinary conversations on the significance of memory and imagination that continued at subsequent Cognitive Futures conferences at the University of Durham and Oxford University, respectively. These interactions planted the seed for what later would become *Quixotic Memories*, which subsequently developed into two essays published in volumes edited by Isabel Jaén and Julien Simon and a third edited by Steven Wagschal and Ryan D. Giles. I thank all of them for their careful reading, helpful suggestions, and impeccable professionalism.

Since that time, my thoughts on memory in Cervantes's work have been refined through numerous conference presentations and other publications. Hence, I would also like to acknowledge the Cervantes Society of America, the Renaissance Society of America, and the Modern Language Association for allowing me to present my ideas at their annual conferences. For their incredible inspiration; unconditional support; and valuable ideas, comments, and criticism, I thank all the *Cervantistas* and other scholars who listened to my talks and offered their encouragement to me along the way. A number of colleagues have been generous with time and inspiration, and so I am indebted to Lina Bolzoni, Frederick de Armas, Edward Friedman, Enrique García

Santo-Tomás, Howard Mancing, and Alan Richardson for their willingness to read and comment on portions of the book. I would also like to express my gratitude to my dear friend and colleague Elisa Rizo for her excitement and kindness throughout this long journey.

I am extremely grateful to Suzanne Rancourt and the University of Toronto Press for their interest in publishing my work and to the anonymous peer reviewers for their enthusiasm, careful evaluation, and fruitful suggestions. Toronto has been thorough and vigilant, and the experience working with the press has been wonderful. I also thank Chad M. Gasta and Heather Dubnick for their amazing work translating sections of my text, correcting my English, and editing the final manuscript.

A project as vast as this could not have happened without the generous funding from my academic home, Iowa State University. From the dean of the College of Liberal Arts and Sciences to the Office of the Provost to the Cassling Family Foundation and the Center for the Excellence in the Arts and the Humanities, I have received wonderful support for my research at ISU. I am also thankful to the Iowa State University Publication Endowment, ISU Foundation, for their support for the publication of this work. I also recognize the Interlibrary Loan Office at Parks Library. Were it not for their remarkable efforts, many of the source materials and other resources for this project would have not been available to me.

I would not be here without the absolute support of my academic father, Robert L. Fiore, and of my beloved Amy Williamsen at my *alma mater,* the University of Arizona. I also want to thank my families in Spain and in Michigan and, most importantly, my husband, Chad, for championing my work and for his words of reassurance and motivation when I needed them most. I am eternally indebted to him. Last but not least, to my two daughters, Sofía and Victoria, for all the times that you rightfully asked me, "When will the book be done?" it is all yours now, *mis niñas.*

QUIXOTIC MEMORIES

Introduction

Obsessions with Remembering

A great and beautiful invention is memory,
always useful both for learning and for life.
– *Dialexeis*
400 BC[1]

Es tan grande el bien que Dios dio a los hombres en darles memoria,
Que, en solos loores de ella y en contar los bienes que se siguen en tenerla,
se pudiera gastar mucho tiempo y papel.
– Pedro Mejía
Silva de varia lección[2]

"En un lugar de la Mancha, de cuyo nombre no quiero acordarme" marks the beginning of a novel distinctively framed by a controlled act of memory. Through this retrospective action, Miguel de Cervantes establishes the act of remembering at the centre of his narrative and puts the early modern reader on notice that memory will play an important role throughout the story, starting with the first words.[3] Indeed, the term *memory* pervades the work, occurring no fewer than 134 times in the course of the novel – not to mention the instances when the term is not explicitly cited but the act of remembering is implicit. This recurrence should come as no surprise, considering that nearly everything the protagonist does comes from ceaseless attempts to access the materials of the past by drawing on his memory of reading, as proven by the frequency of Don Quixote's utterance of the phrase "me acuerdo haber leído" and his proclaimed nostalgia for an old chivalric world that is foundational but obsolete. A persistent practice of deliberately remembering also marks the behaviour of other characters whose own narrativization of their past involves strategies to retrieve and structure their previous experiences through a selective process of (re)telling.[4] For these characters, memory is not just a personal experience but also part of a social practice that impacts individual and collective identity formation. As a whole, the novel is an unfolding act of memory wherein the reader contemplates memory in the making and its many varied processes. Through the pages of *Don Quixote*, the reader is asked to reflect upon the implications of remembering and reveals memory's traps and ellipses, and therefore its unreliability, which simultaneously reflects an ongoing debate regarding the partial nature of memory in the early modern period.

Cervantes was one of the most influential writers in early modern Europe, and his narrative reflects the rich culture of memory in which it was engendered and highlights the ideas and debates surrounding the faculty. His literary work reflects a sophisticated understanding of what memory processes and operations entail, as well as the different theories surrounding the faculty during his time. Amazingly, Cervantes himself was able to remember and accurately cite an impressive number of sources for his novel: 104 mythological, legendary, and biblical characters; 131 characters from chivalric and pastoral novels; 227 historical personages; 21 celebrated animals; 93 books; and 261 geographical places.[5] The fact that he remembered it all without having at hand the original sources like books, manuscripts, or images shows how memory proved essential for creativity and how powerful Cervantes's was. He understood that memory had long been a valued and a powerful faculty but also a fragile instrument[6] whose presence recurs throughout a variety of cultural phenomena in Cervantes's time. In this study, I offer insight into the plurality and complexity of memory's cultural scope through the lens of Cervantes and, specifically, through his novel *Don Quixote*. In the process, I will explore the many spaces that memory created for itself in early modern Spain, particularly in the fields of natural philosophy, medicine, rhetoric, mnemotechnics, visual arts, and pedagogy.

Quixotic Memories: Cervantes and Memory in Early Modern Spain analyses the essential role of memory within the context of the rapidly shifting cultural production during the sixteenth and seventeenth centuries and how memory is central to understanding Cervantes's work. Artists and writers like Cervantes were trained in the philosophical theories of memory from classical antiquity. However, the author was writing at a time of great upheaval brought about by boundless advancements in science and technology, the introduction of new systems of finance and commerce, the institution of global transit, and the development of mass printing and book technologies. This swiftly evolving global state caused European societies to confront information overload by adapting new approaches involving memory that helped Renaissance individuals understand their place in the world – make sense of it all. Furthermore, in a society that was expanding its epistemological horizons, writers sought new ways to come to grips with what was viewed as a cultural revolution in thought and perception. As a result, processes of cognition, such as memory, became subject to reexamination in Renaissance culture.[7]

More than a theme, memory is a system of understanding, an episteme, in Cervantes's world as a result of the major changes that epitomize Renaissance humanist culture and that concurrently will be key in the transition to modernity. For Cervantes and his contemporaries, memory was an essential tool to face this swerve, and new discourses and practices on memory emerge as a response to the demands of early modern culture, as theories were no longer confined to classical rhetoric. Their understanding of theories about how memory worked were adapted to Renaissance culture and the emergence of scientific thought.

Cervantes's fiction acknowledges this new direction and diversified enquiries around memory. As I will examine in the pages that follow, his works drew on extant theories regarding memory that had been developed since classical antiquity and adapted to the specific circumstances of his own time. Such an adaptation was produced in response to the most diverse needs of the time reflected in *Don Quixote*: nostalgia for an earlier period as a means to confront the fears that come with a rapidly changing society; utilizing imagination and memory as powerful tools to detach oneself from society's impositions and instead endorse the right to be forgotten; pedagogical theories that evolved as a response to the intellectual overload and the impositions of the *imitatio*; the role of memory in a society that continued to cling to the oral tradition; the use of powerful mnemonic images in cultural environments; and, finally, the immense power of memory in individual and collective identity formation and, paradoxically, memory's fragility and malleability when faced with social, religious, and cultural demands.

In Renaissance studies, the increasing number and frequency of scholarly works on memory vis-à-vis literary studies speaks to the rising prominence of the topic and its broad spectrum.[8] In recent years, numerous seminal publications regarding memory in the Renaissance period have become essential reading. Publications such as *The Memory*

Arts in Renaissance England (2016) edited by William E. Engel, Rory Loughnane, and Grant Williams or *Memory in Early Modern Europe 1500–1800* (2017) by Judith Pollmann provide context and scope for exposing the significance that memory played in early modern Europe. A great deal of work has been carried out on specific authors of the period, especially William Shakespeare, such as Andrew Hiscock's study on memory in England, *Reading Memory in Early Modern Literature* (2011), Garrett Sullivan's *Memory and Forgetting in English Renaissance Drama* (2005), Jonathan Baldo's *Memory in Shakespeare's Histories* (2011), Raphael Lyne's *Memory and Intertextuality in Renaissance Literature* (2016), and more recently, *The Routledge Handbook of Shakespeare and Memory* (2018), edited by Hiscock and Lina Perkins Wilder. The study of early modern memory therefore has grown immensely and evolved to include a variety of subjects, genres, and authors, among other areas.[9]

These and other recent publications in just the last two decades alone demonstrate the weight and scope of this topic in early modern European literary studies.[10] It is quite surprising, however, that despite the growing numbers of publications on the subject, very little attention has been paid to the study of memory in literary studies in early modern Spain and, specifically, to one of the most important writers in any period or country, Miguel de Cervantes.[11] In her seminal essay "*Don Quijote* y la memoria" (1991), later included in *Cervantes y las puertas del sueño* (1994), Aurora Egido laid the foundations for studying memory as a guiding thread in Cervantes's novel.[12] Nevertheless, in the several decades that have elapsed since the appearance of Egido's article – while studies and theories regarding Renaissance memory have continued to acquire great relevance outside early modern Spanish literature – similar work regarding Cervantes unfortunately remains tangential. In fact, there are only a few – but very significant – studies on the topic of memory with a focus on early modern Spanish literature, mainly the aforementioned work by Egido[13] and a few others by Frederick de Armas, Fernando Rodríguez de la Flor, Fernando Bouza Álvarez, and Luis Merino. Equally remarkable is the fact that the topic of memory in Cervantes's work has never been explored in a book-length study. This study seeks to remedy that problem by demonstrating how memory is pivotal to early modern Spanish culture and played an exceptionally critical role in Cervantes's *Don Quixote*. I hope not only to provide a new reading of Cervantes's novel by tracing the sociohistorical and cultural prominence of memory during the author's lifetime but also to fill in an unfortunate gap in Cervantes scholarship.

The Culture of Memory in Early Modern Spain

Proof of such a broad scope and the different theories and debates surrounding the term during the sixteenth and seventeenth centuries in Spain can be found in the digital archive of the Biblioteca Nacional de España (BNE, National Library of Spain). A search for the word *memory* between the years 1500 and 1700 generates a total of 4,205 single instances of the term in works of the most diverse nature.[14] The majority of these citations are found in printed works in the fields of linguistics and literature (314); religion and theology (194); geography, biography, and history (67); social sciences (40); philosophy and psychology (37); fine arts, shows, and sports (15); applied sciences, medicine, and technology (14); sciences (10); and culture in general (2). It is striking that the highest number of references to the term (940) is recorded from the period 1601 to 1620 – the time that Cervantes published his most important works.

A similar search in the *Diachronic Corpus of Spanish* of the Real Academia Española (CORDE), generates 17,089 cases in 1,672 widely varying documents (only written in Spain).

While the frequency of the term's appearance in archival documents demonstrates the centrality of the term, close examination of the plethora of treatises on memory from the ancient period up to Cervantes's time underscores the significance of memory. From Classical theses about the brain by Galen and Hippocrates, to manuals of rhetoric and pedagogy by Erasmus and Juan Luis Vives, to manuscripts on *albeitería,*[15] *artillería,*[16] or arithmetic[17]. – the many extant sources all aim to praise memory while also providing training on how to strengthen it. The fact that there were so many different perspectives on, interpretations of, and constructions of the status and functions of memory leads one to ponder whether or not memory had reached a zenith of interest at exactly the time Cervantes was writing. This helps explain how intricately the faculty is captured in his work.

Cervantes's contemporaries acclaimed memory as much as – or even more than – we do today. In his popular *Silva de varia lección* (1540), the humanist Pedro Mejía describes the relevance of memory with these words:

> las excelencias de la memoria estriban en ser esta el más acreditado de los sentidos interiores del hombre, tesoro y custodia de todos los demás … Otros llaman a la memoria tesoro de las ciencias: y así dicen que la sabiduría es hija de la memoria, y experiencia: porque la memoria es arca y depósito de todo cuanto entendemos y aprendemos, y vemos. Y lo que desto guarda, y retiene la memoria, esto es lo que nos queda y sabemos.[18]

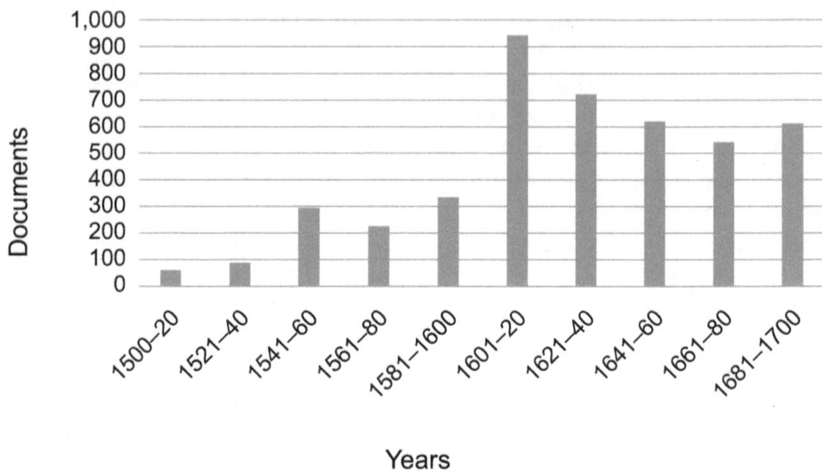

Figure 1 Frequency of the Term "Memory" in the Digital Archive of the Biblioteca Nacional de España between Years 1500 and 1700

As Mejía's words encapsulate, for Cervantes's contemporaries, memory played very important scientific and artistic roles. Mejía specifically highlights memory's place at the heart of all scientific inquiry – it was considered the treasurer of all sciences. Physiologically, physicians believed memory to be an interior sense located very specifically in one of the three ventricles, at the back of the brain, without which neither the brain nor the other interior "faculties," such as intellect and imagination, could function properly. In art, philosophy, and literature, the goddess Mnemosyne was considered the mother of the highly praised nine Muses.[19] As a result of the legacy of the Platonic tradition, remembering was synonymous with knowing; hence, the poet had to be possessed by the goddess to convey knowledge. Ethically, as part of the virtue of *prudentia,* memory was an essential part of the tripartite soul with which man could excel and improve his moral life in future actions. In rhetoric, memory was a critical instrument needed to study, write, and speak properly in public, and pioneering universities such as Salamanca and the various literary academies[20] promoted curricula that included a number of rhetorical manuals. These pivotal institutions of learning and thought provided the tools and cues – inherited from the classic rhetoric and strategies and techniques to perfect memory – to promote memorization in learning. The techniques of memorizing prized committing to memory important texts, speeches, and poems as a means of demonstrating one's intellectual capacity.

Table 1 The Number of Cases in Which the Term "Memory" Appears in the *Diachronic Corpus of Spanish* (CORDE) of the Real Academia Española, Organized by Year and by Text Type

Year	%	Cases	Text Type	%	Cases
1575	10.50	728	Religious prose	17.46	2,985
1605	9.12	632	Narrative prose	16.36	2,796
1535	7.13	494	Historic prose	12.86	2,198
1600	6.95	482	Lyric verse	12.86	2,198
1604	5.47	379	Scientific prose	12.02	2,055
1562	4.67	324	Didactic prose	6.38	1,091
1589	4.46	309	Juridic prose	4.49	768
1554	3.44	239	Society prose	4.31	737
1624	3.04	211	Dramatic verse	4.26	729
Other	45.17	3,130	Other	5.46	934

The scope and diverse nature of the historical records also reveal that to speak of memory in the time of Cervantes is not only to speak of the inner workings of the brain (*natural memory*), the intricacies of the soul, and the construction of the self, but also to address ways to improve memory's capacity through trained recollection (*artificial memory*), powerful mnemonic images, and diverse tools of external memory such as books, libraries, commonplace books, *librillos de memoria*, and objects that attempt to preserve the past. Memory was therefore linked to a humanist pedagogy that promoted different instruments, technologies, and artefacts to cope with the "information overload" of the Renaissance,[21] brought about by early modern Spain's shift from an oral to a written culture stimulated by the advent of the mechanical press. It was also closely connected to life writing and history writing, as ways of narrating, recording, and reconstructing the past, which would become an obsession for the Spanish Habsburgs through their desire to construct, fashion, and impose certain collective memories and erase others. Therefore, it is not surprising that during this time, through private and public records, individual and collective identities are constructed and contested in an increasing number of *espejos*, anatomies, books of memory, chronicles, autobiographies, and memoirs – all using the common thread of memory.

The rapid increase in printed materials and their broad dissemination, particularly through religious institutions, triggered everyday thoughts of instability and uncertainty as contradictory messages yielded contradictory interpretations, leading citizens to question their own existence. From monarchs to civic authorities to individual writers, in all disciplines during the Renaissance there was an increasing need for – an obsession with – remembering, revisiting, and recomposing the past. For Stephen Greenblatt, these transformations in the early modern period brought about "increased self-consciousness about the fashioning of human identity as a manipulable, artful process" that led people to "self-fashioning," the willing manipulation of one's identity so that it corresponded better to a preferred circumstance.[22] Accordingly, for Greenblatt, major authors of the period created fictional self-conscious characters who possessed the capacity for self-reflection. As part of such creation and in line with Greenblatt's notion of self-fashioning, I would add that manipulation of their pasts becomes a crucial component in identity formation. Naturally, Cervantes's *Don Quixote* comes to mind: Alonso Quijano, the gentleman, willingly forgets his country lifestyle to become a knight-errant so that he may correct the world's wrongs. Furthermore, this idea that the past was subject to reexamination provoked anxiety and insecurity. The tension caused by revisiting past narratives is the subject of a great number of studies on the cultural value of memory during the Renaissance. Critics speak to an obsession with memory as a constant "sense of the past" (Burke 1969); a persistent obsession about the past (Bolzoni 2001); an anxiety provoked by the memory and fear of losing it (Hiscock 2011); the fear of forgetting and the tension between the fragility of memory and the different supports that sustain it, such as writing, as a reflection of that same fragility (Chartier 2006); and memory as a "pressing need" (Gómez-Bravo 2013).[23] Donald Beecher summarizes these aspects through the following words:

> For the Renaissance, memory was the focal point of an implicit sense of anxiety over learning, identity, social continuity, the permanence of the soul, and the nature of the mental faculties, all of which figured not only in their philosophical speculations but also in the development of their bibliographical and pedagogical cultures.[24]

Hence, in Cervantes's time, there existed an obvious obsession with the past and an equally palpable fascination with its (re)interpretation, and thus memory emerges as a central component of the debate.[25] For the author's contemporaries, "every aspect of society, learning and the arts entails some dimension of memory."[26] As Kurt Danziger puts it, the writings on the subject of memory during this time frame by such a wide array of professionals such as philosophers, physicians, psychologists, and others ensured the dissemination of multiple and sometimes contradictory beliefs about memory across various disciplines.[27]

Key studies by Frances Yates, Mary Carruthers, and Janet Coleman demonstrate that philosophical theories about memory in the early modern era have their roots in classical antiquity and the medieval period. Specifically, they point to the legacy and impact of Plato's and Aristotle's views and how these ancients' writings were adapted over time as a response to the demands of early modern culture and to the specific practices of memory during that time. Hiscock explains the phenomenon with these words: "For a society that was enormously diversifying its understandings of epistemology and, indeed ontological difference, it was inevitable that key concepts associated with acts of cognition, such as *memoria,* would undergo intense and sustained interrogation."[28] In this regard, Cervantes and his contemporaries, such as Juan Huarte de San Juan and Mejía, who were interested in the process of cognition, based many of their ideas about memory on Plato's and Aristotle's theories as the foundation of the nature of the human condition. In particular several intellectuals and writers embraced Plato's theories on memory, as espoused in *Meno,* where the philosopher writes that memory was key to accessing innate knowledge: "Learning (*mathēsis*) is thus knowing, and knowing is recollection as coming to understand what one has known before (*proteron*) but somehow has forgotten."[29] As stated in his *Phaedo,* by using memory, ideas are (re) discovered and therefore recollected. Similarly, in *Theaetetus,* the philosopher described memory as a block of wax where impressions can be made – a vivid image that became a benchmark for writers and intellectuals in the Renaissance such as Huarte de San Juan, who will use the wax metaphor as visual metaphor to understand how memory works, a notion that also appears in Cervantes's work:[30]

> We may look upon it, then, as a gift of Memory, the mother of the Muses. We make impressions upon this of everything we wish to remember among the things we have seen or heard or thought of ourselves; we hold the wax under our perceptions and thoughts and take a stamp from them, in the way in which we take the imprints of signet rings. Whatever is impressed upon the wax we remember and know so long as the image remains in the wax; whatever is obliterated or cannot be impressed, we forget, and we do not know.[31]

Despite differences in their theories, both Plato and Aristotle agreed that two key concepts are equally important: *mnēme* (remembering) and *anamnēsis* (recollection).[32] For Aristotle, in the first monographic book on memory, *De memoria et reminiscentia,* "remembering" was the act of storing representations of events and things witnessed or learned;[33] it was also a space where images were located and memorization took place; on the other hand, "recollection" was thus the reconstructive process by which something no longer present is recalled. Therefore, according to Aristotle, memory was an integral part of cognition important to general philosophical questions such as truth and untruth, and the overall problem in retrieving memories is that it was a reconstructive process, which Plato similarly observed in *Theaetetus*.

Both Plato's and Aristotle's legacies on memory underscore the faculty's fragility and fragmented character; both philosophers maintained a distinction between memory and recollection – the former being a passive storage location subject to reconstructive process by the latter. The debate over this distinction continues to this day. As the psychologist Daniel Schacter puts it, the stories we tell about our past are not exact copies but (re)constructions of what happened to give cohesiveness to our experiences:[34]

> Like the objects in which we attempt to preserve the past, the fragile power of memory provides us with a general sense of who we are and where we have been, even though it hides many of the specific incidents that helped shape us. We may be profoundly moved by experiences that we remember inaccurately, or by illusory memories of events we only feared or imagined. Our thoughts and actions are sometimes influenced implicitly by incidents that we do not recollect at all. And many of the specific episodes in our lives have vanished from our memories forever. On balance, however, our memory systems do a remarkably good job of preserving the general contours of our pasts and or recording correctly many of the important things that have happened to us. We could not have evolved as a species otherwise. Memory is a central part of the brain's attempt to make sense of experience, and to tell coherent stories about it. These tales are all we have of our pasts, and they are potent determinants of how we view ourselves and what we do. Yet our stories are built from many different ingredients: snippets of what actually happened, thoughts about what might have happened, and beliefs that guide us as we attempt to remember. Our memories are the fragile but powerful products of what we recall from the past, believe about the present, and imagine about the future.[35]

Memory, therefore, is powerful but unstable, and Cervantes was quite aware of this. Time and again in his fiction, he focuses on the impossibility of attaining truth, taking memory, in Ulric Neisser's words, with a grain of salt when considering that it depended on reconstruction – a process that was not always reliable.[36] Such a concern is evident in how Cervantes's fiction insists that the human capacity to recollect the past is always partial and, as a consequence, in his narratives memory is often questioned and contested in the (re)telling of stories. Memory depends on a reconstructive process encompassing traps, ellipses, and competing versions. This is highlighted explicitly in *La gran sultana* where Andrea reproaches Madrigal for "la memoria tenéis dada a adobar, a lo que entiendo, o reducirla a voluntad."[37] As Andrea notes, memory can *adobar* or *reducir*, indicating that there is an obvious malleability or creativity thanks to which memories "adoban" or "reducen." Similarly, in *La Galatea*, Lenio sings a love song in which he describes memory as subject to change: "Un vano, descuidado pensamiento, / una loca, altanera fantasía, / un no sé qué, que la memoria cría, / sin ser, sin calidad, sin fundamento; / una esperanza que se lleva el viento, / un dolor con renombre de alegría."[38] For the shepherd, love is a "thought" or a "fantasy" that memory itself has created. With the choice of the verb *criar*, the author alludes to how memory can be nurtured or nourished; therefore, it can depart from the original experience.

Despite their fallibility and imperfections – or perhaps because of them – memories were an inevitable source of creativity that were also subject to the imposition of a high degree of imagination in the reconstructive process. As a matter of fact, "memory" and "imagination" appear interchangeably in the novel, which follows Aristotle's precepts from *De memoria et reminiscentia*, in which the philosopher determined that memory and imagination belong to the same part of the soul.[39] Consider, for example, at a lexical level, the famous moment when Don Quixote creates a name for his lady, his horse, and himself: "Y así, después de muchos nombres que formó, borró y quitó, añadió, deshizo y tornó a hacer en *su memoria e imaginación*, al fin le vino a llamar Rocinante: nombre, a su parecer, alto, sonoro y significativo de lo que había sido."[40] The repetitive process of constructing, deconstructing, and constructing again demonstrates the lengths to which the knight will go to find the appropriate name for his lady while also underscoring how memory and imagination work in tandem in the creative process of the reconstruction of memories.[41]

A fascination with the processes of cognition and the physical workings of memory in Cervantes's fiction is not surprising given society's active interest in understanding the role of memory in the human condition. This was a legacy passed down by Aristotle, who initially linked memory operations with human physiology and humoralism, an argument I develop in chapter 1, "The Anatomy of Early Modern Memory." Cervantes's contemporaries were aware of the nature of memory as having both somatic and intellectual status, as Lina Bolzoni has argued in *The Gallery of Memory*. As I show in this chapter, although memory and recollection are seemingly intellectual activities, they are nevertheless part of a larger corporeal process. Whereas for Plato memory was an introspective, spiritual action, Aristotle believed memory to be the product of imprinted sensorial experience that materialized in mental images. According to Aristotle memory is an *affectio* "produced by means of perception in the soul and in that part of the body which contains the soul, as being like a sort of picture, the having of which we say is memory."[42] The *affectio* provokes a change that, according to Aristotle, "marks in a sort of imprint, as it were, of the sense-image, as people who seal things with signet rings."[43]

Aristotle's legacy continued in Cervantes's lifetime through the work of the doctor Huarte de San Juan whose *Examen de ingenios* (1575) was strongly influenced by the work of Hippocrates and Galen. A copy of Huarte's work was among Cervantes's possessions, and we can deduce that as a result of reading Huarte, Cervantes at minimum would have been aware of Aristotle's views on memory – if not from having read the Greek philosopher directly. In fact, Huarte admits that his definition of memory and its workings are strikingly similar to those established by Aristotle, even citing the philosopher by name:

> la memoria no es más que una blandura del celebro, dispuesta (con cierto género de humidad) para recebir y guardar lo que la imaginativa percibe, en la mesma proporción que tiene el papel blanco y liso con el que ha de escrebir. Porque, así como el escribano escribe en el papel las cosas que quiere que no se olviden y después de escritas las torna a leer, de la mesma manera se ha de entender que la imaginativa escribe en la memoria las figuras de las cosas que conocieron los cinco sentidos y el entendimiento y otras que ella mesma fabrica. Y cuando quiere acordarse de ellas, dice Aristóteles que las torna a mirar y contemplar. De esta manera de comparación usó Platón cuando dijo que, temiendo la poca memoria de la vejez, se daba priesa a hacer otra de papel (que son los libros) para que no se le perdiese su trabajo, y hubiese después quien se lo representase cuando lo quisiese leer. Esto mesmo hace la imaginativa: escrebir en la memoria y tornar a leer cuando se quiere acordar.[44]

Building on Aristotelian theories, Huarte and his contemporaries believed that the human body and its humours conditioned the sensory perceptions and subsequently the retention of mental images. The physical imprint of memory depended on the softness of the brain, whose quality and nature in turn depended on its physiological constitution and the humours. As I also analyse in chapter 1, melancholy, caused by an imbalance or dyscrasia in the humours, was thought to have a powerful effect on the faculty of memory and, by relation, on imagination. As stated in Aristotle's *De memoria et reminiscentia* and widely believed in early modern Spain, melancholics incessantly recollect images stored in memory and, as I argue, Don Quixote's melancholic state affected the process of remembering.

Pollmann has observed that, as a result of the relationship between memory and the body during the early modern era, individuals structured their memories in line with their physical condition: "In a culture that thought of emotional change as a physical process, the decision to structure memories around the state of one's body was an obvious choice."[45] In Cervantes's work this practice is evident in how characters assemble their memories according to the negative impact they exert on their physical well-being. Hence, in *Don Quixote* memory appears described several times over as "enemiga mortal del descanso."[46] Similar physical effects are observed, for instance, in Cardenio's corporal reaction upon hearing the name of Luscinda: "no hizo otra cosa que encoger los hombros, morderse los labios, enarcar las cejas y dejar de allí a poco caer por sus ojos dos fuentes de lágrimas;"[47] or consider Clara, who, upon hearing the verses that Luis sang, "le tomó un temblor tan extraño como si de algún grave accidente de cuartana."[48] In these examples, a literal physical reaction accompanies the act of remembering.

Since memory could provoke somatic behaviour, it is not surprising that the actual physical location of memory was also a point of debate during the early modern period. As Huarte has noted, ideas about memory inherited from Galenic and Hippocratic theories on anatomy and medicine and later developed by Arabic scholars such as Avicenna and Averroes situated it in a "ventricle" area at the rear of the brain. Like other theorists, Huarte believed the brain was divided into three ventricles – imagination, intellect, and memory – each one having a specific function. The existence of these ventricles was commonly accepted during Cervantes's time, as evident in the multitude of terms used to describe them. In one such example, San Juan de la Cruz called them "cavernas,"[49] a notion repeated in *Don Quixote* when the narrator speaks of the protagonist's "aposentos de la cabeza."[50]

Given its assumed structure and capacity, memory was also thought to occupy a physical storage space that amassed memories and mental images. Lope de Vega, in *El cuerdo loco* (1594), refers to memory as a sort of voluminous collection, like a thesaurus, when the main character asks, "¿Qué es la memoria? Un tesoro de las intenciones es."[51] The idea is repeated in Cervantes's *El rufián viudo llamado Trampagos* when Escarramán talks of stories "dignas de atesorarlas en la memoria."[52] In *Agudeza y arte de ingenio* (1648), Baltasar Gracián describes memory as a "despensa," "magacén," "vestuario y guardajoyas,"[53] where fundamental erudite material was stored. This led to the creation of metaphors that, although not empirical, were continuously employed to visualize both the inscription processes commonly believed to create memories and the storage area to hold them. The storage metaphor made some think of memory as a container such as a birdcage, a box, or a chest but also a purse or a money bag, as Carruthers and others have revealed.[54] Architectural analogies that highlighted physical spaces where mental images reside also became very common: houses, rooms, palaces – like Saint Augustine's "spacious palaces of memory" – as well as a storehouse, a library, or a theatre. Memory was thus a literal and figurative treasure (hence the term "thesaurus"), a subject I develop in detail later in this study.

Since memory was viewed as a priceless faculty, a good amount of medical literature was devoted to how to properly maintain it, which I review in chapter 1. For example, in *Libro intitulado la conservación de la salud del cuerpo y del alma … agora nuevamente impreso con un singular tratado de la firme y tenaz memoria y del bueno y claro entendimiento* (1599), Blas Álvarez de Miraval, a doctor and professor from the University of Salamanca, offers common dietetic remedies to care for one's memory as well as advice on the proper treatment of the body to prevent forgetfulness.[55] Manuals like Álvarez de Miraval's suggested certain food, beverages, and ointments to keep memory healthy. Among recommended self-care regimens were purging, irrigations, and baths with a shaved head; the application of cataplasms made of the powder from deer antlers or beaver bones; the intake of anacardine (mentioned by authors such as Lope and Saavedra Fajardo on several occasions); the consumption of maidenhair; or only eating raisins or almonds for fifty straight nights. Campuzano refers to the latter in the *Coloquio de los perros* when he states that his diet of raisins and almonds allowed him to remember the entire conversation between the two dogs at the hospital: "merced a las almendras y pasas que había comido."[56] Similar patterns can be found throughout *Don Quixote*. When the knight eats properly and gets good rest, his memory and the other cognitive functions improve considerably. For example, he starts his lucid speech about the golden age after sharing a meal with the goat herders, a good night's rest, and remaining hydrated – all of which render his cognitive abilities much sharper than usual. On the other hand, while fasting as part of his penance in the Sierra Morena, the knight shows signs of confusion, depression, and sickliness. Indeed, at the outset of the novel, the reader is told that the hidalgo Alonso Quijano cared more about reading than eating and tending to his own health, leading him to the chivalric frenzy in which he finds himself. The loss of sustenance is perhaps one reason the knight mixes fact and fiction in his memory, sparsely recalling some details more than others.

A number of manuals from the period were dedicated to the maintenance of one's health, and natural memory featured prominently in them. Among these, Luis Lobera de Ávila's *Libro del régimen de la salud* (1551) is of particular interest since the writer recommends a strict regimen (*regimen sanitatis*) meant to improve one's overall well-being. Lobera de Ávila wrote about the need to control the *sex res non naturales*, or the six non-natural elements, known to be air, food and drink, exercise and rest, sleep and wakefulness, excretions and secretions, and other elements that affect one's mood. As already indicated by Plato and Aristotle, one's age and other factors in the process of remembering (*mnēme*) and reminiscing (*anamnēsis*) were equally important, which was highlighted by Mejía in the following way: "Unos hombres tienen las memorias prestas y presto toman lo que les encomiendan, pero no lo guardan durante mucho tiempo. Otras por el contrario, con dificultad lo reciben, pero consérvanlo largo espacio."[57]

Besides the aforementioned medical recommendations, natural memory could also be strengthened with studious mental discipline through a series of mnemonic exercises known as artificial memory or *ars memoriae*. The *ars memoriae*, also called the art of memory, was an ever-increasing and expanding compendium of techniques and strategies used to effectively improve one's memory that was passed down from antiquity and broadly expanded and adapted during the Renaissance in learned circles across Europe. While most early modern writers drew from the art of memory's many strategies for their personal self-enrichment, still others wrote their own theoretical works that expanded the knowledge base on memory in various directions and contributed to the growing number of printed works that make up the art of memory. It is impossible to adequately study memory in the early modern period without exploring the role and impact of the art of memory on culture and society.

Much of the importance of the art of memory was exposed by Frances Yates in *The Art of Memory*. Yates extensively studied the memorization techniques that were immensely popular in ancient Greece and Rome and were adopted by oratory schools where memory was treated as a part of Rhetoric alongside *inventio, dispositio, elocutio,* and *actio*. The main precursors of the art of memory in Rome were Cicero's *De oratore*, Quintilian's *Institutio oratoria*, and the anonymous work *Rhetorica ad Herennium*. The *ars memoriae* system was employed widely to help individuals remember a speech without reading it. In Roman society and later in early modern Europe, reading a prepared speech aloud – rather than reciting from memory – was considered inappropriate. The *ars memoriae* system taught a speaker to mentally design an architectural sketch that included a series of spaces (*loci*), each having a specific meaning and association. As the speaker mentally moved through the spaces, he contemplated the images (*imagines*) stored there, and he was able to more eloquently craft his speech. The images of memory and the combinatory mnemonics become very important in the Renaissance mind. This cognitive strategy asked the individual to actively contemplate images or *phantasms* as part of a network of association. William E. Engel describes the process as an interdisciplinary Renaissance mentality that he calls "mnemonic episteme,"[58] a widely embraced system of memorization that refers to the diversity and ubiquity of a mnemonic culture. As a cultural *contaminatio*, literary works, such as Cervantes's *Don Quixote*, will conceptualize some of their contents in mnemonic terms by including within the text descriptions of architectural designs, paintings, images, tapestries, and other representational devices such as emblems, physiognomies, or symbols of heraldry. These mnemonic devices become pictorial artefacts or well-known places to the reader, and they trigger memories through the Aristotelian laws of association.

Thus, vestiges of the process of the *ars memoriae*, with which readers of the time were quite familiar, are seen throughout *Don Quixote*. Chapter 2, "Mental Libraries: The Places of Memory," reveals the general cultural awareness in early modern Spain of the *ars memoriae* and how its mnemonic system is embedded in Cervantes's novel. Cervantes, like other authors of the period, does not refer to the art of memory directly, but it is clear that he was familiar with its techniques. The art of memory was very significant for the Renaissance mind, and it evolved in myriad forms based on its reception among the intellectual circles of the time. As the art of memory changed, writers began to theorize with a three-dimensionality in literature and to conceive texts in spatial terms. When invoking the memory of his readings, Don Quixote literally travels the places (*loci*) in his mind, stopping to contemplate the images (*imagines*) evoked – the principal technique of the *ars memoriae*, which itself was based on the Aristotelian laws of association. In this process, the reader accesses a gallery of images stored in Don Quixote's memory through the mental wanderings of the character. In fact, the novel repeatedly exhibits an ecological orientation of memory by featuring a progression through the chivalric *loci* stored in the protagonist's mind, which represents a sort of mnemonic exercise. There is also a frequent use of verbs that indicate movement that mimic a mental journey through a series of memory places of the chivalric novels that the protagonist read. Memory processes are constantly described in terms of movement or space; consequently, memories "vienen a la mente" or something "las trae a la memoria." Even the novel's celebrated beginning refers to a place "de cuyo nombre no quiero acordarme," giving memory a special role from the outset, a strategic reference that, according to Egido, "remite a la tradición retórica del *locus* que predicaban las artes de memoria."[59]

In addition to the prominence of the mental places, the mnemonic image will also move beyond the rhetorical treatises and expand its influence on other realms of culture. Book illustrations, board games, paintings, tapestries, playing cards, and other pictorial elements contributed to the plasticity of the Renaissance mind, which was accustomed to interpreting, decoding, and making sense of rich images both symbolically and allegorically. For example, as espoused by Diego Valadés in *Rhetorica Christiana* (1579), playing cards could be used to help students learn Latin by providing visual mnemonic alphabets.[60] The importance attributed to mnemonic images and their frequent appearances in *Don Quixote* are central to my argument in chapter 3, "*Ut Pictura Memoria*: The Mnemonic Power of Images." This chapter examines *Don Quixote* as a product of this iconic culture in which collective memory embraced certain mnemonic images. Cervantes was well aware of the power of such images on society. For example, he penned a sonnet for *Filosofía cortesana moralizada* (1587), a prose work by his friend Alonso de Barros that included a board game with the text. Games were able to "mobilize an entire heritage of cultural, literary and above all, iconographic memory, transforming it into an occasion for play."[61] They had hidden meanings that required a player to use their memory to make quick associations. But mnemonic devices were not for play alone. Pictorial images were also meant to educate, as illustrated in the example of Valadés's playing cards. In *Don Quixote*, there is frequent use of a variety of instructional devices – such as riddles, symbols, emblems, and hieroglyphs – to help the reader reveal the meaning of a particular episode, theme, or character. Consequently, the novel obeys the views of the contemporaneous art theorist Gaspar Gutiérrez de los Ríos, who wrote in his *Noticia general para la estimación de las artes* (1600) that "con las [historias] bien pintadas y relevadas se deleytan los ojos, se recrea la memoria, se aguza y abiva el entendimiento, se apacienta el ánimo, se incita la voluntad y se está, finalmente, encendiendo el desseo, viendo los valores y virtudes de otros para imitarlos, tanto, y aún algunas vezes más, que por las historias escritas."[62]

Outside of literary production, vestiges of the art of memory pervaded civil, social, religious, and political institutions where mnemonic devices were used as visual expressions of a particular point of view. The array of celebratory devices in early modern societies, according to Engel, was far reaching and eclectic: "from temporary triumphal entry arches, to painted emblematic programs within town halls and state council chambers, to commemorative medals, ceiling bosses, marriage chests, signet rings; and of course, the ubiquitous displays of heraldic arms and personal devices or imprese."[63] The pervasion of commemoration through instruments, rituals, and honourific ceremonies were designed with a memorial function in mind, and they were therefore viewed as extensions of memory. The most obvious example from *Don Quixote* is Grisóstomo's funeral, where the narrator poignantly describes the grave surrounded by "libros y muchos papeles, abiertos y cerrados," placed there as a tribute to the deceased shepherd. In *Noticia general para la estimación de las artes* (1600), Gutiérrez de los Ríos explains how the iconography was paramount for honouring the dead:

> Mas, si por las historias escritas se eterniza la memoria de las cosas, también y mucho más se eterniza por medio de las historias relevadas, figuras, estatuas, colosos, medallas y monedas, que está menos sujeto a las injurias del tiempo. Y aun algunas vezes la verdad de la historia escrita, si tiene alguna, se saca por las dichas estatuas, sepulcros y colosos.[64]

Medals seemed to play an especially important role in commemorations. Easy to create, inexpensive in comparison to other memorial forms, and simple to transport, medals were minted to celebrate historic events and heroic deeds, and they usually included hidden messages about the subject that humanists needed to decipher. It was likewise fashionable to include pictorial medals as sculptures on building façades with an iconographic symbolism. As I explore in this chapter, it is within this culture of heraldic devices that Don Quixote understandably demonstrates his knowledge of badges, coats of arms, crests, flags, and military insignia, among several other devices. For example, in the episode of the Battle of the Sheep, the narrator makes clear that the knight was able to recall from memory (and imagination) the particular leaders of both groups with unusual immediacy and impressive details, but it seems he is able to do so mainly because of "sus armas, colores, empresas y motes de improviso."[65] That is, the mnemonical devices are the stimulus for the knight to concoct his version of the unfolding events with astounding detail and amazing creativity.

Even though governments, institutions, and even individual families put mnemonical devices to use for gain, the techniques of the *ars memorativa* had countless implications for Cervantes's cultural milieu, and they were not always accepted by Spanish intellectuals. There were some important thinkers within pedagogical circles who were clearly detractors, such as Vives, Diego de Saavedra Fajardo, and Baltasar de Céspedes.[66] The work of Vives, in particular, is important among writers of the Spanish Renaissance because his writings on education featured discussions of the role of memory. For Vives, as for Plato, memory was essential to learning and was a chief constituent for training intellectuals. In his *De tradendis disciplinis* (1531), Vives develops his theory on pillars of education and advises that knowledge should be acquired through dedication, hard work, and discipline. To do so, he recommends reading aloud in order to learn information through memorization and emphasizes the significance of images in the learning process (following Aristotelian teachings on mental association and visualization). Similarly, Erasmus of Rotterdam valued a healthy memory, and he advised that memory should be cared for and cultivated. But Erasmus, like Vives, clearly disliked many of the tenets of the art of memory that had become popular in his lifetime, such as memorizing instead of learning. In *De ratione studii* (1511), Erasmus opposes simple rote memorization, deeming this to be artificial. Instead, he advocated for using memorization to learn facts. Both writers disapprove of merely acquiring the means to memorize and instead encourage memorization to help learn. Echoes of this apprehension are seen in Cervantes's *El Casamiento engañoso* when Campuzano speaks negatively about certain animals – and, by extension, about humankind – which simply repeat what they have memorized without understanding its significance because it was never learned in the first place: "que bien sé que si los tordos, picazas y papagayos hablan, no son sino las palabras que aprenden y toman de memoria, … mas no por esto pueden hablar y responder con discurso concertado."[67]

Erasmus, Vives, and other humanists of the period recognize that training and perfecting memory is essential to its efficacy as an intellectual instrument, but the dominant processes for improving memory are faulty. Erasmus writes that "the memory required training in order for the aspiring scholar to realize his fullest potential," but he also understands that "inane rote-learning could only have a damaging effect upon the powers of apprehension and retention."[68] There are allusions to the faultiness of such learning strategies through various scholarly characters in Cervantes's work. In particular, the Cousin in *Don Quixote* is an excellent example of the perils of excessive memorization, as I demonstrate in chapter 4, "Information Overload: Stocking Memory in the Age of Cervantes." The Cousin symbolizes how the ever-increasing number of books led to official intents to regulate and control knowledge by imposing new directions in logic and dialectics. During the expansion of Renaissance humanism, the various techniques derived from the *ars memorativa* were utilized to help make sense of the proliferation of texts and new information. Techniques like alphabetizing and indexing prompted the brain to memorize and retain concepts in order to structure knowledge and catalogue memories in much the same way as a library orders its collections. Hence, in *Don Quixote,* when the narrator and his friend discuss how to include a list of authors in the prologue, they opt for alphabetization, just as most Renaissance humanists might: "para ponerlos al principio, como hacen todos, por las letras del abecé, comenzando en Aristóteles y acabando en Xenofonte y en Zoílo o Zeuxis."[69] The problem, as I show in this chapter, is that some scholars like the Cousin have abandoned the rigorous pursuit and publication of original research in favour of printing encyclopedic-type texts that contain fairly useless information – yet these compendia were widely consulted since they were readily available and easy to use. The irrelevant knowledge the Cousin promotes adds to the proliferation of printed materials without really advancing erudition, a situation that Cervantes seems to detest. In this context, the Cousin is representative of the student whose excessive memorization of worthless details becomes a commentary on the questionable pedagogical practices at universities.

In connection with the pedagogical ramifications of memory in Cervantes's time, memory represented past experience and was also the foundation upon which future decisions could be made, converting memory into the basis for knowledge.[70] If one knew to prudently use his past experience, it was believed he could correctly make use of future action to improve his person and society. Pliny expressed it in the following way in his *Historia natural de los animales*:

> Es la memoria una facultad del alma noble y de grande valor por ser la guarda de los tesoros del hombre, que son las ciencias y dotrina que adquiere. Y assí dize Quintiliano: "¿De qué aprovechara aprender si no huviera memoria de lo aprendido?" La memoria haze a los hombres prudentes, sabios, discretos y recatados, porque en ella, como en un archivo, está la esperiencia provechosa y la ciencia saludable.[71]

Memory was therefore considered an essential aptitude for the noble soul of prudent and wise men. It was esteemed for being "guarda de los tesoros del hombre"[72] and was necessary to pursue virtuous action and high deeds. According to Cicero in *De inventione,* memory was closely associated with prudence, one of four moral virtues (along with *iustitia, fortitudo,* and *temperantia*), which allowed one to make wise and moral judgments and plan future action effectively:

> Prudence is the knowledge of things which are good, or bad, or neither good nor bad. Its parts are memory, intelligence, and foresight. Memory is

> therefore that faculty by which the mind recovers the knowledge of things which have been. Intelligence is that by which it perceives what exists at present. Foresight is that by which anything is seen to be about to happen, before it does happen.[73]

The idea of memory as it appears in *De inventione* later would be adopted by theologians to develop a Christian idea of prudence as seen in Saint Augustine's *Confessions*, Thomas Aquinas's *Summa Theologica*, and Albertus Magnus's *De bono*. These authors considered the role of experience – and therefore memory – fundamental to the moral construction of the individual. Their legacy of medieval scholastic memory would endure in Cervantes's time in the concept of "trinidad del alma," previously described in Saint Augustine's *De Trinitate*. For Saint Augustine, memory is part of the spiritual triad along with intellect (*intelligentia*, *cogitatio*) and will (*voluntas*, *providentia*), which, together, were considered a symbol of the Trinity's essence (Father-Son-Holy Spirit). This very same tripartite division of the faculties of the soul can be found in quite a varied list of writings. For example, in a letter to Philip IV, Sor María de Jesús de Ágreda referred to the trinity as a legal court formed in the interior;[74] Bartolomé Jiménez Patón, in his *Elocuencia*, speaks of the crucial role of the faculties of the soul, intellect, will, and memory. Within the triad, Saint Teresa de Jesús refers to memory as something that appears suddenly – a "mariposilla importuna"[75] – and in *La cuna y la sepultura*, Francisco de Quevedo considers memory a faculty "necessaríssima."[76]

As John Weiger has demonstrated, Cervantes, like many Western writers, inherited the legacy of the metaphorical representation of the triad[77] that "underlies much of Cervantes's portrayal of the human struggle for self-realization."[78] References to the three faculties of the soul appear over and over throughout his work. Notice how each of their functions is described in *La Galatea* with a clear moral purpose: "la memoria sólo sirve de tesorera y guardadora del objecto que los ojos miraron, y el entendimiento en escudriñar y conocer el valor de la que bien ama, y la voluntad de consentir de que la memoria y entendimiento en otra cosa no se ocupen."[79] The soul's three faculties were part of teachings that connected to a conduct that reflected moral character. It therefore comes as no surprise that, according to Carruthers, memory was considered a trope of saints' lives that marked their superior moral character.[80] For that reason, theologians and church officials normally characterized the saints as grander individuals because of their exceptional memory. In fact, people with exceptional memories were not only held up as great personages in history, but their mnemonic ability was also viewed as a distinctive mark of that same superior moral character.[81] Training memory was therefore not only a way to improve the means to write or talk properly – as seen above – but also a way to build "character, judgment, citizenship, and piety."[82] Consequently, possessing a superior memory was a mark of celebrated individuals throughout history who had reached their fame through their gifts of remembering:

> La memoria, bien grandemente necessaria a la vida, dificultosamente se puede dezir en quién aya sido mayor, pues muchos han alcançado por ella famosa gloria. El rey Ciro nombró a todos los soldados de su exército por sus nombres, y Lucio Scipión a todos los del pueblo romano. Cincas, embaxador del rey Pirro, el segundo día que estuvo en Roma saludó al senado y a la orden de cavallería nombrando a cada uno por su nombre. Mitridates, rey de veinte y dos naciones, tratando de su administración, en un razonamiento los habló en otras tantas lenguas sin tener intérprete alguno. En Grecia, uno llamado Carneades recitó, como si lo fuera leyendo, los volúmenes de libros que qualquiera autor avía compuesto.[83]

It was common practice in Cervantes's time to enumerate historical figures who became known for their gift of memory, demonstrating once again the importance placed on this ability. In many cases it was held that those who enjoyed an excellent memory were also well behaved. We can point to the example of the protagonist in *El licenciado Vidriera*, whose "felice memoria" made him famous in the university:

> [S]e hizo tan famoso en la universidad, por su buen ingenio y notable habilidad, que de todo género de gentes era estimado y querido. Su principal estudio fue de leyes; pero en lo que más se mostraba era en letras humanas; y tenía tan felice memoria que era cosa de espanto, e ilustrábala tanto con su buen entendimiento, que no era menos famoso por él que por ella.[84]

A similar idea is visible in many treatises and manuals of the period that were designed to teach and train the individual to exercise correct conduct. Perhaps no writer is as clear on this topic as Fadrique Furió Ceriol, who, in the first chapter of *El concejo y consejeros del príncipe* (1559), emphasizes that anyone who advises the prince "con que mejor i más fácilmente se le acuerde de lo passado, entienda lo presente, provea en lo por venir … Es el Concejo para con el Príncipe como casi todos sus sentidos, su entendimiento, su memoria, sus ojos, sus oídos, su boz, sus pies i manos."[85] There are traces of this idea in the advice that Don Quixote gives Sancho before the latter's departure to become Governor of Barataria, a passage in which the use of the word "memory" is constant. As Egido reminds us in reference to this episode, the "memoria de las cosas pasadas" is not only playing out in the mind of the protagonist as he constructs an aristocratic ethos[86] but also in the rest of the characters,[87] and even in Cervantes himself.[88]

Throughout Cervantes's fiction, characters consistently shape their actions in light of their memories and show unusual agility and promptness at remembering. Humillos recites prayers from memory in *La elección de los alcaldes de Daganzo*; Teolinda recalls poetic verses from Artidoro's song in *La Galatea* when "los tomé tan en la memoria que aun hasta agora no se me han olvidado."[89] Preciosa remembers verses from her first encounter with Clemente: "Desde la vez primera que llegaste a nuestro aduar te conocí, Clemente, y se me vinieron a la memoria los versos que en Madrid me diste."[90] In *El juez de los divorcios*, Doña Guiomar laments her spouse's attempts to be a poet who "está haciendo un soneto en la memoria para un amigo que se le ha pedido."[91] There are sonnets that "no se pasan de la memoria,"[92] such as the one Avendaño hears in *La ilustre fregona*. In *Los trabajos de Persiles y Sigismunda*, verses are sung from memory, and Periandro automatically knows the aphorisms by heart. The same happens in *La gran sultana* when Madrigal is proud to admit that he knew a few versos "bien de memoria."[93] In *Don Quixote* many characters appear who recite poems that they "toman de memoria," such as the Cousin or even Don Quixote himself, who composes poetry in his spare time: "en el tiempo que falta de aquí al día daré rienda a mis pensamientos y los desfogaré en un madrigalete que, sin que tú lo sepas, anoche compuse en la memoria."[94] The knight also knows verbatim a number of *romances* such as the one he recites to his neighbour "del mismo modo que había leído la historia en *La Diana*."[95] For his part, the Innkeeper is viewed as a community representative who easily "leía" chivalric romances, thanks to his prodigious memory.

The convergence between orality and writing is also seen in lexical ambivalences of verbs used to refer to what was understood as "reading" at the time. In this regard, Margit Frenk[96] argues that in early modern Spain, "no existía una gran diferencia entre la lectura de un texto registrado en el papel y la de uno guardado en la memoria."[97] This is clearly seen in the title of chapter 66 in *Don Quixote*, "Que trata de lo que verá el que lo leyere o lo oirá el que lo escuchare leer."[98] Thus, one could read a text on paper but also read a text registered in memory.[99] This distinction is therefore key to signalling the existence of both forms of memorization of a text, both existing in Europe before and after the appearance of the printing press. Examples of this process are verbs such as *leer* and *decir* used interchangeably: verses "se dicen de memoria" and texts also "se leían de memoria." Likewise, the etymology of the verb *leer*, from the Latin *lego*, establishes interesting connections with the processes of memory. Carruthers has rightly observed that the Latin verb meant "to collect" or "to select," just as one remembers or "collects" the material in memory.[100] This same distinction also existed during the early modern period. For example, among the many meanings that Sebastián Covarrubias attributes to the verb *leer*, there is that of "enseñar alguna disciplina públicamente," knowing that the one who teaches does so using what he has in memory.

In any case, the ability to recall quotes, legends, poems, or stories depends on one's memory. In the prologue to his thirteenth volume of his *comedias*, the playwright Lope de Vega complained of "poetas duendes" who steal his work: "estos que llama el vulgo, al uno, Memorilla, y al otro, Gran Memoria: los cuales con algunos versos que aprenden, mezclan infinitos suyos bárbaros, con que ganan la vida, vendiéndolas a los pueblos, y autores extra muro, gente vil, sin oficio."[101] Judging by Lope's complaints, the reality in the theatre world was that more than one of his verses was stolen outright based solely on the thief's ability to memorize. Here one must remember that theatregoers and other writers would only have access to the spoken verses by attending the play in question – scripts were not distributed in written form. Such a complaint should not be surprising in a culture still dominated by the oral tradition where memory was paramount for accomplishing just about anything. Lope de Vega thus denounced the effects brought about by the vestiges or orality where memory converted his theatrical parts into a currency of changeable objects that were subject to great transformation and variation by others. The residual of orality that "deforma" the work of the celebrated dramatist is an excellent example of what Frenk qualified as a contradiction of an "época de transición entre la cultura de la voz, la memoria, la variación y la cultura de la lectura silenciosa, del olvido, del texto fijo."[102] In a period when going to the theatre meant to "oír comedias," the prominence of orality reveals a culture in which people necessarily memorized what they heard.

Frenk attributes this wonder regarding memorization in part to the enthusiasm for chivalric romances.[103] The infamous case of Román Ramírez is one illustration of this phenomenon. This *morisco* from Deza drew on his astonishing memory to recite chivalric tales with incredible detail: "tomaba en la memoria ... la sustancia de las aventuras y los nombres de las ciudades, reinos, caballeros y princesas ... y después, cuando lo recitaba, alargaba y acortaba en las raçones cuanto quería."[104] His skill drew suspicion from those who believed the ability must be otherworldly, and he was accused of sorcery by the Inquisition. However, Ramírez did not recall these stories verbatim but rather imitated their content, style, and vocabulary and essentially created his own version that was so close to the original that no one knew the difference. Alonso de Fuentes, a fanatical reader of *Palmerín de Olivia,* claimed that he had more or less memorized the narrative: "lo sabía de cabeza."[105] Such an ability seemed to be fairly widespread. In *Las fortunas de Diana*, Lope writes to Marcia Leonarda that many learned men knew these chivalric stories from memory and did not recall ever seeing them written down: "Estos se sabían de memoria, y nunca, que yo me acuerde, los vi escritos."[106] If *Palmerín* and other chivalric books could be memorized easily enough, there is little doubt that less complex and shorter genres such as short stories, poetry, or letters could be easily memorized, too.[107] In *Don Quixote*, Sancho came to know the crux of some verses from the *Romancero* after hearing them only once – when they were recited to Don Quixote:

> – Pues en verdad – respondió Sancho – que he oído yo decir a mi señor,
> que es zahorí de las historias, contando aquella de Lanzarote,
> cuando de Bretaña vino,
> que damas curaban de él,
> y dueñas del su rocino.[108]

The oral was a therefore significant vehicle for the transmission of memory through songs, poems, sayings, popular expressions, and stories, and the subjectivity of memory becomes important in Sancho's development.

Therefore, any discussion of memory in the Renaissance also requires some examination of the oral tradition and the socialization of memory. What we know, however, is that memory will not always be so faithful. Sancho, for example, continuously reconfigures and adjusts what he remembers throughout the novel, which reflects not only the malleability of memory when it has a particular finality or personal interest but also the fact that memory can be altered by external forces. This is the subject of chapter 5, "Disputes over Memory: Sancho and the Artful Manipulation of Memory," which examines how Sancho organizes, interprets, and narrates the past and how this individual process is subject to social forces to the extent that memory becomes a game of manipulation. In Sancho's case, his memory is impacted by a series of circumstances such as his socio-economic condition as a labourer, his illiteracy, his status as an "old Christian," his unyielding desire to reach his governorship, the influence of other people upon him, as well as the intricate relationship with the oral culture from which he hails – all of which demand that he recall experiences in a certain way. Individual memory is therefore a practice nourished by the surrounding culture and subject to it.[109] As I discuss in this chapter, and drawing again on Greenblatt's observation about Renaissance self-fashioning, the fabrication and manipulation of memories to favour Sancho's intentions parallels an ongoing ethical and pragmatic debate on memory by writers such as Lucas Gracián, Jiménez Patón, and Antonio de Guevara.

Aware that memory was delicate and susceptible to loss, Cervantes's fiction also breaks with the traditional accounts of memory by weaving forgetfulness and forgetting into his characterization of memory. At a time when people experienced massive information overload, remembering became the subject of multiple social anxieties. Within this social paradigm, in a culture where remembering the past becomes an obsession, forgetting and avoidance likewise will have an important function. It is ironic that a novel based on earlier chivalric novels begins with a protagonist who has forgotten his past. Indeed, we know very little about Don Quixote's previous life precisely because, ironically, he forgets most of it. But by forgetting, he constructs and enriches a new identity – his forgetfulness is therefore not without intention. In the epilogue, "Lete and the Laws of Oblivion: Sites of Forgetting in *Don Quixote*," I explore the reasons behind the intentional cases of oblivion throughout the novel, how they serve as examples of the construction of the self, and what impact social practice has on that construction. As I demonstrate, just as memory is at the core of writing history(-ies), oblivion also is central. This notion was advanced by writers in the period such as Juan Velázquez de Azevedo, whose *El Fénix de Minerva y Arte de Memoria* (1626) included a lesson under the title "Del olvido" ("On Forgetfulness") that declared that forgetting was necessary for the correct functioning of memory.[110] Memory is fragile, and its resultant relative value makes it crucial for knowledge while also subject to constant alteration due to forgetting. Just as memory plays a critical role in the novel, so does forgetfulness.

Challenging the principles of verisimilitude and Aristotelian truth that had long been attributed to history writing, throughout the pages of *Don Quixote*, Cervantes stresses the volatile nature of memory. The novel shows that the personal filter of memory is negotiable, making any text that claims to be historical mere fiction. Examples of this tension between fiction and history abound in the novel and are continuously confronted with the real and perceived functions of memory, starting with the very first sentence, "En un lugar de la Mancha de cuyo nombre no quiero acordarme." The opening reminds the reader that the novel is nothing more than methodically selected and ordered material subject to memory's filter.

Chapter 1

The Anatomy of Early Modern Memory

In the year 1030, a Bavarian monk named Arnold was sent by his abbot on a trip to Pannonia, a province of the Roman Empire near the Danube. In his written account of the trip, Arnold describes having the unusual experience of encountering a flying dragon with a head the size of a mountain and a body covered with scales. According to the monk's narration of his experience, the dragon remained in sight for at least three hours and then fled at a great speed disappearing in the distance.[1] This millennial story, almost straight out of a chivalric novel, is recounted by psychologist Schacter in his book *Searching for Memory* to illustrate a defining and fascinating aspect of memory still valid today – its constructive nature:

> Arnold's memory of the giant dragon emerged gradually as he thought about his experience in the context of religious texts and precepts and as he related it to the widely held beliefs of his contemporaries about the meaning and significance of dragons. In other words, Arnold probably did encounter a large bird or creature of some sort of his trip, but *his final memory took time to construct from an assortment of cues and beliefs that saturated his retrieval environment.*[2]

As the psychologist explains, Arnold's memory of the dragon is a fabrication, "an imaginative invention that incorporates information from the present as Arnold tries to make sense of what happened in the past."[3] The monk's inventive creation emphasizes that remembering is a subjective process dependent upon both the existing retrieval setting and a wide variety of other determinant factors. In Arnold's case, his environment was completely full of texts, cultural references, and philosophical and religious ideas about dragons, which actually drove him to purposefully recall a similar creature during his trip. In other words, the context of the present led him to construct a coherent narrative of his past experience that he confidently boasted as accurate.

This very subjective experience of remembering similarly can be found in Don Quixote's fabrication and adaptation of his own memories throughout the novel. Just as Arnold incorporated information from his surroundings to make sense of the past, the knight compiles stories from fragments and previously read texts, to which he adds his own "cues and beliefs" to make sense of his present. In fact, whenever the knight emulates his models, the reader witnesses a recurring pattern: the combined power of memory and imagination engage with his past readings to inscribe new elements upon his current experience and circumstances. Consider, for example, the way he constructs Maritornes, the Asturian servant woman at the inn who the narrator describes as short, hunched-over, and wide in the body and face. In Don Quixote's mind, images of the various courtly ladies he has read about are stored in memory and play a pivotal role in the construction of the appearance of Maritornes and, as a result, "finalmente, él la pintó en su imaginación, de la misma traza y modo, que había leído en sus libros."[4] In yet another example, when the knight is insistently looking for a name for his horse, he once again refers back to his readings and determines that his steed, having the same high attributes as the horses of his fictional heroes, deserves a title as appropriate and high sounding as the heroic horses from those chivalric tales: "Y así, después de muchos nombres que formó, borró y quitó, añadió, deshizo y tornó a hacer *en su memoria e imaginación*, al fin le vino a llamar 'Rocinante.'"[5] These are among the many instances when the reader witnesses how the formidable combination of imaginative invention and memory drives Don Quixote's behaviour.

It was widely believed that the human being possessed fragile but powerful memories that also had great flexibility and creativity.[6] The examples above serve as a reflection of the workings of the early modern brain, the organ where memory and imagination – two of the three revered internal senses during Cervantes's time – work together to make sense of past experience in the act of recollection. The fine line between memory and imagination was part of an ongoing debate during the early modern period when theorists argued whether memory alone was responsible for recall or whether imagination was needed to reconstruct the past. Much of this debate is still unfolding today. As the neurologist Oliver Sacks states in *The River of Consciousness*, memory cannot straightforwardly record events, and so memories are constructed subjectively by the individual. As a result, according to Sacks, the only truth that can be attributed to our past experience is narrative truth: that is, the stories we tell each other that are continually modified over time:

> There is no way by which the events of the world can be directly transmitted or recorded in our brains, they are experienced and constructed in a highly subjective way, which is different in every individual to begin with, and differently reinterpreted and reexperienced whenever they are recollected. Our only truth is narrative truth, the stories we tell each other and ourselves, the stories we continually recategorize and refine.[7]

For Sacks, narrating the past, which assumes some level of fiction, is the only possible approach to "what happened," and in *Don Quixote* this is accomplished by numerous different characters and narrators who (re) tell their past. In order to make sense of past experiences in the constructions of the self, their stories are constantly refined through a very subjective process of recollection that likewise reflects memory's inner operations, which are replete with traps and ellipses. And ultimately, this process reflects the way in which the main story is being narrated in the novel.

As a writer so interested in the psychology of his characters and the construction of their identities, Cervantes witnessed with eagerness the expanding studies on the workings of the mind and, more specifically, the theories on how memory functioned, which was deemed essential for the understanding of human subjectivity.[8] A product of a classical education that included rhetorical training on how to bend memory to one's will, the changing times required new methods for coping with personal experience. Through his travels across the Mediterranean world that included stints in Italy, imprisonment in Spain, and a dreadful captivity in North Africa, Cervantes witnessed first-hand how important memory was in the construction of the self. He understood how the inner workings of the mind convert the impressions of the external world into memories that are key for identity formation. Hence, more than other writers of the time, Cervantes seemed attentive to early modern theories involving the brain and psychology, and he sought to develop a higher degree of consciousness in his characters that reinforced the idea of the modern man.

The writer's fictional works are concerned with a very fundamental question of the time: how the mind converts sensations and experiences into memories and how the resultant experience of one individual differs from that of someone else.[9] Most of the cognitive theories embraced by Cervantes's contemporaries came from ancient philosophers and physicians such as Plato, Aristotle, Galen, and Hippocrates, among others.[10] As part of their legacy, memory in the process of cognition was considered to have both intellectual and somatic status.[11] The ancients' observations on memory, its fragility and partialness, and the difference between the processes of memory (*mnēme*) and recollection (*anamnēsis*) were influenced and consequently affected by human physiology. Defining memory's psychosomatic quality and mapping its inner operations became essential undertakings in the works of prominent doctors and intellectuals during the Renaissance.[12] This understanding of human subjectivity is amply demonstrated in *Don Quixote*, where the main protagonist is a case study for how the human being possessed fragile but potent memories that were essential for great creativity but that could also cause physical changes. The knight is an example of the fascination with the processes of cognition and the physical operations of memory. In particular, melancholy, caused by an imbalance or dyscrasia in the humours, was believed to influence the workings of memory and, by relation, imagination. In *Don Quixote*, the two interior faculties, imagination and memory, are exploited as powerful tools that will help the main protagonist detach himself from society's impositions. This intrinsic correlation between the intellectual and the somatic in the workings of memory will be pivotal in the construction of the character of Don Quixote, as I will develop in the pages that follow.

Cervantes and the Early Modern Mind

Early modern Spanish medical treatises enjoyed prestige and recognition across Europe,[13] and, as with so many areas of science, Cervantes likely was familiar with them through different channels.[14] What can be gleaned from the historical record is that the writer may have been knowledgeable about the early modern conceptions of body and mind from personal study and from family and friends.[15] First, at least five members of Cervantes's immediate family held positions in various medical fields.[16] His grandfather, Juan Díaz de Torreblanca, and his father, Rodrigo de Cervantes, were medical practitioners, and his sister, Andrea de Cervantes, was a nurse. Cervantes also had a number of acquaintances in various medical fields, such as Francisco Díaz, a professor at the University of Alcalá, whose study of urology, *Tratado de todas las enfermedades de los riñones, vexiga y carnosidades de la verga y orina* (1588), included a sonnet by Cervantes. Another close friend was the doctor Alonso López "el Pinciano." El Pinciano was an adept translator of the *Aphorisms* by the Greek physician Hippocrates[17] and was strongly influenced by the ideas of Aristotle and Huarte de San Juan.[18] Another of Cervantes's acquaintances, Antonio Ponce de Santa Cruz, served as a professor at the University of Valladolid and as a doctor in the court of Philip III and Philip IV. Furthermore, it is very likely that Cervantes had a close relationship with Dionisio Daza Chacón, an army doctor charged with the care of Charles V and Philip II, who later became John of Austria's physician. Daza Chacón's *Práctica y teórica de la cirugía en romance y latín* (1580) was held by the writer in his personal library.[19] It is possible that his father's friendships with the doctor Gil Verte and the humanist Juan de Vergara also influenced the writer.

Cervantes's friends and family were not the only ones exerting an influence on his medical knowledge. It is well known that the writer frequently visited the Hospital of Innocents in Seville and the Hospital of Orates in Valladolid, indicating an interest in mental illnesses, their symptoms, and their imbalances. The hospital in Valladolid housed not only mentally disabled people but also disturbed criminals and members of less-favoured classes whom Cervantes portrays in his novels alongside abundant references to mental insanity. He utilizes mental illness as both a literary strategy and a social criticism, not only with his best-known character in *Don Quixote* but also with other secondary characters (Cardenio, Anselmo, Basilio) and those in other narratives such as *El celoso extremeño* or *El licenciado Vidriera*. Different sorts of clinical cases are also abundant in his work, especially those related to mental illness. In this regard, the neurologists José Alberto Palma and Fermín Palma have approached *Don Quixote* from a neurological point of view to demonstrate that there exist copious references associated with a variety of mental issues and the inner workings of the brain: tremors (I, 27; I, 43; II, 32), dream disorders (I, 8; I, 48; I, 1; II, 54; I, 35), neuropsychiatric symptoms (I, 8; II, 32; I, 45), dementia (I, 1; II, 23; I, 7; I, 7, II, 1, II, 1; II, 18), epilepsy (II, 47; I, 20), paralysis (II, 47; II, 19), cerebrovascular diseases, syncopes (I, 21; I, 34; II, 46; II, 53), brain injuries (I, 17; I, 45; II, 60), migraines (II, 2; I, 17), and other compulsive-type mental disorders, such as the *pica*[20] (I, 33).

Cervantes also owned a collection of medical-related books that he inherited from his physician father. These treatises and technical works referenced the emerging interest in Spain and Europe in the operations of the body and mind. According to Daniel Eisenberg, among the 214 volumes that the writer owned in his personal library, there were several well-known medical treatises such as *Libro de las cuatro enfermedades cortesanas* (1544) by Lobera de Ávila, Charles V's doctor; *Práctica y theórica de la cirugía en romance y latín* (1582) by Daza Chacón, mentioned above; the *Practica in Arte Chirurgica Copiosa* (1514) by Giovanni de Vigo, Pope Julio II's surgeon; the aforementioned *Tratado nuevamente impreso de todas las enfermedades de los riñones, vexiga y carnosidades de la verga* (1588) by Francisco Díaz, Philip II's surgeon; and the annotated and commented translation of *De materia medica* by the Greek physician Pedanious Dioscorides, translated by the humanist doctor Andrés Laguna. Among the many reference works Cervantes probably owned, Dioscorides's is the only work he cited, and among its many remedies were herbs and drugs to enhance memory that were very common at the time, such as the intake of raisins and almonds, which the ensign Campuzano mentions in *El casamiento engañoso.* Cervantes likely was mindful of how medicine emphasized the presence of the body and the medicalization of memory, both of which were the subject of numerous treatises of the time, such as that of Álvarez de Miraval, who emphasized the role of physical and psychological dispositions and the therapeutics of memory that boost or weaken recollection. Lastly, the treatise that most influenced Cervantes is Huarte's *Examen de ingenios* (1575), a copy of which Cervantes owned. As we shall see throughout this study, Huarte will exert considerable influence on Cervantes's conception of his protagonist, particularly with respect to the role of memory and how it shapes cognitive and bodily processes that conform to the cultural perception of memory during the early modern period.[21] Furthermore, following Huarte, Cervantes's novel reflects a persistent concern with the proper function of memory as a powerful device for understanding subjectivity.

The Topography of the Early Modern Brain

At the outset of the Renaissance in Spain, aided by the advent and rapid advancements in printing, a number of medical treatises and essays such as those mentioned above circulated across Europe, fueling increased interest in the human condition. Physicians and philosophers alike came to know the various prevailing theories that described human physiology and the functions of the brain, and many set out to add to the scholarship with their own work. Cervantes, it seems to me, shared these interests, not least of all because of the sheer number of medical personnel in his family or the texts he owned or may have consulted. Throughout the pages of *Don Quixote*, an impressive array of topics related to medicine are central, some of which have been explored by a number of scholars in recent years. The novel reflects a particular interest in the anatomical makeup of the brain, the inner processes that unfold therein, and how they impact the psychological development of characters. More specifically and for the purpose of this study, there is an emphasis on understanding and reflecting on the role of the senses in forming memories, how memories are stored and the process for their retrieval, and how remembering can have a physical impact on individuals. In the sections that follow, I review the major medical treatises written during the period that describe memory functions as part of a complex process of storage and retrieval accomplished through imaginative reconstruction. Therefore, the many contemporaneous theories and theorists explored here provide the underlying basis for *Don Quixote*'s impressive engagement with the function of memory.

Cervantes must have had at least a working knowledge about the mind and the processes of perception and cognition, as described in the books that proliferated on the topography of the brain and which he held among his possessions.[22] It is also likely that he was familiar with at least one of the many popular illustrations that pictorially unraveled the mechanisms of the brain, such as the one found in the compilation *Margarita Philosophica* (1503) by the German humanist writer Gregor Reisch. These anatomical drawings were representative of a multitude of similar diagrammatic images during the time that illustrate the structure of the brain and its division into *cellae, ventricles,* or compartments.[23] The illustrations circulated widely in Europe, and in most cases such illustrations divided the brain into three sections, representing the three main faculties or internal senses – *imaginativa* (imagination), *estimativa* (intellect), and *memorativa* (memory) – which, together, were deemed responsible for carrying out the main cognitive functions of the brain.[24] One well-known illustration by the German doctor Hieronymus Brunschwig depicted how the five external senses (sight, sound, smell, touch, and taste) captured sensorial impressions that converged at the *sensus comunis,*[25] the receptor of all sense impressions, so that they could be processed by the interior senses. Brunschwig's illustration of sensorial processes affected many other theorists such that his interpretation became something of a standard understanding of how these processes worked.

In early modern Spain, illustrations and descriptions of the brain featuring the three ventricles and the senses were key forms of considering cognitive function. One of these was Olivia de Sabuco, the naturalist and daughter of the apothecary Miguel de Sabuco. In *Nueva filosofía de la naturaleza del hombre, no conocida ni alcanzada de los grandes filósofos antiguos, la qual mejora la vida, y la salud humana* (1587), she summarizes the sensorial process by emphasizing the concomitant connection between the external and internal senses:

> Entran las especias de las cosas de este mundo por los cinco sentidos, y representándolas al sentido común, que es la primera celda de sesos en la frente: y allí el entendimiento juzga lo presente, y dice a la voluntad, malo

> o bueno es, y en la estimativa (que es la segunda celda de la cabeza) juzga lo ausente sacando las especias de la tercera celda (que es la memoria donde han estado guardadas las especies de lo pasado) y allí juzga lo que está ausente, y dice a la voluntad, malo o bueno es: y luego la voluntad se mueve a querer aquella noticia o aborrecerla, y luego que la voluntad lo manda se mueven los miembros que lo han de hacer. Para tomar una manzana pasa todo esto en vos por la vista, y para comerla por el gusto.[26]

Sabuco fortuitously drafts the early modern psychophysiological theory governing the interrelationship between the external and internal senses as a dynamic, active, and riveting process. Describing the workings and intricacies of the "sesos" and mapping the functions of the internal senses became important undertakings for many scholars, as seen in the work of prominent Spanish physicians and intellectuals. Building on Sabuco's observations, Huarte similarly describes the close connection between external and internal senses. Drawing on ancient philosophers and physicians such as Plato, Aristotle, Galen, and Hippocrates,[27] Huarte will provide one of the most important descriptions of the process of cognition:

> Vese esto claramente en la facultad animal, la cual hace varias obras en los sentidos exteriores por tener cada uno su peculiar compostura: una tienen los ojos, otra los oídos, otra el gusto, otra el olfato y otra el tacto … De este manifiesto y claro que pasa en los sentidos exteriores podemos colegir lo que hay más allá dentro en los interiores. Con esta misma virtud animal entendemos, imaginamos y nos acordamos.[28]

For Huarte, the cognitive process was based on the coalescence of the three internal faculties noted above: *imaginativa, estimativa,* and *memorativa,* respectively. He and most other physicians during the time believed that the three faculties worked independently but together, they formed the basis for understanding how people recall the past.

After seemingly deciphering the function of the sensorial process in human cognition, specialists also sought to identify the physical location where these processes were carried out. The most poignant theory was advanced by Alonso de Fuentes in his *Suma de filosofía natural* (1547), where he describes the location of the internal senses as housed in "cámaras": "En nuestra cabeça ay tres cámaras y una de ellas en la frente, y otra en medio, la otra en el colodrillo."[29] These "cámaras" appear in *Don Quixote* in allusions to "aposentos de la cabeza"[30] or "camaranchones del celebro."[31] Some of the characters are quite aware of having "celebros" or "sesos," such as when Don Quixote speaks of his "cascos" or "sesos" melting: "parece que se me ablandan los cascos o se me derriten los sesos."[32] There are also references in the novel to the posterior part of the brain known as "colodrillo,"[33] where *memorativa* was located and to the "últimos retretes del secreto,"[34] which indicate general knowledge of the location of the internal senses and the physical presence of memory. *Memorativa* therefore would commonly be located in the last of the three cells, therefore occupying the final point along a path or process through the different ventricles of the brain. However, as Huarte states, occupying the last point in the path did not mean it was less important:

> [L]lamamos a la memoria potencia racional porque sin ella no va en nada el entendimiento ni la imaginativa. A todas da materia y figuras sobre qué silogizar, conforme aquel dicho de Aristóteles: *opertet intelligentem phantasmata speculari*. Y el oficio de la memoria es guardar estos fantasmas ... y si esta se pierde, es imposible poder las demás potencias obrar ... porque esta potencia es la que tiene la materia y los fantasmas sobre los que se ha de especular.[35]

Theorists' belief that they had identified how the senses functioned and where they were sheltered in the brain unified the physical and the psychological, which, in turn, gave memory a psychosomatic quality.

Given the belief in memory's mental and corporeal properties, references to the physical site of memory did not involve only the head or brain; they also were linked to another important organ, the heart.[36] According to Carruthers, Aristotle believed that "the two organs were involved in the production of memories: the heart, which received all externally-derived impressions, and the brain, to which this information was relayed and where it was stored."[37] Cervantes, evidently following Huarte, similarly sees the heart and the brain as commingling systems: "dándole a comer cosas confortativas y apropiadas *para el corazón y el celebro*, de donde procedía, según buen discurso, toda su mala ventura."[38] Equally important is how the writer uses "heart" as a metaphor for memory by encoding in words and expressions several allusions to the cardiocentric theory of memory. For example, "recordar" means to recollect, from the common Latin verb *recordari* (from *re* and *cor*) – literally, back to the heart. In other cases, the frequently used "saber de coro" (lat. *Cor, cordis*) denotes knowing, reciting, or saying by heart. In still other examples, words such as "cuerdo," "recordar," and "recuerdo" expose the Latin root of *cor* (heart), an expression similar to the English "by heart." Likewise, the word *pecho* is used equally as "chest" or "heart" to serve as a deposit or archive for memory: "si las ordenanzas y leyes de la caballería andante se perdiesen, se hallarían *en el pecho* de vuesa merced como en su mismo depósito y archivo."[39]

Memory and Recollection

Most of what was known about memory in early modern Spain came from Plato's and Aristotle's theories.[40] Both philosophers were aware of the fragility, partialness, and constructive nature of memory. Following his master, Socrates, Plato amplifies his theory on memory in important works such as *Meno, Phaedo,* and *Theaetetus,* in which he bestowed upon it a prominent intellectual role. Unlike Aristotle, who believed sensorial perception to be the source of knowledge, Plato posits that innate ideas are responsible; hence, as Socrates reminds Meno, all learning is in fact an act of recollection of the knowledge stored in the soul from a previous life:

> The soul, then, as being immortal, and having been born again many times, and having seen all things that exist, whether in this world or in the world below, has knowledge of them all; and it is no wonder that she should be able to call to remembrance all that she ever knew about virtue, and about everything; for as all nature is akin, and the soul has learned all things; there is no difficulty in her eliciting or as men say learning, out of a single recollection – all the rest, if a man is strenuous and does not faint; *for all enquiry and all learning is but recollection.*[41]

According to Plato, when one learns a new idea, the concept is actually being recalled and is then made to be one's own. The same process of "recollecting" or "recovering knowledge" appears again in *Phaedo*: "would not the process which we call learning really be recovering knowledge which is our own? And should we be right in calling this recollection?"[42] Plato's theory on the construction of memory became a referent in Cervantes's time, specifically in regards to the metaphor of memory as a block of wax, gift of Mnemosyne, the mother of the Muses,[43] where memories left their impression, although different from the original: "For do you really suppose that anyone would admit the memory which a man has of an impression which has passed away to be the same with that which he experienced at the time? Assuredly not."[44]

The metaphor of the block is used by Plato in *Theaetetus* and later by Aristotle in *De anima*[45] and more extensively in the latter's first monograph devoted exclusively to the theme of memory, *De memoria et reminiscentia*. In *Theaetetus* Plato proposes the metaphor of memory as a block of wax where impressions are stamped like a seal ring and where the surface of that wax is decisive for the quality and duration of the impression:

> Imagine ... that our minds contain a block of wax, which in this or that individual may be larger or smaller, and composed of wax that is comparatively pure or muddy, and harder in some, softer in others, and sometimes of just the right consistency ... Let us call it the gift of the Muses' mother, Memory, and say that whenever we wish to remember something we see or hear or conceive in our own minds, we hold this wax under the perceptions or ideas and imprint them on it as we might stamp the impression of a seal ring. Whatever is so imprinted we remember and know so long as the image remains; whatever is rubbed out or has not succeeded in leaving an impression we have forgotten and do not know.

According to Plato, memory is consequently a result of a variable individual experience that will determine how mental images are imprinted on the brain. When he refers to the block of wax being "larger," "smaller," "pure," "muddy," "harder," or "softer" or having "the right consistency," he metaphorically alludes to the importance of the physiology of the brain, which originates with Hippocrates and will continue until the 1700s.

It follows that once we have identified how the faculties process information and store it in physical locations in the brain, the next logical step in exposing how we remember is to consider how memories are retrieved. Aristotle makes a fundamental distinction between two important concepts, *mnēme* (memory) and *anamnesis* (recollection), to describe the process of retrieving memories and understanding their reconstructive nature. On the one hand, he considers memory (Greek *mnēme*/Latin *memoria*) as the capacity to store representations of events and things witnessed or learned; memory is also the space where the mental images resulting from the act of perception were located and where memorization also took place; on the other hand, recollection (Greek *anamnesis*/Latin *reminiscentia*) is the reconstructive process by which something is recalled through internal operations. For Aristotle, recollection is an active, intellectual process; memory is a passive, receiving one.[46] Recollection is the process by which one voluntarily seeks in memory what is to be remembered. Memory, on the other hand, is performed naturally and without effort. As I will discuss in this chapter, the active process of searching for a memory is an active reconstruction by which the originally stored memory is reproduced, but in an indirect and partial way.

As Aristotle notes, and Cervantes's contemporaries affirm, memories are reconstructions based on stored mental images: every sensorial perception ends up being an image or phantasm (*phantasmata*) in memory.[47] But, as the philosopher states in *De memoria et reminiscentia*, in the process of recollection, copies (*eikon*) of the object stored in the memory are drawn forth: "memory, even the memory of the objects of thought, is not without an image." However, this image is not an exact copy of what it represents, but rather just a partial fabrication, "like a sort of picture, the having of which we say is memory. For the change that occurs marks in a sort of imprint, as it were, of the sense image, as people do who seal things with signet rings."[48] Hence, the mental image, the "sort of imprint" on the memory, is just a copy of the object being recalled. The process is constructive in its nature, and the resulting image is subjective and partial. Aristotle outlined in this fashion the reconstructive aspect of memory that will evolve for centuries after.

These ideas were very influential in the early modern period. Consider as an illustration the distinction between memory and the reproduction of mental images that Velázquez de Azevedo outlines in *Fénix de Minerva o Arte de memoria* (1626):

> Cuanto a la primera [memoria], las imágenes o simulacros se ocasionan y originan principalmente de los sentidos exteriores, que reciben aquellas ideas o imágenes sensibles y por ellos, que sirven de acueductos, pasan a las estancias interiores que son sentido común y memoria, y allí se afirma y radican … En cuanto a la segunda [reminiscencia], no sólo recibe la memoria las ideas que le han ministrado los sentidos, sino las que habemos dicho que *imagina* y forma la cogitativa, la cual contemplando *las imágenes que están en la memoria, junta una con otra o saca y recoge otras nuevas de aquellas y estas después las vuelve a recibir la memoria.*[49]

Velázquez de Azevedo cannot be more precise in emphasizing the creative process that takes place when remembering where mental images from past experiences "juntan," "sacan," y "recogen otras nuevas." The fact that the process is described in terms of movement – "reciben," "pasan" – emphasizes its dynamism and transformative nature.

This distinction between memory as a passive and natural force and recollection as an active and subjective process will be key in understanding the use of memory in the novel. There is ample evidence that recollection has the capacity to give new form and meaning to the images that are previously stored. Throughout *Don Quixote*, the process first advanced by Aristotle and subsequently described by Velázquez de Azevedo is seen constantly at work, not only in the protagonist and his adaptation of his readings to his circumstances, but also in the characters who (re)tell – and consequently reconstruct – their past experiences through their narrations.

In these reconstructions, images are vital for Don Quixote's process of recollection emphasizing memory's visual quality. As represented in one of the most iconic illustrations of the character, the engraving *Don Quixote in His Library* by Gustave Doré,[50] his memory is overflowing with fictional deeds, heroes, maidens, giants, wizards, battles, and other numerous images – all of which are products of his extensive readings of more than three hundred chivalric books from his library.[51] For Don Quixote, recollection becomes a reconstructive process similar to an act of reading where his memories are not just "read" but also profoundly visualized. In this regard, and as Carruthers points out, the process of *anamnesis* (recollection) is in fact analogous to that of reading letters: "Because it recalls signs, reminiscence is an act of interpretation, inference, investigation, and reconstruction, an act like reading."[52] Similarly, the etymology of the verb *leer* shares a clear connection with the processes of memory; the Latin *lego* means "to collect" or "to select," just as when one remembers or "collects" the material already stored in memory. As an illustration of this analogy in the novel, after the destruction of Maese Pedro's *retablo* and the grief of the puppeteer, Don Quixote explains what went through his mind as the images retrieved were literally read "al pie de la letra":

> – Ahora acabo de creer – dijo a este punto don Quixote – lo que otras muchas veces he creído: que estos encantadores que me persiguen no hacen sino ponerme las figuras como ellas son delante de los ojos, y luego me las mudan y truecan en las que ellos quieren. *Real y verdaderamente os digo, señores que me oís, que a mí me pareció todo lo que aquí ha pasado que pasaba al pie de la letra*: que Melisendra era Melisendra, don Gaiferos don Gaiferos, Marsilio Marsilio, y Carlomagno Carlomagno.[53]

Don Quixote may blame the enchanters for his actions, but the language used in his own justification points to facts derived from the (re) construction and adaptation of the mental images from his readings and transferred to his present circumstances as he "reads" them in his memory.

Other characters in the novel similarly experience the effects of a potentially faulty *anamnesis*. A case in point is Cardenio, who voluntarily escapes to the Sierra Morena in an attempt to avoid the ill-fated memory of Luscinda. When he remembers "el cuento de sus desgracias" after the end of the disastrous relationship with his beloved, the act of recollection, of "traerlas a la memoria," is of no use to him other than "añadir otras de nuevo."[54] By adding new memories and emotions that modify the original experience, he emphasizes the act of recollection as a refined and constructed process affected by his present circumstances. Similar statements appear repeatedly throughout the novel when characters remember experiences and by doing so inescapably change the original memory. The same idea is pointed out once again by Cardenio, who, appealing to the malleable and capricious character of memory, interpolates the "cruel" faculty to represent the image of Luscinda according to "lo que entonces hizo" – which may help him forget her – and not according to her deceiving "incomparable belleza" – which strengthens the persistence of her memory and consequently his pain:

> ¡Oh memoria, enemiga mortal de mi descanso! ¿De qué sirve representarme ahora la incomparable belleza de aquella adorada enemiga mía? ¿No será mejor, cruel memoria, que me acuerdes y representes lo que entonces hizo, para que, movido de tan manifiesto agravio, procure, ya que no la venganza, a lo menos perder la vida?[55]

Cardenio's words bring up another important element to consider during the process: although memory and recollection are seemingly intellectual activities, they are nevertheless part of a larger bodily process as "enemiga mortal de mi descanso" and the impact that remembering exerts on the body, which Aristotle also highlights. According to the philosopher, because of their physical imprint – "a sort of imprint"[56] that leaves a mark – memories also were thought to generate physical changes or affects in the body[57] and vice versa, a point I turn to now.

The Psychosomatic Nature of Memory

In very simple terms, the physical trace of a memory, its imprint on the brain, depended on the softness of the organ. Softer tissue was believed to yield better imprints, which meant that a memory could be better reconstructed later. A crucial factor in the quality of the reconstruction was the individual's physiological constitution, which was believed to be affected by the bodily humours. Most physicians during the period held that all of the faculties were considerably affected by physiological conditions. In *Examen de ingenios*, Huarte, strongly influenced by Aristotle as well as by the physicians Hippocrates and Galen, depicts memory as "una blandura del cerebro, dispuesta con cierto género de humidad, para recibir y guardar lo que la imaginativa percibe, en la misma proporción que tiene el papel blanco y liso en el que ha de escribir."[58]

Huarte's description of the process as writing on paper aligned with the aforementioned idea of the wax tablet developed by Plato in *Theaetetus* and advanced by Aristotle in *De Anima*.[59] Huarte goes on to describe how the appropriate balance in temperature and humidity was necessary for a properly functioning brain:

> [C]uatro condiciones ha de tener el cerebro para que el ánima racional pueda con él hacer cómodamente las obras que son de entendimiento y prudencia. ... buena compostura ... que sus partes estén bien unidas ... que el calor no exceda a la frialdad, ni la humedad a la sequedad ... que la sustancia esté compuesta de partes sutiles y muy delicadas.[60]

The Spanish physician and his contemporaries believed that the human body and its humours conditioned the sensory perceptions, the workings of the internal senses, and subsequently the quality and retention of mental images. Humoural theory was widely embraced during the time as a means to understand the complexity of the brain functions and the process of perception and cognition. With its quaternary division of the four cosmic elements of water, air, earth, and fire corresponding to the four qualities of warm, dry, cool, and moist,[61] the doctrine of the humours established that certain combinations of cosmic elements with one or more qualities were said to yield a variety of phenomena and help characterize a person's general mental and physical state. The Greek physician Galen originally developed the theory with the aim of finding a physiological explanation for human behaviour. According to Galen, the four cosmic elements produce four humours: blood, yellow bile, black bile, and phlegm.[62] Galen classified the four humours according to the aforementioned qualities: blood was warm, phlegm was cool, yellow bile was dry, and black bile was wet. He believed that an excess or lack of the humours in the body (*krasis*) shaped human behaviour: a correct balance of humours (*eucrasia*) or an imbalance (*dyscrasia*) resulted in the four temperamental categories: sanguine, choleric, melancholic, and phlegmatic.

The brain played the central role in affecting the balance of humours and ultimately the processes of perception and cognition, which Sabuco explains in the following way: "La raíz y oficina de todos los humores, buenos y malos, es el cerebro."[63] According to the Hippocratic-Galenic tradition, dyscrasia yielded an imbalance in the brain that impacted all three faculties – intellect, imagination, and memory – but it was the case that two might be reinforced and the third weakened. Huarte, paraphrasing Galen's *De usu partium* XVII, describes the phenomenon with these words: "que cuando en la enfermedad se desbarata el temperamento y buena compostura del celebro, muchas veces se pierden las obras del entendimiento y quedan salvas las de la memoria y las de la imaginativa."[64] This cause-and-effect relation between the humours, their qualities, and the brain explains why the intellect, imagination, and memory would therefore strengthen or weaken at the mercy of these variations: "El ingenio puede diferenciarse por un mayor grado de sequedad en cuyo caso predominará el entendimiento; una mayor humedad para el predominio de la memoria o un mayor grado de calor lo que provocará una gran imaginación."[65] The excess of one humour over another – especially black bile or melancholy – would also explain how imagination and memory are sometimes favoured over intellect. This is clearly the case of Don Quixote as is evident in a well-cited passage from the novel in which the narrator gives full accounting of the knight's consideration of chivalry:

> Del poco dormir y del mucho leer, se le secó el cerebro, de manera que vino a perder el juicio. Llenósele la fantasía de todo aquello que leía en los libros, así de encantamentos como de pendencias, batallas, desafíos, heridas, requiebros, amores, tormentas y disparates imposibles; y asentósele de tal modo en la imaginación que era verdad toda aquella máquina de soñadas invenciones que leía, que para él no había otra historia más cierta en el mundo.[66]

As the narrator notes, Alonso Quijano's reading overexertion "dried up his brain," leading to an overactive imagination.[67] As Guillermo Serés states, the narrator plainly describes Alonso Quijano's situation as one related to an imbalance of the humours: "sólo la imaginativa está destemplada por exceso de sequedad, el entendimiento es el de un hombre prudentísimo. La analogía con el héroe cervantino salta a la vista; y no se trata, como dice Green, de una 'hypertrophy of the entendimiento' sino de una buena templanza de esta facultad, frente a la destemplanza de la otra."[68] For early modern physicians, a malfunctioning imagination meant a malfunctioning memory, the two faculties being so closely related. According to Aristotle, memory occupied the same part of the soul as imagination, and thus both were equally affected when a specific type of humoral unbalance occurred: "It is apparent, then, to which part of the soul memory belongs, namely the same part as that to which imagination belongs."[69] Galen also notes this very close relationship between imagination and memory in *De motu musculorum:* "La parte del alma que imagina, cualquiera que sea, es la misma que recuerda."[70] As an illustration of the correlation between the faculties, the terms "memory" and "imagination" are used equally throughout the novel, and oftentimes interchangeably in the same statement, such as when Sancho reminds Don Quixote about the enchanters: "Creo – respondió Sancho – que aquel Merlín o aquellos encantadores que encantaron a toda la chusma que vuestra merced dice que ha visto y comunicado allá bajo *le encajaron en el magín o la memoria* toda esa máquina que nos ha contado y todo aquello que por contar le queda."[71] Proof of the relationship between the faculties of memory and imagination is the indiscriminate use of both in the novel in expressions such as "al cual en aquel punto se le representó en su imaginación al vivo que aquélla era una de las aventuras de sus libros"[72] or when memories are kept in "el magín o la memoria."[73]

Don Quixote's Memory

It was believed that each temperament matched particular physiognomic traits and specific types of behaviour. As summarized by Mauricio de Iriarte, such combinations explain the physical description of Don Quixote: "alto de talla, largo de miembros, flaco pero recio, seco de carnes, huesudo y musculoso, rostro estirado y enjuto, el color moreno y amarillo, la nariz aguileña, lacio el cabello que antes fue negro y ahora entrecano, abundante vellosidad, venas abultadas, voz ronca; y en conjunto feo y mal entallado."[74] With respect to Don Quixote's psychological traits, as Iriarte notes, based on contemporaneous understanding of the humours, the knight's behaviour was due to an excess or lack of particular qualities that subsequently mark him as choleric and melancholic, which, in turn, impacted his physical well-being. *Melancholia* was widely considered the most representative cases of humoral imbalance during the period, and it exerted a powerful effect on memory and, by relation, on imagination. An excess of *melancholia*[75] was often linked to high-functioning ingenuity, *ingenio*, and it was highly venerated by intellectuals, doctors, and philosophers during the time. Some of the most well-known theories were based on the pseudo-Aristotelian theory found in his *Problemata*.[76] The *Problemata* XXX states that individuals affected by melancholy are prone to a hyper-developed imagination and *ingenio*, consequently relating the dominance of melancholy to philosophy, poetry, and the arts: "Why is it that all those who have become eminent in philosophy or politics or poetry or the arts are clearly of an atrabilious temperament, and some of them to such an extent as to be affected by diseases caused by black bile, as is said to have happened to Heracles among the heroes?"[77] Authors of the period often adopt such beliefs. For example, in Lope de Vega's *La prueba de los ingenios*, Florela refers to the character of the melancholics and the implicit connection to imagination: "Sequedad, melancolía, / acompañan la grandeza / del ingenio, aunque Galeno / estas partes diferencia: / melancolía con cólera / y sangre pura, gobiernan / los ingenios altamente."[78] Melancholy is therefore considered the most appropriate humour for a high-functioning *ingenio,* as seen in Tirso de Molina's *El Melancólico*: "Toda melancolía / ingeniosa, es un ramo de manía; / y no hay sabio que un poco / (si a Platón damos fe) no toque en loco."[79] Needless to say, this is also the case of the "caballero ingenioso," protagonist of Cervantes's novel.

In humoural theory it followed that melancholics like Don Quixote not only have a highly developed imagination but also a stronger-than-usual capacity for memory and particularly for recollection. In his *Rhetorica novissima* (1235), Boncompagno da Signa highlighted the effective memory of melancholics:[80] "Of the four humours, the sanguine and melancholic are the best for memory; melancholics in particular retain well owing to their hard and dry constitution."[81] Albertus Magnus's comment on *De memoria and reminiscentia* also mentioned the relationship and effects of the melancholic temper and memory: "According to the normal theory of humours, melancholy, which is dry and cold, was held to produce good memories, because the melancholic received the impressions of images more firmly and retained them longer than persons of other temperaments."[82] According to Yates, Albertus does not refer here to ordinary melancholy, but rather a different sort, the temperament of *reminiscibilitas*: "Thus the temperament of reminiscence is not the ordinary dry-cold melancholy which gives good memory; it is the dry-hot melancholy, the intellectual, the inspired melancholy."[83] Specifically, the excitability of the reminiscence is in itself the one that Aristotle talks about in his *Problemata* when referring to a type of melancholy *fumosa et fervens* and its effects on memory:

> Such as those who have an accidental melancholy caused by an adustation with the sanguine and choleric [temperaments]. The phastasmata move such men more than any others, because they are most strongly imprinted in the dry of the back part of the brain: and the heat of the *melancholia fumosa* moves these [phantasmata]. This mobility confers reminiscence which is investigation. The conservation in the dry holds many [phantasmata] out of which it [reminiscence] is moved.[84]

Curiously enough, Huarte cited section 1 of *Problemata* XXX sixty times in his works, which would explain Cervantes's possible knowledge of it in the design of a protagonist who suffers from excited reminiscence.[85]

Huarte speaks of three distinctive types of memory in relation to the capacities for memory and recollection, respectively. In the first place, the receptive (but little retentive); second, the retentive (but not very receptive); and finally, the type of memory that receives effortlessly and does not easily forget: "Hay memoria que recibe con facilidad y luego se le olvida; otra se tarda en percebir y lo retiene mucho tiempo; la tercera recibe con facilidad y tarda mucho en olvidar."[86] According to Huarte, having an effective memory depended on the existence of a series of specific conditions in the brain:

> [E]ra necesario que el cerebro tuviera blandura, porque las figuras se han de sellar en él por vía de comprensión y estando duro no podrían fácilmente señalar … [P]ara conservar las especies mucho tiempo, todos dicen que es necesario la dureza y sequedad, como parece en las cosas de fuera, que la figura está impresa en cosa blanda se borra con facilidad, pero en lo seco y duro jamás se pierde.[87]

These conditions explain why Huarte continues to talk about "los que tienen mucha reminiscencia son faltos de entendimiento y tienen gran imaginativa" – clearly Don Quixote's case. This particular aspect would explain why the protagonist stops *storing* memories related to his everyday life and his family's economic welfare: "que olvidó casi de todo punto el ejercicio de la caza, y aun la administración de su hacienda."[88] Instead, he is incapable of stopping the *recollection* of chivalric images. Due to the low humidity caused in large part by age, Don Quixote has little capacity to retain images from his personal life, but he has no problem recollecting those drawn from his books, which have provided a plethora of stories for his new existence. Huarte, paraphrasing Aristotle, explains the phenomenon with these words: "la memoria de los hombres mayores, que, llena de tantas cosas como han visto en el largo discurso de su vida, no les cabe más."[89]

Therefore, it can be said that Don Quixote cannot fit anything else in his memory, but his brain continually reviews the images that he has recollected and repeatedly re-associates them with new or different stimuli. In short, he possesses highly associative powers, a theory Aristotle outlines in *De memoria et reminiscentia* when discussing melancholic people who do not retain new images but who recollect existing ones without control:

> This happens most to melancholic people. For images move them most. The reason for recollecting not being under their control is that just as it

> is no longer in people's power to stop something when they throw it, so also he who is recollecting and hunting moves a bodily thing in which the affection resides.[90]

This associative capacity continues to function nonstop due to the knight's humoural imbalance and its effects on the inner workings of memory. As a melancholic, he recollects constantly and "sabe de memoria todas las ordenanzas de la andante caballeria"[91] while spending entire nights "en sus continuas memorias."[92]

Beyond temperament imbalance and its effects on the faculties, there were also physical processes believed to influence the inner workings of the mind that could also have impacted Don Quixote's memory. The *vermis* (from Latin, literally "worm"), an elongated regulator of the cerebellum, was considered key in the process of memory formation and recollection. Carruthers describes the function of this valve in the following way:

> The path between memory and thinking must be a two way, because memories have to be recalled as well as stored. So a sort of valve was posited, which would allow images to pass into memory, and also to be recalled for cogitation. This was called the vermis, the little worm-like body drawn in the diagram between cogitation and memoria. Moreover, it had been observed that people lower their heads in order to think and raise them when trying to recollect something. This was taken as evidence for the action of the vermis, opening as needed for recollection, and closing for concentrated thinking once one had received from memory the materials one needed. Without such a valve, it was thought, memories could crowd unbidden into the mind, overwhelming and distracting rational thought.[93]

The proper function of this valve would regulate the path of thinking and recollection. Borrowing Carruthers's terms above, Don Quixote's memories "crowd unbidden into the mind," which frequently detracts from his rational thoughts. As the physiological hypothesis goes, the vermis blocked the passage between intellect and memory and therefore impeded rational thinking. This, in turn, helps explain the extraordinary and often erratic changes in Don Quixote's behaviour throughout the novel, as he demonstrates great lucidity whenever not drawing from the chivalric. The physiological existence and general functions of the vermis were often discussed in learned circles in Spain during the early modern period. In *Suma de Filosofía natural* (1547), Fuentes refers to the valve as a "pequeña berruga como peçon de la teta de muger" and provides the following description of its proper function:

> La postrer cámara d'éstas llamamos memorial porque allí está la memoria del hombre y porque el color y figura de la cosa que nuestra ánima a tomado en la cámara primera que es en la frente, la otra mediana la tira assí y lo embía a la postrera por un horado pequeño que está en medio d'éstas dos, al qual agujero cierra una pequeña berruga como peçón de la teta de muger, y quando quiere el ánima encomendar qualquier cosa a la memoria o quiere acordarse d'ella álçase aquella berruga y ábrese el agujero, y hecho aquesto se cierra porque las otras no salgan hasta que el ánima no quiera.[94]

As Fuentes notes, physicians generally believed they understood how the vermis was supposed to work, and the body part's failure to function adequately – as in Don Quixote's case – was linked to partial intemperance. Writers of the period thought that melancholy matched with an improperly functioning vermis could bring about a malfunction of intellect.

In his very own subjective experience of recollecting, Don Quixote's adventures are triggered by cues and hints that unlock his memories in order to make sense of his present circumstances. The process in the novel mirrors what plays out in real life, which aligns with what we know today, according to Schacter: "re-experiencing one's personal past sometimes depends on chance encounters with objects [also smells, sights] that contain the keys to unlocking memories that might otherwise be hidden forever."[95] The notion that one uses past cues to unlock current situations is not new. Cervantes's contemporaries were quite aware of the associative power of memory in which the external senses had a very prominent role. For example, in his *Libro del ejercicio corporal y de sus provechos* (1553), Cristóbal Méndez describes the process this way:

> De manera que la memoria guarda y retiene en sí todo lo que el sentido común ha juzgado o que le vino por los órganos o lo que juzgó de lo que la ymaginativa compuso, y con este exemplo, que es muy bueno al propósito, se dará todo a entender. Tomad un pedazo de oro y dezid a un platero que os haga d'él una fuente, la más rica y más bien labrada que se pueda pensar, con tal condición que todo lo que en ella se obrare sea cosa nueva y que nunca se aya visto.[96]

Examples like this are abundant in the novel. Don Quixote's memories are often determined by cues that, captured by the external senses, act as triggers. Consider, for example, how hearing music defines how and what the knight remembers:

> Y en esto se sintió tocar una harpa suavísimamente. Oyendo lo cual quedó don Quixote pasmado, porque en aquel instante se le vinieron a la memoria las infinitas aventuras semejantes a aquélla, de ventanas, rejas y jardines, músicas, requiebros y desvanecimientos que en los sus desvanecidos libros de caballerías había leído.[97]

In this case, music causes a recall of certain adventures from previous readings. In other cases, it might be a smell or a specific sound that acts as the prompt. For Aristotle, this is how recollection occurs – reminiscence or recollection depends on sequences of associations by similarity, contrast, and contiguity:

> And this is exactly why we hunt for the successor, starting in our thoughts from the present or from something else, or from something similar, or opposite, or neighbouring. By this recollection occurs. For the changes connected with these things in some cases are the same, in others are together, and in others include a part, so that the remainder which one underwent after that part is small.[98]

The laws of association originally formulated by Aristotle will be of utmost importance to thinkers contemporary to Cervantes, such as Vives. In *Sobre el alma,* Vives formulates the concept of associative memory along with its constructive nature: "Las cosas que se han recibido juntas en la fantasía, cuando alguna de ellas se presenta, acostumbra traer de la mano alguna otra."[99] Vives underscores the associative nature by citing his own experience in Valencia: "hallándome en Valencia postrado con la fiebre, y habiendo comido cerezas con mal sabor de boca, siempre que comía esta fruta, después de pasados muchos años, no solo me acordaba de la calentura, sino que parecía tenerla en aquel momento."[100] Another contemporary of Cervantes, the poet Juan Boscán, in his translation of Baldassare Castiglione's *Il Cortegiano* (1528) as *El Cortesano* (1534), describes that associative power of memory with these suggestive and powerful words:

> Y así acaece que un hombre enamorado huelga de ver la ventana donde alguna vez vio a su amiga, aunque la vea cerrada; y todos generalmente holgamos con una sortija, con una carta y en fin con toda cosa que en algún tiempo nos haya traído mucha alegría; asimismo nos alegramos con un huerto o con otro lugar cualquier que sea donde hayamos recebido algún

> placer muy grande; y por el contrario nos entristecemos con un aposiento, por bueno que nos parezca, si hemos estado en él alguna vez presos o padecido algún trabajo o enojo recio y he conocido yo hartos hombres que en ninguna manera bebieran en vaso que se pareciese a otro en que hubiesen tomado algún xarabe siendo enfermos; *porque así como aquella ventana o sortija o carta al uno representa una memoria que mucho le deleita, acordándole que cualquiera de estas cosas fue casi como una parte de sus placeres, así al otro el aposiento o el vaso parece que le traiga juntamente con la memoria la prisión o la enfermedad.* Esta causa creo yo que haga a los viejos decir bien del tiempo pasado y mal del presente.[101]

Recollecting uncontrollably under the associative power of memory was considered a characteristic of melancholics. This is clearly Don Quixote's case. Despite the accolades attributed to Don Quixote's imagination, his ingenuity would be of no use if it were not for the fact that his memory is working at full capacity, where incessant images become the motor and "ordinario remedio" for the protagonist's adventures. For example, after the silk merchants attack Don Quixote, the narrative voice at the outset of chapter 5 plainly states that the knight's response is completely dependent on his chivalric models: "Viendo, pues, que, en efeto, no podía menearse, *acordó de acogerse a su ordinario remedio*, que era pensar en algún paso de sus libros, y trújole su locura a la memoria aquel de Valdovinos y del Marqués de Mantua."[102] Images drawn from literary sources are therefore continually crowding his imagination, as seen in the number of times "imagination" is mentioned as if it were memory, thus emphasizing the relationship between the two faculties: "asentósele en la imaginación," "venir a la imaginación," "revolver en la imaginación," or "imaginando si se le acordaba." In chapter 3, I explore further Don Quixote's profound associative abilities through an examination of heraldic devices, religious imagery, emblems, insignias, and other images that appear in the novel as imaginative prompts for the knight to interpret his surroundings in very specific ways.

During a time when the brain's inner functions captured the attention of philosophers and doctors, they are also one point of departure to develop more dynamic and credible characters. As is the norm in Cervantes's work, his characters vary greatly from the uniform, static, and flat type that was conspicuous in the literature of the time, a prominent departure that marks him as the first major modern novelist. Egido has pointed out that his characters "evolucionan y cambian hasta mezclarse en sus humores, acciones y discursos."[103] The reader witnesses how they process the perceptions of the outer world and make them their own. In this process memory becomes key in the construction of the characters' subjectivity. That is the power of memory, but, as Schacter reminds us, it is a fragile power, affected by many factors, such as the condition of the brain and the body as well as contextual cues and beliefs.

In the particular case of Don Quixote, because of the humoural imbalance affecting the inner workings of his brain, his memory is especially altered yet very distinctive, influential, and imposing in the way he perceives the world around him. In order to make sense of his present circumstances, the protagonist coalesced two of the three internal senses of the early modern brain – memory and imagination: "todo cuanto pensaba, veía o imaginaba le parecía ser hecho y pasar al modo de lo que había leído."[104] But memories are not as accurate as we may think. As Dudai and Carruthers show, memories tend to be reconstructed after the fact in order to provide material for creative thinking: "memories are not direct signature-traces that past experiences leave in the brain. Their function is not to provide an accurate trace of things past, but to provide materials for creative thinking."[105] Thanks to the legacy of ancient philosophers and physicians such as Plato, Aristotle, Galen, and Hippocrates, Cervantes may have been aware of the longstanding debate on the partialness and fragility of memory and likewise understood the processes of *mneme* and *anamnesis* and their relation to imagination. Perhaps none of his characters states it quite like Mauricio, the astrologer in the *Persiles*, who doubted whether or not Periandro's account of his past experience was true: "Essas son fuerzas de la imaginación, en quien suelen representarse las cosas con tanta vehemencia, que se aprenden de la memoria, de manera que quedan en ella, siendo mentiras, como si fueran verdades."[106] Through Mauricio, Cervantes reaffirms the reciprocal relationship between memory and imagination, the reconstructive nature of memory, and its power in the construction of subjectivity. In a world where the emergence of subjectivity becomes an important literary advancement, it is inevitable to think of memory as a key element in that process.

Chapter 2

Mental Libraries: The Places of Memory

Has de fingirte dentro tu misma cabeza,
como que te vas andando por la calle, o por la iglesia.
Por el palacio, o por casa o por el claustro o escalera subiendo de grada en grada.
– F.J. Artiga
Epítome de la elocuencia española[1]

For the backgrounds are very much like wax tablets or papyrus,
the images like the letters, the arrangement and disposition of the images of
the script, and the delivery is like the reading.
– *Rhetorica ad Herennium*[2]

Imaginary Libraries

Several times in *Don Quixote,* the narrator reminds us that books and reading bear the responsibility for Don Quixote's inventive imagination. Calling them "autores del daño," the Priest and the Barber proceed to scrutinize the collection of chivalric tales held in Alonso Quijano's personal library expecting to penalize the culprits of his madness, either by casting them into a fire or putting them out of reach by closing the entrance to the room. As every reader of *Don Quixote* knows, it is futile for the Priest to try and cure the Knight's madness by sealing the entrance to his "aposento de los libros."[3] For some time now, Don Quixote has been carrying his books with him in a rich and intense visual and spatial memory, which has evolved into a memorable graphic gallery of knights, squires, giants, wizards, and chivalric adventures. It is precisely his singular imaginary library that leads the protagonist to incessantly conjure up the images and places that he then correlates to

La Mancha, thus continuously shaping the narrative structure of the novel.

The idea of a mental library was not new to Cervantes or his contemporaries. The concept can be found in the writings of the Franciscan Filippo Gesualdo, who, in the lesson titled "Della Libraria della Memoria" in his *Plutosofía* (1592), describes it thus: "E tanta la forza di questo ricco tesoro della memoria, che diuenta anco Bibliotheca, o Libraria, e con maggior felicitá, e facilitá delle Librarie, nelle quali si gloriano communemente gli huomini studiosi."[4] The humanist Peter of Ravenna boasted of travelling with a "portable"[5] library, and similarly, in Spain, Velázquez de Azevedo, in his *Fénix de la Minerva y arte de memoria* (1626), expressed the difficult and prodigious undertaking involved in "adquirir librería imaginaria en la memoria."[6] Moreover, the Belgian Lambert Schenkel asserted in 1610 that "there are some important men who claim to be able to reconstruct a whole library in their memories (not just the books, but the content of the books); and they show that they are able to transport such a library by sea, over land, effortlessly and at no cost."[7] Such an abundance of references to a creation of a "libraria della memoria" can only be explained within the framework of an epoch in which books were expensive, delicate, bulky, and difficult to carry. Picturing and being able to recall a constructed mental library were one remedy to those limitations, and it became common practice to move mentally through memory – through its spaces, its "librerías mentales."

Schenkel's words above could be perfectly attributed to Don Quixote's own mental library as the knight joyfully transports an assortment of accumulated images and stories throughout La Mancha and beyond. During Cervantes's time, the notion of portable and malleable mental libraries was part of a cultural code based on a science of places and images that was aided by the memorization systems found in the treatises on the art of memory.[8] The main idea behind this art – also called artificial memory, *ars memorativa, ars memoriae,* or local memory – was to create a mental path in memory by following a series of mnemonic techniques that helped an individual visualize a place or set of places and specifically ordering certain associated images with extraordinary intensity. Put another way, according to Bolzoni,

> the idea is to establish an ordered route of places in the mind. To each is assigned through an interplay of associations an image related to the thing to be remembered. Whenever necessary, a practitioner of this art retraces the places of his memory and finds the images that will reactivate the interplay of associations.[9]

Early modern readers were quite accustomed to such exercises of memory that generated mental spaces – in the style of virtual[10] ones today – and that relied on the power of visual imagination, "the mental imagining of a complex architectural structure or landscape in which every chamber or building would contain a piece of relevant information."[11] The result of these mental practices was the creation of highly complex visual systems whose relevance can still be seen today as Joshua Foer shows in his best-selling *Moonwalking with Einstein: The Art and Science of Remembering Everything*.[12]

During Cervantes's time the existence of complex mental systems was one legacy of a humanist education that valued memorization and advocated creating a topographical structure through memorization such as those reflected on in the Augustinian concept of the "*spacious palaces of my memory*"[13] or the spatial disposition in Saint Teresa's *castillo interior*, among others. The historian and humanist Mejía, in his highly acclaimed *Silva de varia lección* (1540), provides one of the first descriptions in Spanish of this art,[14] capturing the essence of the technique while also providing an understanding of what it meant during Cervantes's epoch. Mejía summarized the main principles of the art of memory:

> Que la memoria se puede ayudar e aumentar con arte, es cosa muy cierta y dello escriben muchos auctores ... porque desto también digamos algo, principalmente se han de ayudar de muchos lugares señalados e muy conoscidos, como si en una casa muy grande o camino o calle señalásemos con la imaginación e tuviésemos en la memoria muchos lugares e puertas. Después, por cada uno destos lugares ya conoscidos, se han de poner con el pensamiento las imágines de las cosas que se quieren acordar, poniéndolas por la orden que tienen señalados los lugares según que después se quieren acordar de las cosas. Y hanlas de pintar con la imaginación, cuando las ponen por los lugares, en la manera que cada uno mejor se piense hallar, para que después, llevando el pensamiento por los lugares, por la orden que están puestos, luego se le representan las imágines que allí pusieron y se acuerden de las cosas por que las pusieron. Y, ciertamente, por este arte y manera se puede decir y acordar grande número de cosas sin errar; *y dello tengo yo alguna experiencia*.[15]

As an experienced user of this technique, Mejía understood that memory could be artificially amplified through a kind of mnemonic gymnastics that reinforced mental performance and overcame the pitfalls of remembering even the most basic facts. For Mejía, memory "se puede ayudar o aumentar con arte": that is, memory can be reinforced by means of consciously perfecting and utilizing certain strategies and techniques. Given that natural memory was such a venerated and indispensable capability during the early modern period, an artificial system that helped train and therefore improve natural memory was commonly sought. Theorists generally thought that artificial memory could be a valuable supplement to natural memory. As a result, the distinction between natural and artificial memory was slight, and numerous treatises discussed both in tandem. They often were viewed as mutually dependent. For example, the rhetorician Jiménez Patón noted the variances between the two sorts of memory while underscoring the distinct value of each: "la memoria natural es la que está dentro de nuestras mentes y ha nacido al mismo tiempo que el pensamiento. La memoria artificial es la que sostienen una cierta inducción y sistema de reglas."[16] For most theorists, excellent memory required training, and the use of artificial constructs was essential and practised in an array of fields. In fact, the grammarian Antonio de Nebrija stressed that all work would be useless were it not "por esta especie de aliento."[17]

The strategies dictated by Mejía to reinforce natural memory through artificial means were not new. Such tactics were born in classical antiquity. The ancients who taught oratory stressed the need to develop mental practices that generated spaces through which the orator could move sequentially in order to associate the salient points of a speech to the spaces created. However, unlike the *ars memoriae* of classical times, the Renaissance art of memory was not restricted to storing and retrieving information or strategizing about how to remember certain details. On the contrary, the *ars memoriae* had evolved such that it "actually shaped many Western ideas in a diversity of intellectual domains."[18] In this regard, when providing the context for the tradition of the memory arts from classical times to the Renaissance, Engel, Loughnane, and Williams emphasize its broad dissemination across disciplines in Europe: "Memory training was in fact diffusely influential in several emerging cultural, literary and artistic practices in late medieval and early modern continental Europe."[19] This explains why Bolzoni states that "the treatises of the art of memory are only the tip of the iceberg and … their rules – often dry and repetitive – are just the backdrop of a cultural drama that developed on many levels."[20]

As one of the most representative authors of the period, Cervantes probably drew on the practice of creating mental images and building a topographical structure to enrich his own learning and to shape his writing. Cervantes, like other authors of this epoch, does not refer to the art of memory directly, but the evidence from his writings indicates that he was familiar with its techniques. Rather than seeing the art of memory as a set of rules, I examine it as a reflection of how the protagonist's mind operates, showing the relation of natural memory and artificial memory through his environment. When invoking the memory of his readings, Don Quixote literally travels the places (*loci*) in his mind, stopping to contemplate the images (*imagines*) evoked, and, as he does so, his mind becomes an extension of the chivalric world. In this process, the reader follows Don Quixote through a gallery of images stored in his memory as a theatre of memory or a mnemonic dramaturgy where the past is made present. In fact, the novel repeatedly shows this ecological orientation of memory, a mnemonic progression through the chivalric *loci* stored in the protagonist's mind. This chapter examines the effects of the art of memory on Cervantes's culture, how this art foments a set of mental schemes and attitudes as a result of its evolution through history, and the ways in which its varying ramifications are reflected in Cervantes's work, particularly in the episode featuring Don Quixote's penance in the Sierra Morena. *Don Quixote* reveals precisely those mental habits of the period that constantly appealed to memory, its spaces, and its images.

Cervantes and Artificial Memory

Cervantes – like Mejía, Jiménez Patón, Nebrija, and so many others – recognized the fundamentals of the *art of memory* and how its principles and techniques improved mnemonic capacity. Cervantes was able to memorize extensive quantities of information with a high degree of detail without having the original sources at hand. This fact alone may seem surprising, and it also underscores Cervantes's ample knowledge of the rhetorical tradition from which the *art of memory* emerged. Since antiquity, memory – along with invention, disposition, elocution, and pronunciation[21] – was elevated as an essential constituent of rhetoric. Cervantes must have known some of the many treatises on the subject that circulated during the time as well as the mnemotechnic techniques and mental imaginings espoused by them. According to Yates in *The Art of Memory* (1966), a triad of key classical writers – Cicero, Quintilian, and the unknown author of *Rhetorica ad Herennium* – served as constant references for mnemonic strategies and the art of memory. These authors and their works circulated throughout Europe, and they are *all* explicitly mentioned in the prologue of *Don Quixote*. E.C. Riley has seen in the influence of these three classical authors the origin of Cervantes's extensive knowledge of rhetoric.[22]

On the other hand, and continuing with notable influences that link Cervantes's work to the art of memory, the author also was acquainted with the aforementioned *Silva de varia lección* by Mejía, and he was familiar with Pliny the Elder's *Natural History*. The latter contains an entire section praising the faculty of memory and describing Simonides of Ceos, the founder of the art of memory who "halló y compuso el arte de la memoria ... para que cualquier cosa en oyéndola la pudiesen repetir con las mismas palabras."[23] The impact of Simonides of Ceos is discussed below.

Neither can we ignore the writer's pivotal sojourn in Italy, where he came to know firsthand the social influence of the art of memory as well as the principles of composition of place and arrangement of images that were applied to all the arts, as displayed in works of famous intellectuals such as Cosmas Rosselius, Gesualdo, and Giambattista della Porta, to name a few. De Armas has studied in detail della Porta's possible influence on Cervantes. Della Porta's *L'Arte del ricordare* (1566) was published only three years before Cervantes arrived in Naples, where it already enjoyed popularity, and *L'Arte* was also broadly known in Spain.[24] As de Armas points out, when assessing the impact of Italian Renaissance art and architecture on Cervantes's work, we must also remember how necessary it was for the author to have excellent memory skills including "multiple patterns and images of the architects and painters of the Italian Renaissance ... but he had to recall these many years later."[25] There is plenty of evidence indicating that Cervantes knew the principles of the art of memory as well as its different applications, as I explain here.

The Art of Memory and Its Tradition

In order to understand the presence of the art of memory during the early modern period and, in particular, its impact on Cervantes's work, it is essential to review, however briefly, how the technique evolved from its origins in classical antiquity. The art of memory was part of the classical rhetorical method that, by the seventeenth century, had passed through a variety of medieval and Renaissance enhancements, adaptations, and interpretations.

Most all histories of the art of memory start with the anecdote of its creation, by the poet Simonides of Ceos, and its principal constituent parts: places, images, order, and visualization. Simonides's story takes place around 500 BC, when Scopas, a nobleman from Tesalia, invites the poet to a banquet to sing in Scopas's honour. In his panegyric, Simonides sings a part dedicated to the deities Castor and Pollux, which so angers the host that he refuses to pay the poet his full salary and suggests he ask the gods for their share. At that precise moment, Simonides is informed that two young people are waiting for him outside, but when he gets there, no one is found. Simonides returns to the banquet hall and discovers that the roof has collapsed, killing most of the guests. As it turns out, the mysterious youths who had been waiting for him were Castor and Pollux who, as a show of gratitude for his panegyric, called Simonides away from the banquet hall to spare him from the accident. Because Simonides has recorded in his memory the specific image of each victim and the exact place where they had been seated before the accident, he is able to identify the cadavers. Drawing on this experience, the poet invented the art of memory and its two fundamental principles – the creation of places in memory and the placement of images within those spaces – as a form of iconographic writing in the mind that will continually adapt and evolve until early modern period. Simonides's art of memory became a cornerstone of rhetoric and rhetorical training from that point on. Cervantes might have been acquainted with the story because Don Quixote mentions the two mythological brothers during his experiences in Sierra Morena.[26]

Many Greek rhetorical textbooks recounted the story of Simonides and named him the founder of the art of memory, but most of these texts were lost. Simonides's story was fortunately preserved in Cicero's *De oratore* (55 BC), in which the author recounts how the poet was the first to explicitly recognize a need to facilitate the improvement of memory. As a result, Cicero included memory as one of the five parts of rhetoric (the *officia oratoris*) and evokes Simonides directly: "[Simonides of Ceos] inferred that the persons desiring to train this faculty (of memory) must select places and form mental images of the things they wish to remember and store those images in the places."[27] As promoted by the art of memory (Gr. *techne*, Lat. *ars*), a speaker could perfect his memory and conjure up long speeches thanks to intense visual memorization that was later recalled as he was speaking. The technique required an orator to use his imagination to retrieve images (*imagines agentes*) that he had been previously placed in the memorized places (*loci*). As Cicero describes it, with regular training, any orator could learn to deliver stimulating speeches by drawing forth the images that had been intentionally stored in strategic places created in the memory: "one could thus prepare the mind as a written statement thereby controlling the delivery as though reading from an imaginary text."[28] The practice spurred a preference for memorizing speeches that expanded during the Middle Ages and into Cervantes's time. For example, Huarte, following Cicero's instructions, advises readers not to simply read a speech but to commit it to memory, as there was a certain aversion to the reading of a speech in public: "A propósito de lo que dijo Cicerón, que el buen orador ha de hablar de memoria y no por escrito."[29]

Given the relative importance of Cicero's teachings in the early modern period and the emphasis placed on rhetorical strategies, it is not surprising that the classical text would be integrated into Cervantes's novel. Several times in *Don Quixote* it is possible to see Cervantes's knowledge of the tenets of rhetoric through carefully designed speeches by characters who seem to recite logical and persuasive arguments from memory. Among these are Marcela's opposition to the shepherds and Don Quixote's speech about the Golden Age to the goatherders. In other works, we could consider Scipio's heroic speech in *La Numancia*. It was believed that a meaningful and eloquent speech could only be successfully delivered because of one's great memory. De Armas has pointed out how the great tactician, Scipio, was able to uplift his army at the opening of *La Numancia* because of his impressive ability to "deliver a powerful harangue to his soldiers from memory:" "As a skilled orator he must organize in his mind and remember all the topics and images he wishes to raise."[30] In addition to *De oratore*, among the classical manuals that Cervantes might have had in mind when designing these speeches were two other important Latin sources: Quintilian's classic mnemonic manual for orators, *Institutio Oratoria* (95 AD), and the anonymous Libri IV (c. 80 BC), commonly known as *Rhetorica ad Herennimum*. The latter was the most important of the three and, according to Yates, the one that had the greatest influence in the transmission of the art of memory up through the seventeenth century.

Aristotle's contributions on memory are also essential in the evolution of the art, and the philosopher's works were naturally a well-known source for Cervantes. Aristotle's views would be particularly important in the evolution of the art of memory during the Middle Ages when, inherited from pagan culture, the art would adapt to the demands of medieval Christian culture, which inevitably endowed it with a moral sense. In *De anima* and especially in *De memoria et reminiscentia*, Aristotle lays the foundation for the process of remembering, in which images and a set of associations act as prompts of memory. Following Aristotle, and proceeding also from the Ciceronian doctrines, two of the most important and influential writers about memory during the Middle Ages were Albertus Magnus (*De bono* and his commentary to Aristotle's *De memoria et reminiscentia*) and Thomas Aquinas (in his Aristotelian treatise *In Aristotelis libros De sensu et sensato, De memoriae et reminiscentia commentarium*). Due to the impact of these authors, especially Aquinas, during the Middle Ages the art of memory evolved from being a means to help the speaker remember his speech to a redemptive process that sought salvation by rejecting vice through virtuous action. Yates writes that, over time, the art of memory began to follow Thomistic traditions whereby memorization practices were meant to purify and cleanse the soul and prepare oneself for heaven.[31] Visual cues were routinely placed strategically in symbolic spaces, such as stained-glass windows, sculptures, and frescos of churches and cathedrals, with a didactic and moralistic intention. Images to be committed to memory were moralized in order to instil Christian virtues and vices in the purest style, such as in Giotto's frescos in the Scrovegni Chapel (Yates 92–94). Following Aristotle, and proceeding also from the Ciceronian doctrines, authors closely associated memory with prudence, just as Cicero had done in *De inventione*.[32] As Carruthers has noted, medieval authors came to believe that training memory depended on comprehension of prudence:

> *Memoria* was also an integral part of the virtue of prudence, that which makes moral judgment possible. Training the memory was much more than a matter of providing oneself with the means to compose and converse intelligently when books were not readily to hand, for it was in trained memory that one built character, judgment, citizenship, and piety.[33]

All this had a clear purpose: to engrave the images in people's memory to help them remember a carefully tailored orthodox message, which served also to endow the image with great moral significance.

This exercise, which elevated the search for virtue and exemplary behaviour, could not be dissociated from the search for magnanimous perfection as embodied in many literary works of the medieval and early modern periods, particularly in chivalrous romances. The exhortation of ideal models was already gathered by an expert in the art of memory, Ramon Llull, whose *Llibre de l'orde de cavalleria* formulated the paradigm of the ideal knight that will be extended to *Don Quixote*,[34] whose own chivalric values depended on the role of memory to act prudently. In a thirteenth-century iconographic representation of the ideal knight, in his *Summa de virtutibus et vitiis*, Guillaume Peyraut symbolically portrays a knight protected by the shield of the Trinity and prepared to confront the seven deadly sins. This illustration serves as a catalyst for the characterization of the knight who fights against vice and connects with the mnemonic-didactic system discussed here.[35] In this chivalric world, wise conduct and exemplarity were a must and made possible through the operations of memory that allowed for constant access to materials of the past. As Beecher states, this was reflected in the most representative chivalric works of Renaissance literature, including *Don Quixote*:

> Much of the Renaissance literature culture employs the nostalgia of the quest in which a society seeks to recover through dangerous wandering and hardy exploits the norms and values its attributes to its own earlier manifestations … Humanism, with its lost-golden-age approach to history, curiously fortified the chivalric seizure by nostalgia that prevailed in the more ambitious forms of Renaissance literature: Tasso, Boiardo, Ariosto, Spencer. *Memory was at the heart of it all.*[36]

In other words, chivalric novels sought a return to the past, and memory was decisive in recalling historical deeds and virtuous actions from which ensuing literary protagonists were developed. The characterization of Don Quixote derives then from a monumental framework from which all heroes of chivalric novels depart – a long and venerated list of mythical heroes that Cervantes cites:

> Puede mostrar las astucias de Ulixes, la piedad de Eneas, la valentía de Aquiles, las desgracias de Héctor, las traiciones de Sinón, la amistad de Eurialio, la liberalidad de Alejandro, el valor de César, la clemencia y verdad de Trajano, la fidelidad de Zópiro, la prudencia de Catón, y, finalmente, todas aquellas acciones que pueden hacer perfecto a un varón ilustre, ahora poniéndolas en uno solo, ahora dividiéndolas en muchos.[37]

The passage is an excellent example of Cervantes's tremendous ability to recall authors and works and underscores the breadth of his familiarity with classical texts. As described above, ancient, medieval, and early modern thinkers and writers came to believe that understanding the past was necessary to act prudently in the present, an idea beautifully reflected in Titian's *Allegory of Prudence* (1565–70).[38] Titian's canvas of three faces reflecting past, present, and future is inscribed with an apt expression for the period's comprehension of time that can be easily applied to the chivalric world of Don Quixote. This idea would also be developed in many tracts, manuals, and *espejos* that elicited upstanding individual conduct. Perhaps no one makes it as clear as Furió Ceriol who, in the first chapter of *El concejo y consejeros del príncipe* (1559), declares that the prince must possess good memory: "con que mejor i más fácilmente se le acuerde de lo passado, entienda lo presente, provea en lo por venir … Es el Concejo para con el Príncipe como casi todos sus sentidos, su entendimiento, su memoria, sus ojos, sus oídos, su boz, sus pies i manos."[39] There are traces of this idea in the advice that Don

Quixote gives to Sancho before the latter departs to become Governor, a passage where the word "memory" is constant and purposefully linked to the necessity of acting prudently as a ruler. Similarly, Juan de Funes, in his *Libro intitulado arte militar* (1582), lists memory among the characteristics that a good soldier must cultivate: "Ha de ser el sargento mayor hombre de mucho cuydado, y muy diligente y de muy buena discreción y de gran memoria, porque cuelgan d'él muchas cosas de honra e importancia."[40] Funes's description resonates in *Don Quixote* when the knight describes the qualities and skills of the good soldier. Here, as in other places, memory and discretion are intimately linked, recalling the influence and evolution of the art of memory on which the narrative is built.

The Mnemonic Episteme in the Time of Cervantes

After its evolution through the Middle Ages, the art of memory had neither disappeared nor declined; the art – as well as the many allusions to it in works of diverse nature – continued to be practised and promoted as an essential technique for improving memory. Eventually, in Europe the art of memory evolved into a rich tradition that systematized a similar set of stages and strategies. In France, the tradition of memory systems continued in Pierre de la Ramée's *Dialecticae Partitiones* (1543),[41] Gulielmus Leporeus's *Ars Memorativa* (1520), in England in Guglielmo Gratarolo's *The Castle of Memory* (1562) and Robert Fludd's influential *Utriusque cosmi ... historia* (1617), which contained a section dedicated to the art of memory. Overall, the art of memory tended to follow the same rules dictated mainly in *Rhetorica ad Herennium,* which emphasized the mental composition of places and images, but differed in interpretation and purpose. Yates assures us that every single manual of the art of memory "is repeating the plan, the subject matter, and as often as not the actual words of *Ad Herennium.*"[42]

In Spain, the art of memory became ever more acknowledged in society, and intellectuals of various stripes saw the great utility of its techniques and principles, as studied extensively by Rodríguez de la Flor and Merino.[43] Among the most renowned works were the treatises by Pedro Ciruelo (*De arte memorativa,* Alcalá, 1528), Juan de Aguilera (*Ars memorativa,* Salamanca, 1536), Miguel de Salinas (*Rhetorica en lengua castellana,* Alcalá, 1541), Benito Arias Montano (*Rhetoricum Libri IV,* 1569), Francisco Sánchez de las Brozas (*Artificiosa memoriae ars,* Amberes, 1582), Jiménez Patón (*Mercurius Trimegistus ...,* 1621), Velázquez de Acevedo (*Fénix de Minerva y Arte de Memoria,* Madrid, 1626), Juan Gutiérrez de Godoy (*Disputationes Philosophicae et Medicae super libros Aristotelis 'De memoria et reminiscentia' duobus libri*, Jaén, 1629), and Miguel de Vargas (*Tesoro de la memoria y del entendimiento y arte fácil y breve para toda sabiduría*, Madrid, 1658).

These works were affiliated mainly with two predominant Renaissance currents closely tied to mnemonics. On the one hand, following the scholastic tradition of the Middle Ages as described above, images acquired a moral purpose that would be fully utilized by the religious orders for whom memory was conducive to virtuous Christian behaviour. The ethical necessity of the art of memory would be crucial to the Council of Trent (1545–63), particularly in Spain, where memorial practices were carefully integrated into ecclesiastical teachings that served to bolster Counter-Reformist arguments for orthodox practices. The *ars memorativa* would hold special importance for even the staunchest supporters of the Counter-Reformation such as the Jesuits, who believed in the *compositio loci* and mnemonic power of images for religious conversion. As a result, certain places became fully charged with great symbolism. For the Jesuits and other religious groups, Paradise and Hell emerged as contrived places in memory that served as either a warning or a reward.[44] For example, in his *Thesaurus Artificiosae Memoriae* (1579), Florentine Dominican friar Rossellius featured diagrams designed to visually recollect the road to salvation in Heaven or to condemnation in Hell. Similarly, in the celebrated *Congestiorum Artificiose Memorie* (1520) by the German Dominican Johannes Romberch, one again observes Paradise, Purgatory, and Hell as unmistakable *loci* of memory to which he and others also add many other mnemonic images including the abbey, the human body, alphabets, and spheres, among other details. The juxtaposition of key Catholic images alongside major orthodox metaphysical concepts points to explicit techniques to train memory. In Spain, as Rodríguez de la Flor has emphasized, one cannot deny the weight that such mnemonic strategies possessed: "esta versión cristianizada de la memoria tiene en toda la literatura espiritual del Siglo de Oro hispano y, de modo singular, la conexión evidente que existe entre el método de meditación por imágenes y lugares (la *compositio loci* ignaciana) y las secciones dedicadas a la mnemotecnia en las retóricas clásicas."[45]

On the other hand, and in contrast to the scholastic influence on the systems of artificial memory during the Renaissance, another tradition emerged in the work of the aforementioned Franciscan Llull, persuaded by Augustinian and Platonic thought. Here, representations of memory acquired a more symbolic and occultist value. In Llull's works, compiled in his *Ars Magna* (1305), the combination of symbols, such as movable figures, diagrams, and trees of science, created an entire classification of systems of knowledge that exercised a great influence in Renaissance in the teachings of Neoplatonism, magic, occultism, and astrology and in the hermetic trends for obelisks, cubes, and pyramids.[46] Mnemonic systems included, for example, the style of Llull's concentric circles, Giordano Bruno's zodiacs, and Giulio Camillo's famous theatre of memory.[47] These and many other examples connected an occultist character of the art of memory to the Renaissance Hermetic tradition for which man is the "great miracle" in the Hermetic *Asclepius*: "If man's *mens* is divine, then the divine organization of the universe is within it, and an art which reproduces the divine organization of the universe in memory will tap the powers of the cosmos, which are in man himself."[48] For humanists like Camillo, memory was a "teatro del mundo" wherein all knowledge was condensed symbolically like a pansophy: "the theatre is that which makes visible, which projects outward, the stage spectacle overseen by memory inside of man."[49] The notion of one's mind having the capacity to learn and store all knowledge was linked to an Augustinian conception of the mind as an extension of the immensity of the universe. In this world view, memory was the key for connecting humankind with the infinite possibilities beyond our everyday lives.

The influence of Llull, Camillo, Bruno, and other prominent figures on the art of memory can be seen in early modern Spain, particularly in the context of a turn towards Neoplatonism.[50] Neoplatonism provided, as Egido recognized, "un riquísimo campo para la configuración mental de *picturae* y *loci* en estrecho paralelismo con las artes memorativas."[51] Llull and his contemporaries, as well as several other writers and theorists, recognized the importance of the art of memory as developed in earlier literary works. In his *Tesoro de la memoria y del entendimiento y arte fácil y breve para toda sabiduría* (1658), Vargas comments on the influence of Llull's *Liber ad memoriam confirmandam* (1308). Similarly, in his official approval of Vargas's book, Fray Francisco de Mendoza referred to Fray Agustín Núñez Delgadillo, a great admirer of Llull, whose *Breve y fácil declaración del artificio luliano, provechosa para todas facultades* (1622) he described as "artificio admirable." Another well-known author deeply influenced by Llull was Pedro de Guevara, whose *Arte general y breve, en dos instrumentos, para todas las ciencias* (1584) drew on ideas put forth in Llull's *Ars magna* and whose *Nueva invención en seis instrumentos, intitulada juego y exercicio de letras de las Serenissimas Infantas Doña Isabel y Doña Catalina de Austria, con el qual en muy breve tiempo se aprenderá de todo el artificio y estilo de las gramáticas impressas* (1577) was a manual meant for the instruction of the infantas Isabel and Catalina that likewise benefitted from Llull's perspectives on the art of memory. Following the Llullian model, Guevara incorporates movable wheels to visualize learning and to create infinite possibilities within the text. Rhetorical wheels like Camillo's *artificiosa rota* were popular in Spain – in fact the origin of the expression "rote memory" might have something to do with these wheels, *rota*. This spatial disposition situates the reader in a multidimensional space through which he or she follows a mental process explained in terms of movement[52] through the text, another important element in the art of memory that will also be reflected in Cervantes's work, as I develop below.

Based on different implementations and forms as well as the expansive reception it enjoyed among intellectuals of the time, the art of memory and its varying applications were very important for the Renaissance mind. Yates's monumental *The Art of Memory* offers the best in-depth study of the art of memory's connections to rhetoric, religion, ethics, philosophy, and psychology, among other areas. According to Yates, Renaissance humanism emphasized the search for encyclopedic knowledge concentrated in palaces and theatres, as was demonstrated in emblems and *exempla*, art, and literature. Given the art of memory's ubiquity and permeability, Engel speaks of an early modern emblematic and mnemonic mentality of interdisciplinary character that he calls "mnemonic episteme." According to Engel, in the early modern period, an epistemological shift "fostered a mental ecosystem conducive to cultivating the memory arts"[53] whose diverse ramifications were clearly observed throughout Europe:

> the memory arts may encompass in some form or another the liberal arts; the art of rhetoric; the art of logic; *ars poetica*; the arts of genre; *imitatio*; memoir; Ramism; the art of printing; iconographic arts including emblematics, painting and allegory; *ars historia*; antiquarianism; the scriptural arts such as typology and numerology; the art of meditation and devotion; *ars notaria* and the occult art; alchemy; Lillian *ars combinatoria*; horoscopic astrology; *ars moriendi*; the funeral art, burial rites and monuments; the architectural arts; the juridical arts; the medical arts, etc.[54]

The art of memory's influence was so ubiquitous that its importance extended beyond intellectual endeavours. It transcended literature and the studio arts within public domain: physicians, preachers, ambassadors, students, and professors all became adherents of techniques advanced by the art of memory – as did card players, debt collectors, and merchants. The art of memory as a social phenomenon showed how mnemotechnics and their mental systems penetrated "into the lives of the urban middle classes, and even [play] a role in shaping one's daily habits."[55]

The evolution of the art of memory and its advent in the Renaissance in Spain helped writers theorize about the three-dimensionality of literature where multiple places and images competed within narrative structures, making a work of literature much richer and more complex. As Egido points out, artificial memory undoubtedly facilitated the production of mental schemas reflected in both artistic and literary works that led to endless possibilities: "los ingenios de la máquina mnemotécnica produjeron un sinfín de posibilidades combinatorias, y favorecieron en la literatura toda clase de espacios alegóricos."[56] This influence on literature should come as no surprise since artificial memory was widely embraced in society to such a degree that it became a part of the instruction in the literary academies where poetic mnemonic exercises were carried out.[57] One of the most celebrated examples in this tradition is San Juan de la Cruz, who, as a result of his classes on logic, rhetoric, and mnemonics at the University of Salamanca, devised his *Cántico espiritual* mentally in prison, where he memorized the first thirty stanzas of his work and later put the poem to text.[58]

Another important consequence of the *ars memoriae* was the emphasis on building topographical structures of memory. Texts began to be perceived in architectural terms, as reflected in the use of titles such as *Plaza ... Jardín ... Teatro ... Hospital ...* revealing an underlying "spatial and architectural model" (Bolzoni, Gallery 212). As Bolzoni notes, the use of such terms promoted by the *ars memoriae* "answered multiple needs, whether it was used for encyclopedic enumeration or debased for grotesque and moralizing ends."[59] Texts were similarly perceived as physical spaces, occupying the space of the page, a phenomenon that would proliferate with the advent of the printing press and the changes it generated in the perception of the world. Moreover, as Bolzoni argues, the book as a physical construct and the particular placement of the written word were perceived as places:[60]

> In the age of the printing press – more so than during the age of writing – the text is perceived as a set of places, as something that is positioned in space. The human faculties that generate the text (that is the mind, memory) are perceived in an analogous fashion ... The text is constructed (and read) in the space of the book in the same way that one constructs in the spaces of memory a set of places to which images are assigned.[61]

As one of the most representative authors of his time, Cervantes was not immune to the cultural *contaminatio* of the arts of memory and their evolution. Like other contemporary literary works, his narratives are marked by a rich myriad of applications and possibilities that the art advanced in his time. This is particularly the case with *Don Quixote,* in which numerous traces of the mnemonic schemes of artificial memory can be found. Cervantes constructs the text in much the same way that Don Quixote constructs in his memory the places and images from the chivalric world. In what follows, I develop how the mental disposition dictated by the arts of memory allowed Cervantes to conceive his novel in spatial terms in much the same way that Don Quixote imagines his world as a sequential series of physical places full of specific memories.

Sierra Morena: The Vast Territories of Memory

When Don Quixote invokes the memory of what he has read, he "traverses" the places in his mind, stopping to contemplate the images that he had previously formed from his readings.[62] He then transposes these recollections to the current reality of La Mancha. This "memoria andante," as Egido calls it,[63] is an active and repeated progression that allows the knight to move physically through spaces that are affected, even deformed, as he calls forth his bookish memories and superimposes them on his current situation. Whereas the method of invoking memories based on the Aristotelian laws of association is a constant and repeated process, each journey associates current sensorial cues with stored memories to create a new adventure that plays out before him. Because Don Quixote constantly creates his present situation by summoning specific past memories, the adventure seems new and fresh to him, but the reader will note a repeated pattern of behaviour. Hence, his invocation of past readings tends to follow a similar outline: adapting the reality that surrounds him, he first equates the existing visual and physical site of a *locus* (inn, forest, field, etc.), wherein he begins to visualize the mental images that he associates with similar places from his readings (knights, princesses, dwarfs, rival adventurers, chanters, giants, etc.).

Don Quixote's penance in the Sierra Morena is replete with passages that depend on memory, and the episode is an excellent example of how the pattern of applying memories from readings to the current situation plays out. Very little in this adventure is not driven by memory: Don Quixote and Sancho discover Cardenio's abandoned *librillo de memoria,* a text designed to record past events for future recall; when they finally meet Cardenio, he demands to be allowed to tell his story without disruption, a prompt for the knight that elicits Sancho's similar storytelling practices in the telling of the tale of Torralba;

when Cardenio is subsequently interrupted, his story is suspended, a narrative strategy that reminds us of Don Quixote's fight with the Basque, which the narrator halted intentionally to turn his attention to the discovery of the remaining pages of the novel; when Cardenio later resumes his story, Luscinda's memory provokes Cardenio's pain. In this episode, the constant and repeated appeal to previous thoughts and readings will ultimately form the setting for Don Quixote's mock penance in imitation of his literary heroes: he carefully chooses a place, frees Rocinante, and begins to meditate and compose poetic verses just as his heroes had – all according to what he has read but now applied to his present condition. There is similarly an especially acute emphasis on the necessity of sight and seeing in this episode, such as when Don Quixote demands that Sancho, who is illiterate, memorize the letter he has composed to his beloved Dulcinea. The squire's subsequent memory lapse is an indication of how memory works but also signals the relative insignificance that memorial exercises may have played among the non-learned classes.[64] These episodes are great examples of the mechanisms and principles of memory established by the *ars memorativa*.[65]

What makes the Sierra Morena episode unique to our purposes is the wide array of techniques and strategies that seem clearly derived from the art of memory: the use of repetition to consolidate what was remembered from Don Quixote's readings, a text designed in spatial dimensions meant to reflect the knight's mental imaginings, the development of a topographical memory, the protagonist's highly associative capacity, the imitation of memorized models, his rhetorical elocution, and the two key elements of the mnemonics – the composition of the place and the mental images. As a result of these developments, when reading these episodes, the reader is transported beyond the real space of the Sierra Morena into the "memoryscapes"[66] of the protagonist. Such overlapping of places – real and imagined – yields a text conceived in multidimensional spatial terms. Cervantes thus generates his text in a way that parallels the process used by the knight who conceptualizes and constructs the places and images from his chivalric world.

The escape to the Sierra Morena mountains not only marks a stark change in landscape whose frontier brings the protagonists to the fringes of La Mancha and Andalusia, but also establishes a change in the structure of the narration. The very act of entering into a new space with a completely different and unfamiliar scenic backdrop provides opportunity to develop new adventures and characters within different spatial dimensions.[67] The bucolic – almost Arcadian – location is in fact the trigger for a series of associations that will generate a chain of detailed memories that lead the reader to question whether Don Quixote had been there before:

> Así como don Quijote entró por aquellas montañas, se le alegró el corazón, pareciéndole aquéllos lugares acomodados para las aventuras que buscaba. Reducíansele a la memoria los maravillosos acaecimientos que en semejantes soledades y asperezas habían sucedido a caballeros andantes. Iba pensando en estas cosas, tan embebido y transportado en ellas, que de ninguna otra se acordaba.[68]

As soon as he sets a foot in the mountains, he identifies the place fit for his adventure ("lugares acomodados"), whose rough terrain and solitude activate an association to other places where long-ago celebrated knights acted out their customary penance. In this particular instance the narrator goes to great lengths to expose to the reader the frantic mental activity following the knight's fixation on a specific place within the larger symbolic area. The verb used, "transportado," denotes a sort of movement that carries him to his memories. This transportation is almost metaphysical and explains why Don Quixote speaks, particularly in this episode, as if he were "seeing" the passages narrated in his novels. In fact, there is repeated stress on the act of visualizing the surrounding landscape: "daba contento a los ojos que le miraban" and "así en viéndolo."[69] The reader is asked to literally see the space through the protagonist's eyes and share with him in the experience. By their doing so, Don Quixote's adventure gains depth, which would otherwise be less believable because of the fictional nature on which the knightly penance is drawn. In the process, the current penance connects to those performed by fictional knights, using the present situation as a cue for recalling the former. By seeing through Don Quixote's eyes, the reader is being prepared for the series of characters and adventures that will develop further on.

The narrator expends a great deal of effort in repeatedly describing the idyllic characteristics of the Sierra Morena. By doing so, he provides a justification for the protagonist's choice of this particular setting for his penance while also forcing the reader to return to visualize the space over and over:

> Llegaron en estas pláticas al pie de una alta montaña, que casi como peñón tajado estaba sola entre otras muchas que la rodeaban. Corría por su falda un manso arroyuelo, y hacíase por toda su redondez un prado tan verde y vicioso que daba contento a los ojos que le miraban. Había por allí muchos árboles silvestres y algunas plantas y flores, que hacían el lugar apacible.

> Este sitio escogió el Caballero de la Triste Figura para hacer su penitencia, y, así, en viéndole comenzó a decir en voz alta.[70]

With such emphasis on the natural features of the location – as if it were a *locus amoenus* out of a book – Sierra Morena is portrayed lyrically with emphasis on its natural elements: a "lugar apacible" with "alta montaña" as "peñón tajado" that features a "manso arroyuelo" surrounded by "un prado verde y vicioso." Given this beauty and serenity, who could argue with the choice of this particular location? Yet the narrator must have felt the need to justify the choice. In fact, the space is described rhetorically in still another passage, this time by the protagonist: "– Este es el lugar, ¡oh cielos!, que diputo y escojo para llorar la desventura en que vosotros mesmos me habéis puesto. Este es el sitio donde ..."[71] The repeated references to the area – first by the narrator, then by the protagonist – serve to create the perfect setting for the penance, all of which is based on the memories Don Quixote holds from his readings of what his surroundings should look like. The reader, once again, is asked to play along and embrace the choice of the space and, by extension, the decision to undertake the penance.

It is not accidental that such emphasis is placed on describing the location of Don Quixote's penance for the reader, nor is this just good narrative strategy. The art of memory taught to carefully select and describe specific spaces (*compositio loci*). There was a distinction in the *ars memorativa* between *topotesia* (imaginary places or *ficta loca*) and *topographia* (real or typical places). Don Quixote intentionally takes fictional locations drawn from chivalric texts and popular myth and sets them against a real topographical backdrop. The real place is presented, therefore, as a reflection of the knight's *loci mentales*, where both the physical and mental topographies[72] overlap as the knight traverses them. Several authors interested in the art of memory promoted the combination of real and fictional spaces. In his *Ars memorativa* (1536), Aguilera examined their permutation as "mixed" places that were to be used in the art of memory. Velázquez de Azevedo, in his *Fénix de Minerva* (1626), describes the three types of places with these words:

> Tres suertes hay de lugares, verdaderos, fictos y mixtos. Verdaderos son los que realmente tienen ser y forma y los habemos visto así como los imaginamos. Fictos son los lo que no teniendo ser las imaginamos y pintamos a nuestra voluntad, fantasiando y fingiendo. Mixtos son aquellos que se componen de los unos y de los otros.[73]

The amalgamation of seemingly different places was no doubt integral to the art of memory, but it also served the purpose of further blurring the boundaries between reality and fantasy.

The arts of memory dictated that places could be "naturally or artificially set off on a small scale, complete and conspicuous, so that we can grasp and embrace them easily by the natural memory."[74] Examples in the art of memory include a house, a room, a vault, and the aforementioned library, among many others, resembling in many cases contemporaneous architecture. Also common in the various treatises on memory were peculiar devices and apparatuses such as cabinets and spheres, like the cosmos and the zodiac that Romberch recommended in his *Congestiorum Artificiose Memorie* (1520) and the images of Heaven and Hell proposed in Rossellius's *Thesaurus Artificiosae Memoriae* (1579), mentioned earlier. In spite of their wide variety, these virtual spaces always followed the same dictates of the *Rhetorica ad Herennium* with respect to illumination, cadence, order, and symmetry for the creation of spaces and arrangement of images. In the Spanish literary tradition, there existed numerous examples of mnemonic places that referred to memory, such as the interior castle of Saint Teresa's *Las moradas*[75] or Quevedo's hell in his *Sueños*.

Unlike the various architectural constructions in which space appears controlled, the knight seems to have preference for uncontrolled places "determined by nature," such as the forest and the mountain, in which the dimensions of nature lend themselves to other interpretations. The symbolism acquired by specific places during the Middle Ages and Renaissance – such as Hell,[76] a forest,[77] or a labyrinth – were widely studied by critics. The Sierra Morena falls into this category and acquires a symbolic and allegoric value and has an extensive multiplicity of meanings that recall some of the common *loci* of the arts of memory. Against Don Quixote's idyllic vision of the place chosen to carry out his penance, Sancho describes it as "Hell" and "Purgatory":

> Volveré por los aires, como brujo, y sacaré a vuestra merced deste purgatorio, que parece infierno y no lo es, pues hay esperanza de salir dél, la cual … no la tienen de salir los que están en el infierno … ¿Purgatorio le llamas, Sancho? – dijo don Quijote – Mejor hicieras de llamarle infierno, y aun peor, si hay otra cosa que lo sea.[78]

In many of his narratives, Cervantes uses metaphorical spaces full of symbolism, such as the black forest in which a large part of the action of *La casa de los celos* develops, the valley of the Cypresses in *La Galatea*, and the Cave of Montesinos. The cave, in particular, has been studied by Egido as a place forged with memory, given its particular emphasis on *loci e imagines* of the *ars memoriae*.[79]

The Aristotelian principles of association also play an important role in the choice of surroundings to carry out the penance. As already noted, Don Quixote recalls a place or an image from his stored memories and closely aligns it to his present circumstances. The process echoes Aristotle, whose laws of association dictate in what manner memory is elicited: "this is exactly why we hunt for the successor, starting in our thoughts from the present or from something else, and from something similar, or opposite, or neighbouring. By this means recollection occurs."[80] Don Quixote associates something he encounters in his path – places and images – to the memories treasured in his memory regardless of their similarity:[81] "y pues estos *lugares* son tan acomodados para *semejantes* efectos, no hay para qué se deje pasar la ocasión, que ahora con tanta comodidad me ofrece sus guedejas."[82] The knight therefore adheres to the premises of *De memoria et reminiscentia* in which Aristotle warns that memory does not always occur spontaneously, but rather must be knowingly activated "mediante una suerte de investigación que obliga al individuo a recorrer los elementos que preceden o siguen a lo olvidado."[83] For Aristotle, the physical surroundings act as a trigger, a starting point for association: "And thus whenever someone wishes to recollect, he will do the following. He will seek to get a starting-point."[84] The starting point for Don Quixote is provided in the text by the frequent use of the verbs *buscar* and *hallar* in the adventures in the Sierra Morena as noted by Horacio Chiong Rivero.[85] These verbs propel the story as the protagonist uses active memory search that will yield a suitable association. Through the process of reminiscence, Don Quixote goes about recovering images that do not arrive spontaneously, but which instead require a major search effort through which thoughts and perceptions appear in sequence. The scenario plays out over and over again in the novel and follows the basic principles of association that generate an entire chain of memories that will simultaneously compose the text.

Once Don Quixote has "los lugares acomodados para las aventuras que buscaba," he will go about placing and arranging the pertinent images as they are treasured in his memory – not as one would normally expect them to be associated to his concurrent situation.[86] Thus, for example, as he debates whether to imitate Roldán or Amadís, the rich images associated with both heroes follow each other unceasingly. He recalls the "alfiler de a blanca" that can only kill Roldán "por la planta del pie" or Roldán's "zapatos con siete suelas de hierro" taken from the story of Bernardo del Carpio. Similarly, Don Quixote incessantly recalls the fictional narrative of Amadís de Gaula, who, "sin perder el juicio y sin hacer locuras" and "por verse desdeñado de su señora Oriana … se retiró a la Peña Pobre en compañía de un ermitaño."[87] After debating and discussing in his own mind, he finally opts to follow the memory of Amadís, to whom he refers over and over in the novel and whom he imitates the most: "Viva la memoria de Amadís, y sea imitado de don Quijote de la Mancha en todo lo que pudiere."[88] Because Amadís emerges as the model knight whose daring feats and accomplishments are so embedded in Don Quixote's memory, it is natural that Don Quixote would seek to emulate the fictional knight's penance. Emulating his hero, Don Quixote makes a rosary, prays, and commends himself to God; writes and engraves verses in tree bark; and invokes images traditionally associated with specific landscapes found in the Amadís narrative – forests and meadows along with their fawns, sylvans, and nymphs: "En esto y en suspirar y en llamar a los faunos y silvanos de aquellos bosques, a las ninfas de los ríos, a la dolorosa y húmida Eco, que le respondiese, consolasen y escuchasen, se entretenía."[89] The entire process invokes memories of Amadís.

Through this imitation, Don Quixote seeks chivalric perfection, another trait linking the narrative to the art of memory. Specifically, the art of memory called for moral perfection through imitation, as the protagonist himself recognizes: "el caballero andante que más le imitare estará más cerca de *alcanzar la perfección de la caballería*."[90] Although this is not a penance for his sins, the act recalls the virtuous practice in ascetic literature that shared some of the techniques from the *ars memoriae*.[91] Rodríguez de la Flor has seen in the practice of solitude and recollection the attitudes of classical rhetoric.[92] In that tradition, medieval asceticism confers a moral character on memory, which is further enhanced through solitude and recollection; for example, in *La Galatea*, loneliness is portrayed as "despertadora de memorias tristes o alegres" (I, 182). Once within the solitude of the setting and talking to himself – this will be the second time that Don Quixote appears alone in a place – all his memories of his readings will come and go incessantly in "mnemónica incontinencia"[93] initiating his particular "autopenintencia sin culpa."[94]

With Don Quixote's decision to honour the memory of the fictional Amadís over the historic Roldán, memory is once again essential in the process of the *imitatio*:[95] "Ea, pues, manos a la obra: *venid a mi memoria*, cosas de Amadís, y enseñadme por dónde tengo de comenzar a imitaros."[96] Through the imperative "venid a mi memoria," Don Quixote combines the practices and exercises of mnemonics, and the phrase exemplifies that which is called in rhetoric *memoriae mandare*, in the *compositio loci* where images – "cosas de Amadís," in Don Quixote's words –

are summoned together in the mind. This and other expressions used by Cervantes appear frequently throughout his work to denote the spatiality of memory. Phrases such as "encajar en la memoria," "ocupar la memoria," "depositar en la memoria," "caber en la memoria" (*memoria tenere*), and "tener en la memoria" (*habere in memoria*) all work to underscore that memory was believed to have space and size. These expressions also refer to one of the two existing types of conceptual metaphors describing how memory has volume as a receptacle, repository, warehouse, room, archive, or treasury of mental images.[97] In these instances, memory is presented not as an Aristotelian model of inference but rather as an Augustinian repository of images "with its secret and unimaginable caverns"[98] where "a person's own depths unfold like a memory palace or landscape."[99] Such a conceptualization of memory as a storehouse came from the treatises on classical rhetoric in which memory appears commonly described in terms of its spatiality (such as Aristotle's *Topica* in the Greek tradition) and is conceived as a space divided into *loci* where images are positioned in a precious treasure, a thesaurus [Lat. *thesaurus*]. Thus, in the *Rhetorica ad Herennium*, the anonymous author conceives of memory as "treasure-house of the ideas supplied by the invention … guardian of all parts of rhetoric,"[100] and Quintilian refers to it as "treasury of eloquence." Cervantes utilizes descriptions and examples effectively, illustrating how memory was conceived in spatial terms. For example, in *El rufián viudo llamado Trampagos*, Escarramán speaks of a story "digna de atesorarla en mi memoria,"[101] and in *La Galatea* memory is "tesorera y guardadora del objeto que los ojos miraron."[102] In *Don Quixote*, before his departure for the governorship of Barataria, Sancho listens carefully to the knight, trying to "conservar en la memoria sus consejos, como quien pensaba guardarlos."[103]

Since memory was regarded as something arranged in space, mental processes were perceived and described in terms of movement – another prominent element in the *ars memoria*. Don Quixote's memories constantly "vienen a la memoria" or something "los trae a la memoria,"[104] together with the use of other verbs that denote the same idea, such as *llevar*, *perseguir*, or *trasladar*,[105] when referring to the mental activity of the memory. Moreover, expressions such as "*iba y venía* con el pensamiento por mil géneros de lugares"[106] are frequent in the novel. Something similar happens with the verbs used to express *olvido*, such as *pasarse*, *irse*, or *caerse* from memory, a topic I will deal with in depth the epilogue to this book. From the earliest episodes, Don Quixote initiates action with a memory, resorting incessantly to "su ordinario remedio que era pensar en algún paso de sus libros,"[107] like the time that "su locura *trajo* a la memoria aquel de Valdovinos y del marqués de Mantua."[108] The process tends to employ the same expressions throughout the novel whenever a new adventure is about to start: "fue que le *vino* a la memoria"[109] or "Mas *viniéndole* a la memoria."[110]

Therefore, the spatial conception of memory reverberates in the text as endowed with depth and dimension. As a consequence, the text begins to be perceived in terms of space and movement. The ebbs and flows in the text likewise can be considered a reflection of Don Quixote's mind: real places and fragments from memory are fused and superimposed, contributing to the augmentation of an entire series of correspondences between the physical dimension and the mental disposition, a displacement of the planes between interior and exterior space through which the protagonist incessantly moves, which also reflects the way the text is conceived. These memory practices reflect the specular relationship between writing and mind pointed out in the *Artificiosa memoriae ars* (1582) by Sánchez de las Brozas who, speaking of places and images, says: "Los lugares sustituyen la página y las imágenes las letras. La disposición de las imágenes equivale a la escritura y su recitado a la lectura."[111] It is not surprising that Velázquez de Azevedo very aptly summarized the art of memory as "escribir imaginario."[112]

During Cervantes's time, the *ars memoriae* emulated the spatial dimension of natural memory through a mental journey. A similar process unfolds in *Don Quixote*, as illustrated in the episodes in the Sierra Morena. As the knight reconstructs the past by imitating his heroes, memory (re)creates the spaces and images of the *ars memoriae* and superimposes them on the situation in which Don Quixote finds himself. A writer like Cervantes, who, without sources at hand, was forced to recall his own readings, had to be familiar with the techniques of composition of *loci* employed by the abundant versions of the *ars memorativa* of the epoch along with its architectural and pictorial principles. In fact, his protagonist becomes the best exponent of these techniques to stimulate memory by means of an exercise of intense mental visualization. Thanks to these techniques, the catalogue of places and mental images drawn from his readings, treasured in the space of his memory, brings literature to life. The novel features highly visual "memoryscapes" that shape Don Quixote's spatial memory and that also contribute to the creation of a text conceived in spatial terms.

In much the same way that the mnemonist physically appears within the system he composes, Don Quixote becomes a sort of stage director of the theatre of his own memory. I use the word "theatre" here echoing Camillo's usage as cited by Bolzoni: "the theatre is that which makes visible, which projects outward, the stage spectacle overseen by memory inside of man."[113] During Don Quixote's penance in the Sierra Morena in particular, the reader witnesses the locative projection of the protagonist and his spatial disposition in which he inserts multiple images, converting the episode into a theatre of mental imageries following the dictates of the art of memory. By projecting his interior space towards the exterior, the protagonist opens up his mental theatre to the reader, who shares the protagonist's experience and participates in his mental and physical journey through the Sierra Morena. Cervantes does this by composing a text that functions in a fashion parallel to the way memory works. The analysis from the perspective of theories of memory allows one to see these episodes as a cycle of images, much in the style of the times, in which texts are seen as edifices, palaces, and galleries.

Don Quixote's narration projects an entire gallery of images reminiscent of Galileo's words "upon entering" in Ludovico Ariosto's *Orlando Furioso*, which he described as a splendid gallery characterized by the rarity of his objects, "almost projecting it in the gallery of the Ufizzi."[114] Like Galileo, the reader of *Don Quixote* enters the textual space that is an observatory for the display of images that populate the protagonist's interior spaces and that surfaces as an iconological repertoire, rendering *Don Quixote* a sort of Wunderkammer of immense visual intensity. There is no doubt that the writer had great mastery to "paint" in his works all kinds of characters, settings, and plots that his readers later recalled in astonishing detail, which I turn my attention to in the following chapter.

Chapter 3

Ut Pictura Memoria: The Mnemonic Power of Images

The art of memory was a creator of imagery
which must surely have flowed out into creative works of art and literature.
– Frances Yates
The Art of Memory[1]

A variety of woodcuts that illustrate *Los quatro libros de Amadis de Gaula nuevamente impressos y hystoriados en Sevilla* (1526) appear repeatedly in the pages of this chivalric narrative, even when a specific illustration does not directly describe the episode or the text it accompanies.[2] Such frequency and repetition must have had a triggering effect on the memory of early modern readers who, like Alonso Quijano, were very habituated to associating the recurring images with particular passages, specific contexts, and characters' traits,[3] all within a visually charged and stimulating printed page.[4] In *Reading in the Renaissance: Amadis de Gaule and the Lessons of Memory*, Marian Rothstein has pointed out that the specific placement and reiteration of artworks alongside texts was a common associative strategy in the Renaissance that prompted early modern readers to better remember the stories since "[r]everbalizing events from a visual prompt cannot but increase their retention; *given the importance of visual images in Renaissance systems of artificial memory, the stimulus was probably more powerful than we are equipped to feel.*"[5] For the culture of the Renaissance, this persistent prominence of the image, its powerful mnemonic value, its characteristics and effects will be put to use by painters, sculptors, and writers who, following the principles of the art of memory, understood how to invoke the power and persuasion of imagery in the creation of their works.

As an early modern reader himself, Cervantes must have been accustomed to recollecting, retrieving, and associating images, a process that he also fosters in his own construction of *Don Quixote*. Mindful of the mnemonic power and impact of visual stimuli, Cervantes incorporates images into his fictional work through detailed and innovative textual description in order to help his reader paint in the mind's eye a portrait of the unfolding events. The arrangement and structure of the *loci* espoused by the art of memory exerted an influence on the spatial conception of some key passages in the novel, specifically for his protagonist in places like Sierra Morena and the Cave of Montesinos. In the pages that follow, I explore the power of another key element extracted from the art of memory, the mnemonic image. Specifically, this chapter focuses on the nature of the image, its characteristics and ubiquity, and its place within the mind of the protagonist. I also examine how images that appear within the novel become part of the collective memory of protagonists within the text and readers outside of it. This dual operation of the mnemonic image in Cervantes's works reflects some of the paradigmatic memory practices of the time, whereby images continually move within the psychological plane while, at the same time, their external manifestations are encountered along a wide cultural spectrum[6] where "mnemonic images assumed a kind of autonomy that permitted them to pass from context to context, gathering accretions."[7] In this sense, the novel is an example of how memory was both an individual and social practice simultaneously, thus capturing the many "visual expressions of Renaissance mnemonic culture."[8] Hence, in *Don Quixote*, Cervantes explores in varying and distinct ways how the art of memory intersects with collective memory in painting (iconography, canvases, tapestries), rhetoric (*ars praedicandi*), literature (engravings, illustrations, ekphrasis), the use of emblems (*empresas*, hieroglyphs, heraldry), and physiognomy (where the descriptions of the characters follow specific physical traits congruent to their psychological ones). Through these techniques, each explored herein, the visual dimension of narrative is explored, and readers perceive and recall images in pictorial terms. In what follows, I explore how Cervantes creates mnemonic images within the mind of his characters, particularly Don Quixote himself, while developing inner techniques that impose intense visual imagery in the mind of his readers. In doing so his work exemplifies how it, as other literary works of the time, "actively targeted the mental faculties of spectators, audiences and bibliophiles in order to leave a lasting rhetorical, political or moral impression, consonant with the period's views on psychology."[9]

Visual Expressions of Mnemonic Culture in the Age of Cervantes

As we have seen thus far, the art of memory evolved expansively from its once-limited affiliation to the field of rhetoric towards other cultural realms, reaching its highest potential during Cervantes's time.[10] As stated by Engel, this expansion included some paths whereby the main rules of memory training, now distanced from rhetorical handbooks, came to affect "subject behavior, cultural phenomena and institutionalized practices."[11] In other words, the pervasiveness of the art of memory transcended learned circles to impact social behaviour and the operations of institutions. During the sixteenth century in particular, the art of memory's widespread presence resulted in a general awareness that was conducive to what several critics have called "mental ecosystem"[12] and a "cultural code"[13] displayed in multiple dimensions in the society of the time. As a result of the evolution and expansion of the art of memory, the mnemonic image will escape from the rhetorical manuals into the general cultural sphere and subsequently adopt multiple forms:[14] "Whether as picture, icon, simulacrum, emblem, sign, symbol, idée fixe, hieroglyphic, riddle, or mimetic representations, images went into circulation like viruses seeking replication and confirmation in the collective memory."[15] Images thus evolve as prompts for memory, each with different purposes displayed through various manifestations and practices abundant in the daily life of Cervantes's contemporaries. Within the context of Spain, Rodríguez de la Flor describes a "diafanización de las estructuras mentales creadas artificialmente,"[16] in which mental systems originally derived from the mnemonic tradition became more observable to the public. All this evolved from the various treatises in the tradition of the art of memory that had become ingrained in the conception of everyday life. Thanks to different cultural, literary, and artistic practices and, inevitably, the role of the printing press,[17] the art of memory came to play a more significant role in a diversity of cultural domains ranging from iconography to architecture.[18] Major construction projects of the time such as the emblematic Globe Theatre[19] in London or Philip II's masterwork, El Escorial, bore architectural features in their design that harkened to the principles espoused by the art of memory.[20] According to César Chaparro, the art of memory created for itself very distinct spaces that encompass multifarious cultural expressions closely affiliated with the influence of the image during the age of Cervantes:

> El arte de la memoria se mueve igualmente entre el andamiaje retórico y las alcobas y moradas de la piedad y de la devoción barrocas, entre los

> cielos de la astrología judiciaria y los números cabalísticos, entre el neoplatonismo y las ruedas y árboles de Lulio, entre las enciclopedias del saber total y los teatros y palacios renacentistas, entre los emblemas de Alciato y los jeroglíficos egipcios, entre las biografías y los *exempla*, entre epigramas, adagios, proverbios y apotegmas, entre medallas y monedas, entre ideogramas, *artefacta* y *stemmata*, y *figurae*, *imagines* y *signa*.[21]

As the power of the mnemonic image evolved from the *ars memoriae* and aligned with the distinctive plasticity of the Renaissance mind, according to Yates, the transcendence of the art of memory was paramount in the creation of images that emerged in art and literary works of the time: "For when people were being taught to practise the formation of images for remembering, it is so difficult to suppose that *such inner images might not sometimes have found their way into outer expression*."[22]

Given the importance of the creation of images within this cultural environment, the mental processes taught in the art of memory espoused the creation of strong images in art, a reciprocal practice that will be mimicked and shared in literature: vivid imagery created by writers transcended literary works to take their place in art.[23] The connection between the visual and the verbal, poetry and painting, is a classical leitmotif that had been adapted by artists and writers during Cervantes's time, and consequently, many scholarly works have studied this mutually beneficial relationship.[24] As a matter of fact, Cervantes himself is aware of this symbiotic connection as seen when Don Quixote illustrates the relationship in his words: "Pintor o escritor, que todo es uno."[25]

However, and as Bolzoni states, one aspect that scholars have mostly overlooked in this relationship is memory's role in connecting words and images.[26] The importance of memory in this relation was established, according to Plutarch, by the lyric poet Simonides of Ceos, the creator of the art of memory. Simonides likened the connection of word and image to the relationship of the plastic arts to literature by stating that "painting is silent poetry and poetry spoken painting."[27] Horatio later would turn Simonides's statement into his famous *topos "ut pictura poësis"* – precisely to point out that both the poet and the painter share in the creation of images (*eikon*) of reality. For Simonides, "discovering and practicing the art of memory involves becoming an expert in the quality and the extraordinary operational capacity of mental images."[28] By the same token, by thinking in visual images, the poet, the painter, and the practitioner of the art of memory rely on the supremacy of the sense of sight and the relevance of visualization in the process.[29] Through the interaction of linguistic and iconic expressions, the ancient theory of *ut pictura poësis* acquires various and extraordinary forms converted into powerful *imagines agentes* of high mnemonic value, such as the emblem, the motto, or the hieroglyph.[30] It is not surprising, therefore, that the power of visual elements and the optical function led José Antonio Maravall to describe the age of Cervantes as a "cultura de la imagen sensible"[31] where literature, painting, and mnemonics incessantly share the value given to the image and where "los códigos se alimentan recíprocamente, los estímulos son continuos, palabras e imágenes están conectadas, se entrelazan e influencian."[32]

Therefore, during the Renaissance, becoming an expert in the creation of powerful and vivid mnemonic images was a common practice among most humanists – particularly writers and painters – many of them well-acquainted practitioners of the art of memory and its techniques. As an illustration, Giambattista della Porta in *L'arte del ricordare* (1566) frequently refers to *De pictura* (1435) by the artist Leon Battista Alberti to recommend the use of strong images characterized "by pronounced gestures, by histrionic expressivity" precisely because, as he reminds us, "[w]e remember the paintings of Michelangelo, Raphael, Titian more readily than the paintings of a mediocre artist."[33] Della Porta's constant references to passages from *De pictura* reflects a shared tradition among painters and writers to draw on collectively gathered iconological repertories to create images in their works.[34] According to de Armas, Cervantes became cognizant of della Porta's work during his stay in the city of Naples, where, just as in the rest of the country, the techniques of the art of memory were widely practised in intellectual circles. In his treatise, dedicated to Philip II, della Porta develops certain ideas that would have an impact on Cervantes's writings, such as the preeminence of places for memory images, the comparisons between the art of memory and the theatre, and the significance of resilient images well suited for memorizing.[35] In another similar treatise, *Secretum de thesauro experimentorum ymaginationis hominum* (ca. 1430), Giovanni Fontana compares the art of memory and the art of painting[36] by emphasizing that "there is no art or science that is more similar to painting than artificial memory. Both need places and images, and one follows the other, and for this reason it is helpful to use examples taken from painting. Indeed we are painting when we construct images to be positioned in the places."[37] For his part, Iacobo Publicio, another Renaissance master of the art of memory, suggests taking images from the visually enriching descriptions offered by poets: "The good images … are hidden in the texts … and they need to be extracted in order to be used again."[38] Another humanist and theorist of painting, Ludovico Dolce, openly declares that painters and poets are highly prepared and capable of practicing the art of memory: "Every good poet and painter will use the office of this art with greater ease for the readiness that he will have in forming such images for memory."[39] Well-known theorists of painting in Spain such as Francisco Pacheco and Vicente Carducho unequivocally recognize the importance of mental images in the artistic process.[40] In his *Diálogos de la pintura,* Carducho departs from the images stored in memory in order to initiate the process of painting: "Las manos (pintor externo) no hazen más que copiar la pintura que le da la memoria o imaginativa."[41] In Spain there are similar confluences between the art of memory and painting well into the eighteenth century as one of the most famous books on theory of painting, *Arcadia pictórica* (1789) by Francisco Preciado de la Vega, is organized on the principles of mnemotechnics.[42]

Cervantine Mnemonic Inflections

Cervantes and his contemporaries lived in an age when culture in all its forms persistently cultivated memorial practices to remember more accurately and vividly,[43] hence the fascination of writers and artists with including strong mnemonic images in their works "whether as pictures, words, or hieroglyphs to fix in the mind those things they name or represent."[44] As the use of images became a common practice, artists and writers like Cervantes continually encouraged early moderns to read images "as mnemonic inflections."[45] For example, Barros's *Filosofía cortesana moralizada* (1587), a "metaforización político/cortesana del juego en la corte,"[46] was accompanied by a board game, in the style of the "juego de la oca" – very popular in Italy at the time. It has been described as a "pliego grande con ciertas figuras y letras" but is lost to us today. The board game twisted marvellously into a spiral form of sixty-three spaces along a path where concepts, stanzas, riddles, allegories, emblems, and hieroglyphs resulted in an iconic representation of the wheel of Fortune.[47] This visual metaphor was meant to allude to the political fortunes of the court and therefore had a clear didactic and moral purpose. According to Barros's succinct instructions, to complete the game, players must be able to effectively draw on their memory to recognize the board's images. It reflected the common triangular relationship between memory, the visual image – in this case, through emblems – and games in the time of Cervantes: "emblemática, poesía, juego, representación, imágenes y alegorías invaden esta oca serpentoidal, donde la literatura se proyecta sobre la representación icónica."[48] The use of the image in this board game is a clear example of the way in which the mnemonic image was making its way into pastimes, monuments, paintings, and book illustrations with the purpose of triggering memories.[49] Of particular significance to my argument here is the fact that since Cervantes wrote an encomiastic sonnet[50] as part of the preliminaries to Barros's work, he knew about the game board and probably also saw it. Barros's intentions were not lost on Cervantes who, continuing with this interplay between text and image in his poetic tribute, captures the intersection of visual literacy and iconographic memory by unifying the metaphor of the sea to that of the labyrinth, an image commonly used to describe the board game in question. The originality of the board, as well as the playful use of the image within it, must have drawn the writer's attention, despite the fact that he was very accustomed to this type of mnemonic combinations in his works.

Putting his training into practice and aligning himself with well-known writers of the time, it seems to me that Cervantes purposefully creates vivid images with a marked mnemonic intention. *Don Quixote* in particular frequently engages with the techniques from the art of memory and the interaction between literature and art mentioned above. As Riley states, the writer had an extraordinary ability to create images of pronounced intensity that have remained in the memory of his readers throughout the centuries: "a piece of verbal discourse (and initially nothing else) has evoked an image in the minds of individual readers clearly enough for them to recognize immediately visual reproduction."[51] In fact, the power of such evocative images is seen in the impact that Part One of the novel had in the memory of its early modern readers. The notable and ubiquitous silhouette representations of Don Quixote and Sancho alone are evidence of the writer's ingenious ability to firmly establish iconographic details in the reader's mind, which have transcended the text and the time. But there are numerous other lesser-known examples. When talking about the success of the first part, Sansón Carrasco himself illustrates the relationship between word and image by distinctly stressing the effect that reading the original work of 1605 had on its readers' associative capacity of memory "que apenas han visto algún rocín flaco, cuando dicen: 'Allí va Rocinante.'"[52] As Sansón notes, the visual image Cervantes created of Rocinante has transcended the book such that his name is applied to real-life horses. Even the protagonists themselves are aware of the posterior mnemonic power of their own image for future readers' recall as noted in the following exchange:

> – De esta manera me parece a mí, Sancho, que debe de ser el pintor o escritor, que todo es uno, que sacó a luz la historia de este nuevo don Quijote que ha salido: que pintó o escribió lo que saliere.

> – Yo apostaré – dijo Sancho – que antes de mucho tiempo no ha de haber bodegón, venta ni mesón o tienda de barbero donde no ande pintada la historia de nuestras hazañas; pero querría yo que la pintasen manos de otro mejor pintor que el que ha pintado a éstas.[53]

As exemplified in the use of the verb *pintar*, the text appeals to the visual and mental exercise of images transformed into words and vice versa with an eye on later recollection. Furthermore, the choice of specific words in the passage is rather significant, as it captures the role of memory in the symbiotic relation between text and image, as exemplified in the use of "escritor" and "pintor," respectively, and Sancho's prophetic words anticipate the visual traces of both characters in posterity. Such details created in Part One will be etched in memory and easily recalled when readers take up Part Two.

Additionally, this practice clearly aligns with the writer's tendency to use ekphrasis and artistic descriptions throughout his work as de Armas has brilliantly studied. De Armas, indeed, points out how in terms of form and function ekphrasis – with its multiple subjects – can serve as a mnemonic device,[54] which in the case of Cervantes's oeuvre is frequently accomplished to aid and guide readers' memory in the development of the narrative. As an illustration of this technique in *Persiles*, for example, Egido has observed the significance of painting as a form of narration that synthesizes the story as a visual lesson containing *loci* and *imagines*:[55]

> A un lado pintó la isla Bárbara ardiendo en llamas y allí junto la isla de la prisión, y un poco más desviado, la balsa o enmaderamiento donde le halló Arnaldo cundo le llevó a su navío; en otra parte estaba la Isla Nevada, donde el enamorado portugués perdió la vida; luego la nave que los soldados de Arnaldo taladraron; allí junto pintó la división del esquife y de la barca.[56]

In this manner, the canvas becomes a "recopilación que les escusaba de contar su historia por menudo"[57] as well as a clear memory aid technique that serves to trigger reminiscences for the readers. Once again, the frequency of the use of the verb *pintar* forces the reader to distinctly visualize what it is being described for easy recall. Furthermore, the canvas's mnemonic function is significant not only for the reader but also for other characters who use the same technique in order to remember past events within the narration, as when Arnaldo tells that a "mancebo peregrino" is effectively composing "una comedia de los sucesos de Periandro y Auristela, que *los sabía de memoria por un lienzo* que había visto en Portugal, donde se habían pintado."[58]

This type of visual expression is representative of an early modern mnemonic culture that is similarly abundant in *Don Quixote*. The novel introduces almost identical elements to trigger mnemonic activity in both characters and readers. It is not surprising that Egido views *Don Quixote* as an "arsenal de memorias pictóricas y emblemáticas."[59] Consider, for example, the engraving found in the *cartapacio* by the so-called second author in Toledo's Alcaná and his open refusal to believe that "tan curiosa historia estuviese entregada a las leyes del olvido."[60] The picture, as we know, recounts the battle between Don Quixote and the Basque at the time when the narration was suspended for lack of additional material. The image depicts the two in the same postures with their swords raised, along with Rocinante and Sancho looking on, exactly at the point when the reader is told that nothing else is available:

> pintada muy al natural la batalla de don Quijote con el vizcaíno, puestos en la mesma postura que la historia cuenta, levantadas las espadas, el uno cubierto de su rodela, el otro de la almohada, y la mula del vizcaíno tan al vivo, que estaba mostrando ser de alquiler a tiro de ballesta. Tenía a los pies escrito el vizcaíno un título que decía "Don Sancho de Azpetia," que, sin duda, debía de ser su nombre, y a los pies de Rocinante estaba otro que decía "Don Quijote." Estaba Rocinante maravillosamente pintado, tan largo y tendido, tan atenuado y flaco, con tanto espinazo, tan hético confirmado, que mostraba bien al descubierto con cuánta advertencia y propriedad se le había puesto el nombre de "Rocinante." Junto a él estaba Sancho Panza, que tenía del cabestro a su asno, a los pies del cual estaba otro rétulo que decía "Sancho Zancas."[61]

In this particular multilayered episode, the reader witnesses an impromptu and thus far unknown author who employs his own memory in the recognition of an image that subsequently triggers the recall of the past episode for both him and the reader at the exact point where the story was interrupted. The richly ekphrastic and mnemonic description of the scene is the result of combinatory reminiscences that serve as locus for recapitulation, where the Aristotelian laws of association and the significance of visualization are working at high capacity and where images inevitably trigger others through a game of mnemonic associations. By drawing attention to a visual re-presentation of a scene previously narrated, Cervantes not only reshapes, refreshes, and re-narrates past episodes and events within the story, but he also compels his readers, as in an exercise of mental gymnastics,[62] to recall and mentally visualize previous sections of the text in a parallel fashion. In this particular case, he does so as if the reader were actually "seeing" the depiction of the battle, now recast by the hand of the second author. Likewise, this representation of a previously narrated episode also functions as another way to offer a different perspective on the events, which clearly aligns with the reconstructive nature of memory that occurs repeatedly through the work.

The Mnemonic Power of Images: The *Imago Agente* in *Don Quixote*

The effects of creating vivid and intense images in literature that were capable of remaining in the memory of his readers beyond the present is notable in Cervantes's fiction, but it has not always been easy to identify and describe how the author does it. As Ana Laguna states very aptly in *Cervantes and the Pictorial Imagination,* "whereas the visuality of Cervantes's narrative technique is almost unanimously recognized, the identification of the strategies used to achieve this effect is more taxing."[63] Laguna underscores Cervantes's knowledge of rhetoric as the basis for the writer's technique on visualization. Indeed, his solid command of rhetoric plays a significant role in his use of techniques and strategies linked fundamentally to the art of memory that emphasized the creation of strong images. The author seems to be following the guidelines from the *ars memoria* on the formation of images that, as seen above, form part of a cultural patrimony widely shared by artists and writers that Cervantes knows well. After all, since antiquity, both the basis of memory and the art of memory was the image, as stated by Aristotle in *De memoria et reminiscentia*: "Memory, even the memory of objects of thought is not without an image."[64] Following such premises, classical sources of the art of memory in fact describe mental techniques that will depend on visual impressions of great intensity and where the sense of sight will be key, as emphasized by Cicero in *De oratore:* "The most complete pictures are formed in our minds of the things that have been conveyed to them and imprinted on them by the senses, but that the keenest of all our senses is the sense of sight."[65]

The way that Don Quixote remembers is fully in line with the process detailed by the anonymous author of the *Rhetorica ad Herennium*: a memory for things (*memoria rerum*) and a memory for words (*memoria verborum*) that, together, are the basis for mnemonic image formation. The first refers to the arguments, notions, and content to be remembered: that is, the subject of the discourse. For example, on a number of occasions, Don Quixote invokes "las cosas de Amadís" as a means to emulate and create new adventures. Here, "las cosas" are meant to be understood as the general tendencies and characteristics that mark

Amadís as a literary work as well as those that describe the character. The second, the *memoria verborum*, refers to the specific use of words, "the language in which that subject matter is clothed."[66] Thus, for example, the letter the knight writes to Dulcinea in the *librillo de memoria* is full of archaisms and expressions that appeared in other letters found in chivalry books: *no es en mi pro*: "not in my favor"; *afincamiento*: "humiliation"; *maguer que*: "although"; *asaz de sufrido*: "capable of suffering"; *acorrerme*: "help me."[67] The use of such terms, while anachronistic and perhaps not immediately definable to the early modern reader, would nonetheless prompt one to think back to their sources, in this case the chivalric romances. Again and again the protagonist himself overtly invokes this sort of imitation "al modo de los que sus libros le habían enseñado, imitando en cuanto podía su lenguaje."[68] For example, when Sancho asks the meaning of the term "albogues," Don Quixote provides the etymology of the word with the consequent enumeration of several other terms of Moorish origin. The chain of words serves to illustrate the power of association that links one term to the next and exposes Don Quixote's thought process – how he links one idea to another. After the extensive explanation, Don Quixote seems to be fully aware of the associative power of memory though language since, at the end of his discussion, he returns to the word in question and provides an explanation for why he has listed so many other concepts:

> – Albogues son – respondió don Quijote – unas chapas a modo de candeleros de azófar, que dando una con otra por lo vacío y hueco hace un son, que, si no muy agradable ni armónico, no descontenta y viene bien con la rusticidad de la gaita y del tamborín. Y este nombre albogues es morisco, como lo son todos aquellos que en nuestra lengua castellana comienzan en al, conviene a saber: almohaza, almorzar, alfombra, alguacil, alhucema, almacén, alcancía y otros semejantes, que deben ser pocos más; y solos tres tiene nuestra lengua que son moriscos y acaban en í, y son borceguí, zaquizamí y maravedí, alhelí y alfaquí, tanto por el primero como por el í en que acaban, son conocidos por arábigos. *Esto te he dicho de paso, por habérmelo reducido a la memoria la ocasión de haber nombrado albogues.*[69]

The passage is a wonderful example of how the memory of our protagonist is presented as a formidable tool that transfers the composition of mental images to verbal utterance. The process is similar to what Carlos Brito Díaz has called *mnemonic myopia* or the constant use of a mimetic language of the high style of chivalric novels.[70]

Perhaps the most revealing example of the recitation of imitated words can be found at the beginning of the knight's second sally when, speaking to himself, he draws forth the language of mythological dawns:[71]

> ¿Quién duda sino que en los venideros tiempos cuando salga a la luz la verdadera historia de mis famosos hechos, que el sabio que los escribiere no ponga, cuando llegue a contar esta mi primera salida tan de mañana, desta manera, "Apenas había el rubicundo Apolo tendido por la faz de la ancha y espaciosa tierra tendido por la faz de la ancha y espaciosa tierra las doradas hebras de sus hermosos cabellos, y apenas los pequeños y pintados pajaritos con sus harpadas lenguas habrían saludado con dulce y meliflua armonía la venida de la rosada aurora, que, dejando la blanda cama del celoso marido, por las puertas y balcones del manchego horizonte a los mortales se mostraba, cuando el famoso caballero don Quijote de la Mancha, dejando las ociosas plumas, subió sobre su famoso caballo Rocinante y comenzó a caminar por el antiguo y conocido campo de Montiel."[72]

The classification of the images in this passage links his present circumstance and hoped-for glory to the referent from which he draws his inspiration, the chivalric books of his library. The classification of the images was also made in relation to the same referent, and Don Quixote seems to undertake this process just as the manuals of the day would propose. Thus, for example, in his *Fénix*, Velázquez de Azevedo distinguishes between real, symbolic and arbitrary images: "Reales son cuando las mismas imágenes se significan a sí mismas, como espada por espada, sombrero por sombrero. Simbólica es poner una figura que simboliza con la idea o con su nombre.... Arbitrarias son las que uno elige y fantasía según arbitrio."[73] As Velázquez de Azevedo shows, the rules for creating images were actually very similar to the rules that governed the creation of *loci*. Accordingly, for example, one of the *imágenes de las cosas* illustrated by Aguilera in his *Ars memorativa* (1536) sets a certain parallelism in the way Don Quixote remembers and brings to memory the characters taken from the novel associated to *loci* in La Mancha: "Si quieres acordarte de algo corpóreo, previamente conocido, por ejemplo del rey, del papa o del obispo, te has de representar su figura asociada a algún lugar *e imaginarla como si realmente estuviese en el lugar elegido.*"[74] Don Quixote associates the place where his adventures take place with the characters who, in a parallel way, correspond to that place in his novels. For example, when viewing the inn as a castle, he transfers the fictional ladies, musicians, dwarves, etc., of the novels to the place before him.

The instances in which the writer translates words into images and vice versa are interestingly emblematic of the techniques of memory. In addition to transposing fictional characters from the past onto real, contemporaneous places, Cervantes successfully renders mental images of Don Quixote into words on the page, a process that de Armas has called *ur-ekphrasis*: that is, "the description of the creation of an art object in the character's mind."[75] Through the rich and detailed descriptions of such images, readers literally visualize the evocative force of mental images and their effects on the protagonist. At the same time, through Cervantes's intense writing, readers access a gallery of memories, or *imagines agentes* – images of an extraordinary visual intensity that have been kept in Don Quixote's memory and that, as we certainly know, he actively recalls many times over. Moreover, this process shares common traits found in the *ars memoria*. In other words, it is not sufficient that the novel vividly depicts the places and people the knight meets; the narrator also goes to great lengths to penetrate Don Quixote's mind to illustrate things seemingly only available to the protagonist. Such techniques were commonly advocated by the *ars memoria*, but not all writers successfully mastered them. To that end, when creating powerful images, Cervantes's fiction exemplifies the psychological reasons espoused in the *Rhetorica ad Herennium*, where the anonymous author establishes a series of characteristics with which the image must be endowed so that it remains longer in memory:[76]

> We ought, then, to set up images of a kind that can adhere longest in memory. And we shall do so if we establish similitudes as striking as possible; if we set up images that are not many or vague but active (*imagines agentes*); if we assign to them exceptional beauty or singular ugliness; if we ornament some of them, as with crowns or purple cloaks, so that the similitude may be more distinct to us; or if we somehow disfigure them, as by introducing one stained with blood or soiled with mud and smeared with red paint, so that its form is more striking, or by assigning certain comic effects to our images, for that, too, will ensure our remembering them more readily.[77]

In order to be able to create images that "adhere longest in memory," they must have a set of characteristics that endow them with extraordinary intensity to facilitate their mental visualization and also a great power of persuasiveness. According to the *Rhetorica ad Herennium*, the most effective method to help memory is through images that are not ordinary but rather surprising, novel, and active:

> Now nature herself teaches us what we should do. When we see in everyday life things that are pretty, ordinary, and banal, we generally fail to

> remember them, because the mind is not being stirred by anything novel or marvelous. But if we see or hear something exceptionally base, dishonorable, unusual, great, unbelievable, or ridiculous, that we are likely to remember in a long time.[78]

Similar theories were repeated by other authors almost verbatim during Cervantes's time. For instance, Sánchez "El Brocense" emphasizes this very same approach in his discussion of the creation of mental image. According to El Brocense, mental images should be associated with unusual things precisely because memory "acostumbra a despertarse sólo con lo novedoso y sorprendente": that is, "lo extraordinariamente feo, deshonesto, inhabitual, importante, increíble o ridículo que vemos u oímos."[79] Nebrija, one of the most influential humanists of the time, explains a similar process:

> [S]i en la vida vemos cosas insignificantes, comunes, habituales, no solemos recordarlas porque nuestro espíritu no se conmueve sino ante cosas novedosas y extraordinarias. Y por el contrario, cuando vemos o escuchamos algo en grado extraordinario indigno u honesto, especialmente increíble, grande, ridículo, acostumbramos a recordarlo durante mucho tiempo.[80]

For Cervantes, offering his readers surprising and novel plots and interestingly vivid characters that were far from ordinary was one of his major achievements. Few writers during the period possessed such talent at developing plot and characterization in such magnanimous ways. But, beyond the textual level, the ability to delve into the imagination of his characters and expose their thoughts to the reader puts the novelist in a category by himself. This is obvious from the many occasions when Don Quixote transforms the prosaic reality of La Mancha into unusual and unbelievable visions: conventional windmills that turn into ferocious giants, calm flocks of sheep converted into armies of fearless fighters, ordinary women become beautiful ladies of the court, and so on and so forth. Cervantes does this by endowing his protagonist's mental images with extraordinary force and very distinctive characteristics through penetrating facial expressions, dramatic body gestures, and powerful movements – which the author goes to great lengths to describe in detail for the reader.[81] Such techniques were in fact highly regarded and frequently used by the practitioners of the art of memory.[82]

It is also the case that Don Quixote acutely remembers his chivalric readings with great agility due to the powerful emotion he bestows upon the images as he stores them in his own memory. For Aristotle, the strength of mental images is due in part to the care and dedication with which they have been constructed as well as to the primacy of the sense of sight and the power of visualization. The philosopher compares the creation of mental images to the very same processes in the creation of images in the art of memory: "for it is possible to put things before our eyes just as those do who invent mnemonic and construct images."[83] For Alonso Quijano, who read and re-read his books with care and profound enthusiasm, it was impossible not to visualize the stories he read. Each reading cemented in his mind certain images and their accompanying storylines with meticulousness to be later recalled more readily at precisely the moment when something in his world matched a past image stored in memory. In fact, when he and the canon exchange contrasting opinions on the impact of literature on the reader, the knight seems to explain that memory recall is deliberate. For Don Quixote, reading chivalric novels requires the visualization of mental images as part of the reading process, but he is an established expert reader, and so the process is so greatly enhanced that he takes this visualization one step further to see images actually materialize before his very eyes: "¿Hay mayor contento de ver, como si dijésemos: *aquí ahora se muestra delante de nosotros* un gran lago de pez hirviendo a borbollones, y que andan nadando y cruzando por él muchas serpientes, culebras y lagartos, y otros muchos géneros de animales feroces?"[84] Whereas a skilled reader visualizes the story she or he reads, here Don Quixote plainly admits that the conversion of reality into fantasy is more agreeable than the referent itself, which demonstrates how his reading process has progressed beyond mere visualization in the mind. The fact that the protagonist is explicitly affected by his own vehemence and spirit finds its echo in a passage that appeared in a very popular text during the sixteenth century, *De sublime*, a Greek work on rhetoric attributed to Longinus: "as a result of enthusiasm and emotion, it appears that you are gazing at the things that you are describing and that you are setting them before the eyes of your listeners."[85] The visualization of images is key in the description given by the knight. As illustrated in the following quote, Don Quixote's defence of chivalric novels abounds with visual prompts described as if, following Longinus's words, the knight was actually gazing upon them:

> [A]llí le *parece* que el cielo es más transparente y que el sol luce con claridad más nueva. *Ofrécesele a los ojos* una apacible floresta de tan verdes y frondosos árboles compuesta, que *alegra a la vista* su verdura, y entretiene los oídos el dulce y no aprendido canto de los pequeños, infinitos y pintados

> pajarillos que por los intricados ramos van cruzando. Aquí *descubre* un arroyuelo, cuyas frescas aguas, que líquidos cristales parecen, corren sobre menudas arenas y blancas pedrezuelas, que oro cernido y puras perlas semejan; acullá *ve* una artificiosa fuente de jaspe variado y de liso mármol compuesta; acá *ve* otra a lo brutesco adornada, adonde las menudas conchas de las almejas con las torcidas casas blancas y amarillas del caracol, puestas con orden desordenada, mezclados entre ellas pedazos de cristal luciente y de contrahechas esmeraldas, hacen una variada labor, de manera que el arte, imitando a la naturaleza, parece que allí la vence. Acullá de improviso *se le descubre* un fuerte castillo o vistoso alcázar, cuyas murallas son de macizo oro, las almenas de diamantes, las puertas de jacintos.[86]

The continuous application of words that patently point to the sense of sight reveals how Cervantes assists readers in successfully concretizing images drawn from memory: *parecer*, *ofrecer a los ojos*, *alegrar a la vista*, *descubrir*, or *ver*. The passage is a clear example of the power and effect of visual images in the protagonist's mind. Moreover, Don Quixote succinctly and chronologically orders the process for recall and visualization, a tactic also described by Aristotle in *De memoria et reminiscentia*, whereby "el ojo de la mente recorr[e] las imágenes de una manera lenta, ordenada y analítica."[87]

Affectio and the Corporeality of the *Phantasmata*

For Don Quixote, however, these images are more than mere tools of memory; they come to life once they inhabit the spaces of the mind, and their power is such that they are able to imprint changes in his body since the personal emotions he connects with them clearly have a physiological effect. In addition to a succinct ordering of images, the author of the *Rhetorica ad Herennium* advocates for helping memory "by arousing emotional affects through these striking and unusual images."[88] The idea of arousing emotional effects (Lat. *affectio*) compares favourably to the aforementioned suggestion by Longinus to evoke great excitement in the reader. In other words, remembering is acutely reinforced by an emotional connection. According to Carruthers, images are a sensorial product endowed with a strong emotional charge: "the representation [in the memory] produces an emotional response; since it is an *affectio*, it is an experience as genuine as what initially produced it."[89] *Affectio* was a way to ensure that the image was more easily recorded in memory, but it was also a means to recall it (*intentio*) and trigger an emotion. A well-known example is that of Ravenna who, in his *Phoenix, sirve artificiosa memoria* (1491), one of the most popular mnemonic treatises in the Renaissance, associated what he wanted to remember with images of beautiful women.[90] The anecdote suggests that to create images that will remain a long time in memory, it is necessary to connect them with an original attribute: physical beauty, specific garb such as crowns or dresses, or even some ridiculous or farcical trait. In Cervantes's world, this might mean Don Quixote's aged armor, the knight's donning of Mambrino's helmet, or even Sancho's portly stature atop a donkey. Such physical attributes, which the novelist goes to great pains to describe in astonishing detail, render the characters more memorable and identifiable and are chiefly responsible for our recall of them through the centuries. Similarly, for some followers of the art of memory, the pathos of the image – denoting it with fear or violence – was an especially good means to guarantee the image's place in memory, an association that will have serious consequences for the protagonist's behaviour, as I will develop below.

Huarte, aware of the attraction and popularity of the chivalric novels during the time, specifically highlights how this genre, more than any other, is able to generate the powerful images as part of the reading process. In his *Examen de ingenios*, Huarte underscores the tenacity and the overwhelming force of the fantastic images in these novels such that readers "se pierden por leer en libros de caballerías, en Orlando, en Boscán, en 'Diana' de Montemayor y otros así; porque todas éstas son obras de imaginativa."[91] By calling them "obras de imaginativa," Huarte seems to be quite conscious of the effect of reading and the overwhelming influence of the mental images created during the process. Huarte's words definitely find an echo in the process Don Quixote follows in the construction of commanding mental images. When the knight "se pierde por leer en libros de caballerías" – using Huarte's words – the process by which the protagonist creates and fixes in his memory the images from his readings is actually the same being portrayed here. Once images from these texts adhere and inhabit the spaces of the mind, they seem to come to life, exerting an effect on Don Quixote's body and mind while the reader may experience a similar phenomenon during the reading process. The knight, already susceptible to exceptionally strong visual and sensorial abilities that bring forth sharp and precise images and their concomitant emotions, simply cannot control this recall process. Therefore, one of his problems resides in the fact that for the knight, images come to life and gain autonomy, and he transposes them on the *loci* of his surroundings. This is precisely de Armas's point when he writes that "Don Quijote strives over and over again to impose the images from his memory and imagination upon the reality of La Mancha."[92] The protagonist throws himself into a past not his but one of his making – brought about by vivid images from his bookish memory – and turns it into a lived experience: that is, into images with such force that they seem to be present: "Todo cuanto pensaba, veía o imaginaba le parecía ser hecho y pasar al modo de lo que había leído."[93] Don Quixote indeed feels fully involved in his adventures, as if he were living and experiencing them firsthand: "Y en la mitad de este caos, máquina y laberinto de cosas, *se le representó en la memoria de don Quijote* que se veía metido de hoz y de coz en la discordia del campo de Agramante."[94]

In the conception of his protagonist, Cervantes seems to be very aware that images can possess overwhelming force such that they are mistaken for reality. This somatic notion of memory was already described by Aristotle and subsequently by theorists of the art of memory who had warned of the perils of the persistence of images when talking of individuals who, like Don Quixote, cannot control the recall process.[95] Bolzoni highlights how, in the treatises on the art of memory, images had a physical and intellectual dimension, halfway between the body and the psyche: "As they begin to inhabit the spaces of the mind – beyond those of writing – the images of memory take on a life of their own."[96] In Spain, Velázquez de Acevedo, in his *Fénix de Minerva o Arte de memoria* (1626), referred to the phenomenon of the corporeality of images with these words:

> la memoria se ocupa y llena con lo que en ella guardamos y con las ideas o imágenes que allí depositamos, diciendo que por no ser corpóreas no pueden ocupar lugar, [pero] lo cierto es que la memoria se divierte y distrae y está restringida al órgano corporal, mediante el cual obra y así se cansa y ofusca y *hay unas más capaces y fuertes que otras*.[97]

The capacity of these images to come to life and consequently escape control was also noted in Fray Luis de Granada's *Guía de pecadores* (1555), in which such lack of control was seen as a consequence of the force of mental visualization, a product of the intensity with which mental images were created.[98] Similarly, the Jesuit Luis de la Puente warned those who were "muy imaginativos" about the power of the images they created:

> Los muy imaginativos han de estar sobre aviso, porque sus vehementes imaginaciones pueden ser ocasión de muchas ilusiones, pensando que su imaginación es revelación *y que la imagen que dentro de sí forman, es la misma cosa que imaginan*, y por su indiscreción suelen quebrarse la cabeza, y convierten en su daño, lo que tomado con moderación puede ser de provecho.[99]

The fact that so many testimonies warned of the impact of the image confirms that there was widespread belief that images could be all consuming, and some writers came to believe in their autonomy, something Aristotle noted early on. In his discussions on the art of memory, Aristotle writes that mental images, especially in dreams, re-enact and have a life of their own, as if they were performing.[100] Consequently, Aristotle highlights the independence and potency of mental images and their capacity to act internally to influence the senses. Since most writers of the period were familiar with the art of memory, they, too, were accustomed to dealing with the potentiality of such images in their writing. The notion that one could be possessed by images coming to life, known as *phantasmata*, actually existed during Cervantes's time:

> There is a rich tradition of classical philosophy and medicine that conceives of images through which we know and remember as *phantasmata*, as something that acts internally but also retains a sensory status ... [I]t is easy to imagine how centuries of experience in memory techniques have given scholars some idea of the complex nature of mental images and their capacity to inhabit their creators, to come alive and escape their control.[101]

This corporeality and strength of images and the dangers that they potentially impose could have dominant and overwhelming effects. People even treated them as an affliction. Their potentially uncontrollable nature required iconoclastic means to erase or weaken them, the remedy for which can be traced to the *ars memorativa* and its counterpart, the *ars oblivionalis* (the art of forgetting). While much effort went into improving memory, the mental ability to forget was just as important – particularly for individuals who suffered from overactive imaginations. As studied by Bolzoni, the belief in the mental capacity to forget was explained in treatises designed to help the afflicted do away with images that haunted them. For example, della Porta advocated for the application of ointments to the back of the brain. Fontana, in *De oblivion*, suggested that one should mentally cover with a piece of cloth images they would like to forget, destroy them in a mental fire, or even visualize them sleeping or dead. Rossellius, in *Thesaurus Artificiosae Memoriae*, preferred to mentally throw them out the window. Lambert Schenkel's *Gazophylacium Artis memoriae* proposed conjuring violent storms or an armed gang that would destroy images or, if that did not work, visualizing the loss of images through their suicide. Gesualdo in *L'Arte di scordare*, drawing on xenophobic fears from the period, suggested that images be hunted by Turks or pagans. Without a doubt, the most astonishing and dangerous of all these remedies was the idea of reheating the back of the skull to melt the image and make it disappear.[102] As these examples reveal, it was believed that both mental and physical remedies could resolve afflictions that were mostly psychological in nature.

The Circulation of Images in Cultural Artefacts

As the discussions around it show, different groups in society, particularly within ecclesiastical and pedagogical sectors, became acquainted with the authority of the mnemonic image and the effects it undoubtedly exerted on individuals. Institutions began to exploit the power of images to affect subject behaviour. As an illustration, in his *Discourse on Sacred and Profane Images* (1582), the cardinal Gabriele Paleotti, archbishop of Bologna, refutes the Protestant condemnation of Catholicism's widespread use of sacred images in religious settings.[103] Instead, in order to prove how images indeed have an effect on human behaviour,[104] Paleotti refers to their influence in the classical art of memory to make the point that imagery can both disavow Protestant opposition and enhance Catholic orthodoxy: "As to memory, what shall we say? We know that so-called artificial memory consists mostly in the use of images. Thus, it is no wonder that sacred images refresh the memory all the more."[105] Arguments like Paleotti's had an impact in Counter Reformation circles in Spain:[106] "The Catholic teachers of memory reappropriate the techniques of the art of their religious enemies and recycle them as useful ingredients of their little theaters of the mind."[107] Therefore, in an exercise parallel to the expansion of the art of memory towards other realms of culture, the initiatives of the Council of Trent advocated for the use of images to indoctrinate and move to piety.[108]

This promotion of the use of the image in Catholic practices explains their rise in sermons and meditation practices in Counter-Reformation Spain and, in turn, will favour the integration of iconography in the arts and literature. Given his knowledge of the workings of memory and aware of the complex nature that the effects of a memory could have on his protagonist and readers, Cervantes captures the different ways in which the influence and intensity of images were used in religious circles several times over in his work while also reflecting the typical nature in which such images were displayed. As an illustration, the episode that narrates the encounter of Don Quixote with wooden images of saints connects memory to institutions like the Catholic Church and reveals the effect of images on individuals. In this episode, after the stay at the Duke and the Duchess's palace, the knight and his squire stumble across a group of farmers peacefully eating. As the narrator notes, the group held something hidden out of sight: "[j]unto a sí tenían unas como sábanas blancas con que cubrían alguna cosa que debajo estaba: estaban empinadas y tendidas y de trecho a trecho puestas."[109] Carried along by his curiosity, Don Quixote enquires about what lies underneath the sheets, to which one of the farmers responds: "Señor, debajo de estos lienzos están unas imágenes de relieve y entalladura que han de servir en un retablo que hacemos en nuestra aldea."[110] Don Quixote asks to see the figures, and the farmer agrees to unveil them since "verla ha por vista de ojos,"[111] emphasizing once again the importance of the sense of sight. What follows in the course of the narration is a repeated pattern that emphasizes the Aristotelian laws of association in what seems a playful game at guessing the identity of the saints: first, the narrator provides a description of each of the images as the farmer unveils them, followed forthwith by Don Quixote's reaction and immediate recognition of the image in question, thanks to distinctive objects and marks commonly associated with each saint. Starting with the first image, the narrator tells us, "mostró ser la de San Jorge puesto a caballo, con una serpiente enroscada a los pies y la lanza atravesada por la boca, con la fiereza que suele pintarse."[112] The specific image traits would be immediately recognizable to early modern readers, and the identity of the saint is confirmed as soon as the knight sees the image: "Este caballero fue uno de los mejores andantes que tuvo la milicia divina: llamóse don San Jorge y fue además defendedor de doncellas."[113] Clearly, the knight has identified San Jorge because of some of the realia adjacent to his image: in this case, the serpent, since the saint was always portrayed with either a snake or a dragon, which served as a symbol of sin. As the farmer unveils the second image, readers witness the same process: that is, first the narrator says, "Descubrióla el hombre, y pareció ser la de San Martín puesto a caballo, que partía la capa con el pobre,"[114] and, just as with the first image, Don Quixote identifies the saint from the distinctive action of his cape: "Este caballero también fue de los aventureros cristianos, y creo que fue más liberal que valiente, como lo puedes echar de ver, Sancho, en que está partiendo la capa con el pobre y le da la mitad."[115] The third image is described by the narrator as "la imagen del Patrón de las Españas a caballo, la espada ensangrentada, atropellando moros y pisando cabezas,"[116] and it is unmistakably identified by Don Quixote as "Diego Matamoros" because of the common image of the saint on his horse ferociously killing his enemies. As the narrator tells us, the last saint represents "la caída de San Pablo del caballo abajo, *con todas las circunstancias que en el retablo de su conversión suelen pintarse*,"[117] signalling Don Quixote's immediate identification. The entire sequence of the unveiling of the images reinforces the significance of religious iconography and, more importantly for this study, demonstrates how memory and the laws of association work together to connect distinctive details to the life story of the saints.

Mnemonic technique that demanded that viewers connect certain established character traits with cultural iconography was prominent in early modern Spain. The ubiquity of the technique was so widely practised by writers and painters that people came to easily associate specific iconography to certain social classes, professions, or geographical locations:

> The images for remembering the saints are generally characterized by the attributes used to identify them in iconography. The treatises of memory pass on lists of the names of saints and their respective attributes that vary on length and that can be extended at will. An analogous technique is used to remember the different trades and professions each is represented with a characteristic tool of the trade or the typical attire of the profession. Countries, cities, and social classes are memorized in the same way.[118]

Returning to the passage cited above, Don Quixote easily recognizes the objects and circumstances frequently attributed to these saints "con las que suelen pintarse." Like errant knights of the divine militia, Don Quixote immediately connects distinct articles and insignias of each saint to their chivalrous deeds. The use of symbolic articles was part of the numerous catalogues of insignia highly recommended in the *ars memoriae* in order to secure more successful and lasting memorization. As noted in Aguilera's *Ars memorativa,* insignias and other objects create effective and durable images that excite the memory: "cuando Aguilera propone recordar el combate mediante las imágenes de una lanza, una espada o cosas similares, utiliza insignias pertenecientes al ámbito de los objetos."[119] Iconography was an especially adept means to engage the reader. In this case, early modern readers were trained to associate certain objects with the specific agonies and ecstasies of the saints and martyrs. Cervantes draws on the Catholic iconographic tradition to invoke a reaction in the reader that is closely akin to that experienced by the knight. In this sense, the reader actively participates in Don Quixote's response through the power of association.

The episode is also an example of the long Catholic tradition of using images for didactic purposes to uphold orthodox teachings in memory. Through paintings, engravings, *cartelas*, catechisms, and other objects in Spain and the New World, the Catholic Church in Spain took very seriously the visual strength of images. According to Rodríguez de la Flor, the use of the image will also be reinforced thanks to the artificial systems of memory and its relation to Christian sermons and meditations. The greatest proponent of meditations was Ignatius of Loyola, the founder of the Society of Jesus, whose *Spiritual Exercises* was devised as a means to teach followers how to contemplate Church teachings and commit to the institution's principles. *Spiritual Exercises* is an example of what Julián Gállego calls a "sensibilidad óptica"[120] that conceals a deep knowledge of mystical psychology along with the power of mental images and the *compositio loci.*[121] According to Jesuit tradition, the composition of place and the use of mental images led to more profound gradations of meditation. It is worth remembering that Cervantes was a product of Jesuit education,[122] and Jesuit visualization strategies can be detected in his work.[123] For example, Karl Ludwig Selig[124] noted a direct reference to the writer's Jesuit schooling in the *Coloquio de los perros.* In the story, one of the main narrators, the dog Berganza, retells his service to a couple of pupils attending a Jesuit primary school where, Berganza explains, mental visualization exercises are an important part of the pedagogical system. Berganza recalls an emphasis on verbs such as *pintar* and *dibujar* to refer to the methodology used by the dedicated teachers who "les pintaban la fealdad y horror de los vicios, y les dibujaban la hermosura de las virtudes." The Ignatian spiritual exercises placed a strong emphasis on visualization practices adopted from the art of memory and then used in their sermons.

For the Jesuits, meditation *per imagines* and through the *compositio loci* provided effective means to advance their indoctrination. In a conversation with his wife, Sancho seems to directly reference this Jesuit method. He confesses to have learned about the mental visualization of images in memory from the village priest during a sermon for Lent: "el cual, si mal no me acuerdo, dijo que todas las cosas presentes que los ojos están mirando se presentan, están y existen en nuestra memoria mucho mejor y con más vehemencia que las cosas pasadas."[125] In his study on the vestiges of contemporary preaching in *Don Quixote*, Robert Ricard underscores how people like Sancho come to gain knowledge as a result of "lo [que] dicen por esos púlpitos," which is then retained in memory.[126] Ricard very aptly points out how Church sermons[127] taught illiterate listeners like Sancho through visually enriched *exempla* that in turn possessed great mnemonic value.[128] Sancho easily recalls the priest's sermons and cites them as examples in his conversations with Don Quixote. The frequency underscores both the effectiveness of such sermons in the squire's daily life and the overall influence such homilies have in society. Examples are numerous in the novel, such as when Sancho reflects on death, "y a nuestro cura he oído decir que con igual pie pisa las altas torres de los reyes como las humildes chozas de los pobres"[129] and in the moments when he remembers popular stories and proverbs, "cuanto más que yo he oído predicar al cura de nuestro lugar, que vuestra merced bien conoce, que quien busca el peligro perece en él."[130] In the first example, the reference to towers and kings would very much incline unlearned listeners to take note of the significance of the message while in the second, easily remembered wise sayings helped fix ideas among the populace. Very much in line with the preference of post-Tridentine imagery, the techniques and methods first developed by the Jesuits came to be promoted throughout Spain by other religious orders, brotherhoods, and congregations such as the "Slaves of the Blessed Sacrament," to which Cervantes belonged. Moreover, all these institutions developed a cult of the image through banners and flags in order to be easily memorized and remembered by those who contemplated them. I will return to the use of these type of symbols momentarily, particularly in the relationship of the heraldry with the art of memory and the novels of chivalry.

The Catholic church is, of course, not the sole institution in early modern Spain to depend on the power of the image to persuasively effect the behaviour of individuals. Cervantes's cultural atmosphere was one where memory was constantly induced to recall through visual expressions, and consequently the mnemonic power of the image will be utilized by other sectors and organizations. This is especially the case in the political and moral arenas, where carefully chosen categories of images were widely used to induce people to associate particular viewpoints or messages with the institution in question. In many of these cases, the chosen form was the emblem. Whether coats of arms, flags, insignias, or monograms, heraldic emblems were widely used to represent a particular family lineage or social or political association while also instilling in specific terms a moral, political, or heroic message about the entity represented by the essentially mnemonic device. With respect to the emblematic tradition in Spain, Giuseppina Ledda has pointed out how emblems sought to cement moral teachings by offering distinct visual qualities that operated based on a certain method "that isn't removed much from the intent of the memorative technique derived from the classical rhetoric throughout the medieval period and handed down, known with diverse modalities and intents in the 16th and 17th centuries."[131] As Engel points out, the wide array of emblems collected in emblem books became instruments of memory, depositories, and models of the mind during Cervantes's time:

> This backlog of collective cultural memory images informs and shapes the interpretative strategies of the Renaissance emblem, fundamentally

> mnemonic in nature ... Whether or not the mnemonic image was used to convey timeless truths of the human condition, appropriated for commerce or law, or employed simply to recall something of domestic or personal value, its efficacy depended on a process of commemoration and recollection. Such symbolic forms therefore are indices to and manifest expressions of a commonplace way of conveying and translating thought-images into graphic practices, and back again into mental figments.[132]

The format of the emblem (*pictura, motto,* and *subscription*) facilitated its memorization, and the images demanded from their readers a plasticity of mind[133] that would be exploited by writers and artists. Emblem books such as Andrea Alciato's *Emblematum liber* (1531) became instruments of memory that collected the most well-known images accumulated at the time.[134] As Bolzoni has noted, the great iconographical repertories of the late sixteenth century, including Alciato's but especially that of Italian iconographer Cesare Ripa's *Iconologia* (1593), were part of a practice connected to the art of memory that could also be "swallowed up by mnemonic practices," hence becoming in turn "a convenient reference point for the construction of *imagines agentes* intended for those who work with the interaction between words and images."[135] Ripa's work served as a source of memory images for a very heterogeneous readership: "orators, preachers, poets, designers of emblems and devices, sculptors, painters, draughtsmen, actors, architects, and creators of scenery to represent all that can befall human thought with the proper symbols."[136]

Several writers of the period recognized that memory was essential in both the composition of the corpus of these works and their later dissemination and use. In Spain, the reform-minded *arbistrista* writers, diplomats, and other significant political and economic figures frequently use emblems intended to make their messages more easily learned through an explicit mnemonic intention meant to "grabar más hondamente sus consejos en la memoria del soberano."[137] The Spanish diplomat Saavedra Fajardo attested to the interconnection between the art of memory and the moral character of the emblem at the beginning in the prologue to *Idea de un príncipe político cristiano, representada en cien empresas* (1643). Addressing himself to the prince Baltasar Carlos directly, Saavedra Fajardo clearly notes the importance of a prince being fully informed and advocated for the enhancement of artificial memory supported by images:

> Propongo a vuestra alteza la idea de un príncipe político cristiano, representada con el buril y con la pluma, para que por los ojos y por los oídos –

> instrumentos del saber – quede más informado el ánimo de V.A. En la sciencia del reinar y *SIRVAN LAS FIGURAS DE MEMORIA ARTIFICIOSA.*[138]

Based primarily on the moral use of the emblem, and similarly to other works of the time that overlap mnemonics and emblems,[139] Saavedra Fajardo closely connects his work to the art of memory. This connection can equally be observed in Juan de Horozco y Covarrubia's *Emblemas morales* (1589) when the author makes explicit reference to "las pinturas" (to be understood as the image in the emblem) that "ayudan a la memoria."[140] Likewise, Velázquez de Azevedo advises in his *Fénix* that "también para la invención de las imágenes es muy provechoso leer emblemas, como las de Alciato y Ausonio y las de Horozco y también jeroglíficos como los de Pierio."[141] In short, authors and theorists concerned with circulating a particular message or viewpoint clearly viewed the emblem as an effective means because of how easily it remained in one's memory.

Given the abundance of emblematic material in his work, it is clear that Cervantes knew how to reflect the visual and the symbolic richness of the time evoked through the use of emblems to create strong images and trigger successful recollection. Bernat Vistarini states that the writer was acquainted with the most popular books of emblems as well as the emblematic motifs collected in *polianteas*.[142] According to Vistarini, it is likely that Cervantes consulted the books by Alciato, the *Triunfos morales* by Francisco de Guzmán, the *Empresas morales* by Juan de Borja, the *Emblemas morales* by Horozco, and many others. As Carmen Pinillos has stated, "Cervantes se muestra enormemente aficionado a este modo de expresión, y no se limita a evocar emblemas concretos, sino que también construye sus propias secuencias narrativas, poéticas o teatrales, según estos modelos."[143] These resources were so deeply rooted in society that even Sancho himself makes use of them at various times in the novel, as when he recalls a frequently used example from several books of emblems – a bald woman with just a few hairs on her forehead: "así, tomaba la ocasión por la melena en esto del regalarse cada y cuando que se le ofrecía."[144] The example would have been known to Cervantes's readers, illustrating how deeply rooted the emblematic tradition was in Spain thanks to the memorization of such images. It would be the author's task to describe with words what people were more accustomed to seeing in visual form.

The influence of the culture of the emblem on Cervantes's work exemplifies the rich interplay between text and image during the time. As pointed out by Ludwig Pfandl, in addition to the emblematic practice described above, there is the tendency in Cervantes's narrative to anthropomorphism – to represent abstract concepts through psychomachia: that is, the use of allegorical personifications that will trigger early modern readers' recollections.[145] Yates has written that there exists a connection between the arts of memory and the use of personifications.[146] Similarly, Aguilera in his *Ars memorativa* (1536) recommends that "si quieres acordarte de algo previamente conocido, pero incorpóreo, tanto que se trate de una sustancia como de un accidente, has de fingir una imagen sensible y corporal."[147] For his part, Ciruelo uses specific rules and examples to attribute corporeal images to both the arts and sciences: "que suelen ser representadas como ciertas niñas vírgenes con sus insignias, como la gramática con la vara, la aritmética con la tabla o el cálculo, la geometría con el compás, las astrología con el cuadrante o el astrolabio, la música con la lira o el órgano, la perspectiva con el espejo."[148]

A comparable iconographical influence drawn from the art of memory is seen in the allegorical figures used by Cervantes in his theatrical works. In the prologue to his *Ocho comedias y ocho entremeses nuevos* (1615), Cervantes declares himself to be the first "que representase las imaginaciones y los pensamientos escondidos del alma, sacando figuras morales al teatro" through bodily figures very much in line with the mnemonic tradition.[149] Cervantes will not only carry out this practice on the stage; he will also use these types of representations throughout his narrative. In *Don Quixote*, for example, Cupid appears as a "rapaz ceguezuelo,"[150] and in *La Galatea* he portrays the blindfolded boy more in line with established the emblematic tradition:

> [N]iño, desnudo, alado, vendados los ojos, con arco y saetas en las manos, por darnos a entender, entre otras cosas, que en siendo uno enamorado, se vuelve de la condición de un niño simple y antojadizo, que es ciego en las pretensiones, ligero en los pensamientos, cruel en las obras, desnudo y pobre de las riquezas del entendimiento. Decían asimesmo que entre las saetas suyas tenía dos, la una de plomo y la otra de oro, con las cuales diferentes efectos hacían, porque la de plomo engendraba odio en los pechos que tocaba, y la de oro, crescido amor en los que hería, por sólo avisarnos que el oro rico es aquél que hace amar, y el plomo pobre aborrecer.[151]

Likewise, Death is either portrayed as a "señora" who is "nada asquerosa: de todo come y a todo hace, y de toda suerte de gentes, edades y preeminencias"[152] or with her traditional image carrying a scythe: "No es segador que duerme las siestas, que a todas horas siega, y corta así la seca como la verde yerba."[153] Similar emblematic representations appear in the choreography orchestrated on the occasion of the celebration of Camacho's wedding, where once again an emblematic atmosphere permeates the episode[154] and in the personifications of the river Guadiana and the Ruidera lagoons in the episode that narrates the adventure in the Cave of Montesinos:

> ellas, las convirtió en otras tantas lagunas, que ahora en el mundo de los vivos y en la provincia de la Mancha las llaman las lagunas de Ruidera; las siete son de los reyes de España, y las dos sobrinas, de los caballeros de una orden santísima que llaman de San Juan. Guadiana, vuestro escudero, plañendo asimismo vuestra desgracia, fue convertido en un río llamado de su mismo nombre, el cual cuando llegó a la superficie de la tierra y vio el sol del otro cielo, fue tanto el pesar que sintió de ver que os dejaba, que se sumergió en las entrañas de la tierra.[155]

In each of these instances, Cervantes is able to draw on the well-established origin stories of these personifications while endowing them with meaning for the larger episode he is developing. His strategy is to connect the reader to the larger narrative featuring Don Quixote and Sancho while also offering rich textual descriptions that demonstrate narrative sophistication while targeting the memory of his readers.

The emblematic world that Cervantes develops also underscores the importance of corporeal movement and gestures. In order to create *imagines agentes,* Velázquez de Azevedo, recommends they exhibit extraordinary gestures and striking facial expressions,[156] and Leon Battista Alberti observes that "the movement of the mind is understood through the movements of the body."[157] In short, Cervantes was faced with engaging the appropriate means to vividly narrate bodily movements in order to reveal to his reader the unfolding actions. As an illustration, when Don Quixote claims to have seen Amadís, he describes the character according to a physiognomy that coincides with the general characteristics commonly assigned to errant knights, and he admits these are also very well known to readers:

> La cual verdad es tan cierta, que estoy por decir que con mis propios ojos vi a Amadís de Gaula, que era un hombre alto de cuerpo, blanco de rostro, bien puesto de barba, aunque negra, de vista entre blanda y rigurosa, corto de razones, tardo en airarse y presto en deponer la ira; y *del modo que he delineado a Amadís pudiera, a mi parecer, pintar y describir todos cuantos caballeros andantes andan en las historias en el orbe,* que por la aprehensión

> que tengo de que fueron como sus historias cuentan, y por las hazañas que hicieron y condiciones que tuvieron, *se pueden sacar por buena fisonomía sus faciones, sus colores y estaturas*.[158]

The knight's admission serves two purposes: it reveals Don Quixote's overactive imagination, which does not just visualize figures and events in his mind but rather turns fiction into reality, and it reminds us that many fictional traits were shared across several characters, thus revealing something of an acknowledged character typification. Within the chivalric culture in the Middle Ages from which fictional heroes like Amadís derive, a representational system emerged that came to be a precedent to the uniforms, coats of arms, and crests that were so popular in the sixteenth and seventeenth centuries. Medieval chivalric codes were fixed to certain royal houses, cementing in memory a particular association between the origins of the action and the family supposedly known to be illustrative of that action. The visual representation found its way into a family's coat of arms and crests, for example, where a specific icon, colour, or form might remind of a particular deed performed by an ancestor or of a general character trait, which, passed down through the years, was supposedly representative of that family. Early modern citizens clearly associated the iconography with certain noble houses, and the connection served as an example of exemplary behaviour for those who contemplated it.[159] Within the extensive emblematic catalogue captured in *Don Quixote*, one cannot deny the use of iconic heraldry that triggers immediate memory associations for the knight. One of the more well-known examples from the novel is the Battle of the Sheep, in which the knight describes a number of qualities associated with the warriors of each army for which they came to be known:

> – Aquel caballero que allí ves de las armas jaldes, que trae en el escudo un león coronado, rendido a los pies de una doncella, es el valeroso Laurcalco, señor de la Puente de Plata; el otro de las armas de las flores de oro, que trae en el escudo tres coronas de plata en campo azul, es el temido Micocolembo, gran duque de Quirocia; el otro de los miembros giganteos, que está a su derecha mano, es el nunca medroso Brandabarbarán de Boliche, señor de las tres Arabias, que viene armado de aquel cuero de serpiente y tiene por escudo una puerta, que según es fama es una de las del templo que derribó Sansón cuando con su muerte se vengó de sus enemigos. Pero vuelve los ojos a estotra parte y verás delante y en la frente destotro ejército al siempre vencedor y jamás vencido Timonel de Carcajona, príncipe de la Nueva Vizcaya, que viene armado con las armas

> partidas a cuarteles, azules, verdes, blancas y amarillas, y trae en el escudo un gato de oro en campo leonado, con una letra que dice "Miau," que es el principio del nombre de su dama, que, según se dice, es la sin par Miulina, hija del duque Alfeñiquén del Algarbe.[160]

In his essay on Cervantes and emblematism, Selig relates the power of ekphrasis to the importance of the catalogue of divisas found in this episode, both of which share their antecedents in the art of memory.[161] There are several other lesser-known examples in the novel where insignias and crests play a role in the development of the chivalric themes. For example, when Don Quixote decides to adopt the title of "Caballero de la Triste Figura,"[162] his conversion cannot be complete without painting "su escudo o rodela como había imaginado."[163] It is also clear that Don Quixote is trained to recognize such insignias: he makes special reference to the crest worn by the Knight of La Blanca Luna, and in the braying episode he decides upon the origin of those who carry the banner by recognizing their "insignia":

> Bajó del recuesto y acercóse al escuadrón tanto, que distintamente vio las banderas, juzgó de las colores y notó las empresas que en ellas traían, especialmente una que en un estandarte o jirón de raso blanco venía, en el cual estaba pintado muy al vivo un asno como un pequeño sardesco, la cabeza levantada, la boca abierta y la lengua defuera, en acto y postura como si estuviera rebuznando; alrededor de él estaban escritos de letras grandes estos dos versos: No rebuznaron en balde / el uno y el otro alcalde. Por esta insignia sacó don Quijote que aquella gente debía de ser del pueblo del rebuzno, y así se lo dijo a Sancho, declarándole lo que en el estandarte venía escrito.[164]

In Don Quixote's description, certain colours play important roles in the composition and later recognition of an insignia. In fact, the symbology of colour was one paramount recommendation from the manuals of the art of memory. For example, in his *Ars memorativa*, Aguilera recommended the use of certain colours to remember numbers and Acevedo, on the other hand, to remember grammar and morphology aspects such as "el caso en el que están los nombres o tiempos de los verbos."[165] We see in the novel many cases such as the braying episode mentioned above or in the adventure in the Cave of Montesinos where the Cousin claims to have composed a book of liveries:[166] "donde pinta setecientas y tres libreas, con sus colores, motes y cifras, de donde podían sacar y tomar las que quisiesen en tiempo de fiestas y regocijos los caballeros cortesanos, sin andarlas mendigando de nadie, ni lambicando, como dicen, el cerbelo, por sacarlas conformes a sus deseos e intenciones."[167] According to Rico's edition of *Don Quixote*, these "libreas" to which the Cousin refers were festive courtly uniforms or decorations of various colours that featured allegorical drawings glossed with poetic verses, and therefore they were symbolic adornments.

As the mnemonic image moved beyond the rhetorical treatises and expanded its influence on other realms of culture, authors like Cervantes perfected the use of images in the construction of plot and characterization while also connecting their narrative to the previously held assumptions of the early modern reader and building an extensive collection of images such as those held in the emblem books.[168] During this time, the arts of memory adopted external forms channeled through various social and cultural expectations and reached their apogee during the Renaissance, thanks to artists who, like Cervantes, knew how to externalize their complex mental operations. Due to the level of autonomy reached by mnemonic images, according to Beecher, they were able to pass from context to context:[169]

> Yet by a simple reversal of optics, the mnemonically inspired image, more than any other, was both representationally compelling and ideologically pregnant ... it too passed into the mind as a simulacrum, a species of phantasm ... The images circulating in cultural artefacts are potential forms and matrices for the images of the mind.[170]

Cervantes will not only use the mnemonic force of the image to guide the actions of his protagonist, but he will also test its effect on the reader and on the development of the narrative. Laden with literary memory that is part of the larger cultural spectrum of "everyone's internal landscape,"[171] *Don Quixote* becomes an iconological repertory where the construction and dissemination of memorable images derive from the precepts of the art of memory.

Chapter 4

Information Overload: Stocking Memory in the Age of Cervantes

Mi memoria, señor, es como vaciadero de basuras.
– Jorge Luis Borges
"Funes el Memorioso"

With the words in the epigraph, Ireneo Funes, the protagonist of the short story "Funes el Memorioso", describes his exhausted and full memory as mimetic and devoid of creativity that has turned into a "vaciadero de basuras."[1] When the character in Jorge Luis Borges's famous tale utters these words, he evokes key events in the history of memory; when the narrator visits him, Funes is reading the chapter on memory in Pliny the Elder's *Natural History*, which contains a long list of illustrious memoirists from classical antiquity[2] that have subsequently appeared in manuals and treatises on memory:

> Ireneo empezó por enumerar en latín y español, los casos de memoria prodigiosa registrados por la *Naturalis historia*: Ciro, rey de los persas que sabía llamar por su nombre a todos los soldados de sus ejércitos; Mitrídates Eupator, que administraba la justicia en los 22 idiomas de su imperio; Simónedes, inventor de la mnemotecnia; Metrodoro, que profesaba el arte de repetir con fidelidad lo escuchado una sola vez.[3]

Like the characters in the history he is reading, Funes has been endowed with an astonishing memory capacity, but he comes to understand that the storage of vain and expendable knowledge, without any use or benefit, has deprived him of his ability to think clearly and "olvidar diferencias."[4] As the narrator tells us, Funes is thus submerged in the folly of a "inútil catálogo mental de todas las imágenes del recuerdo."[5] Funes's never-ending mental cataloguing is similar to that of another outstanding "memorioso" created by Cervantes: the Cousin, an unnamed character who accompanies Don Quixote to the entrance to the Montesinos Cave.[6] Despite the centuries that separate the characters, the two have several remarkable traits in common: they both espouse a deep love for unremitting reading of all sorts of texts, they have an innate desire to accumulate encyclopedic knowledge very similar to the work of the historian Pliny, and each character has an excellent ability to store voluminous facts – albeit mostly useless.

Confronted by a rapidly expanding knowledge base brought about by scientific and technical advances such as the printing press, the Cousin emerges as a literary example of what happens when people are faced with a vast array of information that scarcely can be intelligently managed by even the most learned. Cervantes seems to be acknowledging this predicament by describing in great detail the Cousin's elaborate commitment to writing compilations and lists. The Cousin's literary works include writings in the style of *polyantheas* and miscellanies, compendia of assorted facts and figures. The genre cultivated by the character mimics the work carried out by numerous scholars who dedicated their time to the writing and reading of encyclopedic works in order to facilitate intense learning and constant memorization. However, many of these miscellanies and repertoires were panned as empty erudition – useless knowledge – and they were not held in high regard in learned circles. Chief among these were prominent figures in pedagogy such as Erasmus of Rotterdam and Juan Luis Vives, who favoured creative invention over the limited but pragmatic role of rote learning and mimicry.

In this chapter, I address the implications of memory in the pedagogical and cultural debate through the figure of the Cousin. His purpose is to compile the products of his saturated memory – whatever he has read or heard from unrelated sources – into bound volumes that he plans to continually expand as new publications as new information becomes available. He appears in this episode specifically to record information about Don Quixote and Sancho, given that he has already read the first part of their adventures. Cervantes's portrayal of this character, however, articulates concern for the functions, processes, and limits of memory while also questioning the incessant appearance in early modern Spain of unnecessary books that symbolize the issues surrounding the figure of the intellectual. In an age of constant expansion of learning, the ability to remember was not only a primordial element within humanistic culture but was also synonymous with intellectual prowess and an example of the pressure to which the scholar was subjected. Despite the Cousin's so-called erudition and what seems like a clear case of uncontrollable hypermnesia, the long hours of study, reading, and writing expose the pressure of the pedagogical environment of the time and the scholarly apprehension the intellectual faced. The character embodies, therefore, the effects that the widespread growth and structuring of knowledge had on a humanist's exhausted and saturated memory as well as the sociological impact on the intellectual landscape at a time when excessive use of sources, lack of creativity, and memories full of data – useless in many cases – were everywhere.

The Anxiety of the "Labyrinths of Letters"

We have all been there: that pressing anxiety we experience in this digital information age when confronted with pages and pages of Google search results and reading and taking notes from multiple books, articles, newspaper stories, blogs, archival databases, image repositories, and encyclopedias – among so many other sources. However, this information overload is not a new phenomenon. As early as 1621, Robert Burton, a contemporary of Cervantes, stated the following in his opening pages of *The Anatomy of Melancholy*: "As already, we shall have a vast chaos and confusion of books, we are oppressed with them, our eyes ache with reading, our fingers with turning."[7] To illustrate the immediacy and proliferation of printed materials in everyday life, Ann Blair has pointed out the number of pictorial works that began to flourish after the fifteenth century that portrayed intellectuals surrounded by books and manuscripts in their studies: "Early modern paintings of scholars on the other hand usually depict manuscripts and closed books and manuscripts spread out on desks, shelves and floor, even to the point of messiness."[8] A similar state can also be seen in the Prado Museum's catalogue of paintings where numerous artworks depict comparable scenes, thus indicating that the intellectual in Spain must have experienced a situation similar to that described by Burton and which we confront today.

It is therefore not surprising that, faced with the constant increase in printed materials and accompanied by the desire to learn as well as the status that was bestowed upon the intellectual, humanistic preparation acquired a certain urgency: urgency to learn all that one could, urgency to distinguish oneself from scholarly peers, urgency to stay current with emerging knowledge, urgency to develop new methods to systematize knowledge, urgency to adopt memory training techniques to facilitate remembering what had been read and to reaffirm what has been learned. This phenomenon had immediate consequences for learning and memorization as a result of the tension produced between, on the one hand, the immense textual production – "the labyrinths of letters"[9] as Erasmus called them – and, on the other, measured learning: that is, the limits that make learning more achievable. The Cousin's profession and works result from the information overload that characterized the high modern age, analysed in great detail by Blair in *Too Much to Know: Managing Scholarly Information before the Modern Age*. Blair studies the effects that the invention of the printing press and the consequent abundance of information and books had on the work of scholars and students during the sixteenth and seventeenth centuries in Europe.

This explosion of information in turn brought changes in the attitude of the intellectuals of the time, who paradoxically saw it as both "a subject of wonder and anxiety."[10] An example of this paradox that characterizes the situation of the humanist intellectual is provided by the Swiss bibliographer Conrad Gesner, who, in the preface to his important *Bibliotheca Universalis* (1545), complains about the confusing and distressing proliferation of books facing intellectuals, for which reason he will carry out his imposing bibliographic work.[11] Similar anxious reactions arise in Spain, as recorded in *Colloquios de Palatino y Pinciano* (1550) by the jurist Juan de Arce de Otálora:

> Mas el que estudia ha de acordarse de lo que vio ayer y anteayer y la otra semana y agora un mes y agora un año y agora diez y toda su vida. Y no solamente ha de acordarse pero *ha de tenerlo en la memoria y ver más y querer saber más*, y ha de tener siempre ocupadas en el oficio las tres potencias del alma, memoria y entendimiento y voluntad.[12]

Arce's description becomes palpable in the character of the Cousin, who during his interaction with the knight and his squire continually wants to know more so that he may add additional information to the knowledge he already has memorized and so that he may incorporate it into his future books.

The problem posed for writers, artists, and students by the ever-increasing number of books in turn caused a complex contradiction in humanist pedagogical theory. Simply put, there was a lot to learn, but limited time and capacity to do so and, for this reason, all kinds of devices were conceived to help remember everything, a phenomenon that Beecher describes as the "humanist anxiety over the deficiencies of memory in need of artifice to increase performance."[13] The scholar's anxiety and fatigue during this epoch is captured by Saavedra Fajardo in his *República literaria* (1616). Just before entering the city, Polidoro sees fields of hellebore and anacardium – the former to be used to remedy the headaches caused by intense study and the latter understood to cultivate and promote memory:

> Por el camino fui notando que aquellos campos vecinos llevaban más eléboro que otras yerbas, y, preguntándole la causa, me respondió que la divina Providencia ponía siempre vecinos los remedios a los daños, y que así había dado a la mano aquella yerba para cura de los ciudadanos los cuales, con el continuo estudio, padecían graves achaques de cabeza. *Muchos buscaban entre el eléboro la nacardina para hacerse memoriosos con evidente peligro del juicio.*[14]

Besides the remedies to which Saavedra Fajardo alludes, in the face of the explosion of information that characterized the time, methods and techniques to improve memory proliferated which promised to guarantee the possession and control of all that knowledge. Hence, part of the pedagogical programs of the time favoured external memory supports. Cataloguing mechanisms and artefacts emerged such as Augusto Ramelli's original wheel of books (1587) and Thomas Harrison's *arca studiorum* (1640), later described in Vincent Placcius's *De arte excerpendi* (1689).[15] These were built with sheets of paper hung from hooks labeled with thematic headings – up to 3,300 – and easily accessible and visible at a glance from a short distance. Other techniques and tools for organizing material and notetaking included *cartapacios*, like the one the second author finds in the Alcaná of Toledo in *Don Quixote*, and *librillos de memoria* like Cardenio's, which were among the most common recommendations from humanist pedagogues. Both were types of notebooks for containing or taking notes, easily transportable due to their size and quickly accessible for notetaking. Lorenzo Palmireno, in *El estudioso de la aldea* (1571), recommended the *cartapacio* method as a "ayuda de memoria:" "Por perezoso que sea el estudiante, suele tener un libro, donde escribe lo que mas le agrada: a este llaman *Codex excerptorious*, Proverbiador, o Cartapacio. Es la llave de la doctrina, ayuda de memoria, y en fin no puedes estar sin él."[16] Analogously, another contemporary of Cervantes, the Flemish humanist Justus Lipsius, advised storing images and allegories in memory and taking down in one's notebook quotations (*excerpta*), decorative phrases (*ornamentum*), fixed forms of words (*formulae*), and vocabulary (*dictio*) for later use in their writing or for use by other writers.[17] Among other techniques there were index cards, outlining, and branching diagrams; others advocated laying out the text itself with different fonts and colours.[18] Since the subject has been extensively and extraordinarily studied by Sagrario López Poza, I have only briefly glossed over some of the methods used by humanists to gather available information which provides an understanding of the context from which the figure of the Cousin emerges.

Following the recommendations of prominent humanists in the sixteenth century such as Erasmus, Vives, Miguel de Salinas, and Lorenzo Palmireno and later, in the seventeenth century, Baltasar de Céspedes and Lipsius, many systems and devices were commonly used in the structuring and organization of knowledge so that one could effectively recall information.[19] In *De ratione studii* (1511),[20] Erasmus recommended to his rhetoric students a lecture notebook in which to note "las expresiones significativas, arcaísmos, neologismos, argumentos de sutil invención o de acertada disposición, ornatos elocutivos, y los adagios, ejemplos y sentencias."[21] Erasmus also suggested that students write down *notulae* to mark the most significant passages which could serve as "resortes memorísticos."[22] In Spain, Vives, in his extensive pedagogical work *De trandendis disciplinis* (1531), endorsed a method of study that included dividing a notebook into twelve places or *loci comunes*, which he named "nests," whose process of elaboration was illustrated in the following way:

> Así cada uno de los muchachos habrá de tener una libreta en blanco, dividida en algunas secciones, para recoger todo cuanto sale de la boca del maestro, tan precioso como unas gemas. En un apartado colocará las palabras por separado; en otro las expresiones particulares y los idiotismos, sea de uso cotidiano, sea raros, sea no conocidos ni explicados por todos. En otra sección las historias; en otra las fábulas; en otro apartado los dichos y sentencias señalados, en otro los dichos ingeniosos, en otro los proverbios, en otros los hombres famosos y nobles, en otros las ciudades insignes, en otros los animales, vegetales y minerales extraños; en otro los pasajes difíciles de los autores ya explicados, en otro las dudas todavía no dilucidadas.[23]

Like Erasmus, Vives described methods for taking notes, and in his *Epístola segunda: sobre la pedagogía infantil*, he also offers the key to making sense and good use of everything annotated in the notebook: "Y que no sólo lo sepa el libro, te lo leerás y releerás, lo mandarás a la memoria y lo fijarás de manera que no lo lleves menos escrito en tu corazón que en la libreta. Sírvete de ellos tanto como sea necesario; *de nada sirve tener libros de erudición si tienes una mente ignorante.*"[24]

The humanist scholar extracted what was most useful from firsthand readings and organized the information in folders and booklets – such as the *zibaldone* of Cardenio, a specific type of *librillo de memoria*.[25] These mechanisms for organization followed precepts of the art of memory and simulated the functioning and spatial arrangement of memory by categorizing information in physical spaces, *loci comunes*. Each of these places was then assigned a category and number to be used in later writings.[26] This sort of structuring system aimed to facilitate the memorization process and free memory from the saturation of stored data. According to Blair, "this process of 'excerpting' was said to aid the memory in at least two ways: the act of writing itself helped to ingrain the passage in the memory, and the excerpts could then be learned by heart to exercise the memory."[27] As an advocate for these memorization practices in the pedagogical field, Erasmus advised techniques very similar to those used today to memorize and reproduce what was learned:

> Supplement writing by learning by heart upon this latter question, memory depends at bottom upon three conditions: thorough understanding of the subject, logical ordering of the contents, repetition to ourselves. Without these we can neither retain securely nor reproduce promptly. Read, then, attentively, read over and over again, test your memory vigorously and minutely. Verbal memory may with advantage be aided by ocular impressions; thus, for instance, we can have charts of geographical facts, genealogical trees, large-typed tables of rules of syntax and prosody, which we can hang on the walls. Or again, the scholar may make a practice of copying striking quotations at the top of his exercise books. I have known a proverb inscribed upon a ring, or a cup, sentences worth remembering painted on a door or a window. These are all devices for adding to our intellectual stores, which, trivial as they may seem individually, have a distinct cumulative value.[28]

Similar advice is repeated throughout Europe by education advocates. In Spain, Jiménez Patón recommends a method of dividing facts into strategically devised categories "porque el que dividiere bien, nunca errará en el buen orden, aprovecha también deprender por partes."[29] Comparable recommendations come from El Brocense, who considers it useful to include annotations and drawings in the margins to promote visual memory, such as an anchor if one is going to talk about a ship or a flower to denote something related to botany.[30] Similarly, Aguilera, in his *Ars memorativa*, advises using the margins of a book for mnemonic notetaking.[31] Other figures such as Arias Montano advocate writing out what one wants to memorize "para que la pluma escriba en la mente del mismo modo que en el papel."[32] What all these had in common, which Vives emphasizes, was writing as a key to remembering: "más tenazmente se adhieren a nuestra memoria las cosas que nosotros mismos transcribimos que lo escrito por los otros."[33] According to Vives, writing notes helps avoid possible distractions because "nuestro espíritu anda lejos de pensamientos livianos y torpes."[34]

The Cousin's passion for capturing and cataloguing information highlights the importance of many of these mnemotechnical systems which also represent the cultural practices and anxieties related to memory and learning in early modern Spain. The character is a reflection of what Beecher calls "the transition from the humanist's zeal for honing and training the human brain to an emerging awareness that the information anxiety of that era could only be allayed through extended and improved repositories of external memory."[35] The Cousin's seemingly innocuous scholarly work exposes the apprehension of the age when external supports for memory were paramount if humanists were to make sense out of their world and come to grips with a rapidly changing globalized society. Just as too little information can lead to poor understanding, too much information can be fraught with danger as well.

Pedagogy, Mnemonics, and the Limits of Humanist Education

At the heart of the Cousin's appearance in the novel is an interest in the Erasmian model of pedagogical humanism that responded to the ostensible demand for knowledge within pragmatic limits. Among these practical tenets was to move away from the teaching practices espoused by the art of memory. For Erasmus, the art of memory maintained a connection to a bygone era from which humanists of his stature wanted to dissociate themselves.[36] Consequently, memory and its mechanisms became a recurring theme in Erasmus's work insofar as he sought to train memory for reasonable and appropriate use, rather than for worthless memorization or excessive learning. In this regard, Beecher explains how the Erasmian pedagogical dictates attempted to control memory and protect it from empty contents:

> Memory was to be disciplined, but at the same time protected from second-rate knowledge. Excessive learning he deemed a threat to the mind; knowing everything is not only impossible but undesirable. Hence, in the manner of the firm but compassionate schoolmaster, Erasmus addressed the place of memory in the context of education. His considered approach enabled him to contain the information explosion, build attitudes of wit and understanding through discipline, sidestep the idle speculations

> based on mnemonics, and create an economy of mind that balanced reason and care with industry ... stocking the memory would remain his principal concern.[37]

According to Erasmus, memory, as the treasure of what was learned, had to be reinforced through repetition and practice, which should serve as the basis for all intellectual activity. But he understood that memory should be perfected to handle what was vital and what could be controlled since it was not infinite. The idea that memory's storage capacity was not enough was generally presented as a threat: "I am well aware what an ocean of parallels could be got together from the whole realm of nature, from all the fields of knowledge, all the poets, the historians, the orators. *But an attempt to pursue the infinite would be mere madness.*"[38] For Erasmus, it was impossible to know and memorize everything, and he advocated for a practical approach to learning. To do this, he would attend to two specific factors that are clearly represented in Cervantes's character: on the one hand, the limits of human memory and, on the other, the danger that knowledge was not always adequate or necessary. This is certainly the case with the Cousin, who certainly cannot know everything, but this fact largely amplifies his anxiety of not knowing and drives him to a relentless pursuit of answers. For example, faced with Sancho's question about who the first tumbler in the world was, the anguished Cousin cannot give him an answer at this time because, perhaps embarrassingly, he has yet to study it: "En verdad, hermano ... que no me sabré determinar ahora, hasta que lo estudie. Yo lo estudiaré en volviendo adonde tengo mis libros y yo os satisfaré cuando otra vez nos veamos, que no ha de ser esta la postrera."[39]

Erasmus's educational model gave memory an important role as a treasure of useful knowledge, linked to experience, to the benefit of society, and always with a practical purpose. A cultivated memory meant being able to access relevant information and perhaps expand on it, despite one having access to all sorts of material. However, confronted with the information explosion, heated debates arose about how to effectively memorize and store information. The increase in the circulation of books and the consequent information overload had great consequences that provoked "a methodological crossroads concerning memory and mnemonics, especially where humanist training was concerned."[40] Although there were a significant number of intellectuals who opposed the use of the art of memory, their opposition was mainly against its dry rules and the tendency towards rote memorization. In other words, the art of memory maintained its preeminence in learned circles and evolved into various cultural spheres, but some specific techniques such as rote memorization became the subject of debate. Indeed, the number of references to the art of memory's techniques, either from a critical perspective or one of praise, clearly underscores its pervasiveness and acceptance in society. This explains why there were, on the one hand, those who clung to more traditional methods of memorization such as those found in the art of memory and, on the other, those who began to express some apprehension towards such mnemonic systems, such as Erasmus and Francis Bacon. Mnemonic excesses were increasingly looked down upon in intellectual circles, whose members failed to see the functional utility of memory systems.[41] Most of them complained about the effects that these systems had on memory, overloading it with useless associations and, in many cases, causing mental imbalances.[42] For this reason, some intellectual humanists and pedagogues became reluctant to use the arts of memory in their classes, as was the case with Philip Melanchthon, who, in his *Rhetorica elementa* (1534),[43] prohibits his students from using mnemonic instruments that hinder learning and the ability to think critically. A similar animosity transpires from the words of Erasmus himself at the end of *The Praise of Folly*, where he denounces a useless memory: "There is an old saying, 'I hate a fellow-drinker with a memory' and here's a new one to put alongside it: 'I hate an audience which won't forget.'"[44] This condemnation was due in part to the fact that the art of memory and its systems of frames and repetitive schemes did not always promote invention and creativity. As noted by the intellectual Cornelius Agrippa, the art of memory is more spectacle than substance: "este arte sirve más a la pompa del ingenio y a la ostentación del saber que a procurar el saber mismo."[45] This manner of thinking explains why, in *The Vanitie and Uncertaintie of Artes and Sciences*, he even described the methodology of the art of memory as "monstrous."[46] Bacon shared similar ideas, describing this type of system as "ostentation prodigious" and "devoid of pragmatic usefulness."[47]

In Spain, echoes of these reflections could be found equally in the humanists Sánchez de las Brozas (*editio princeps* of *Ars dicendi*, 1556) and Vives (*De ratione dicendi libri* III). Conscious of the renovation of pedagogical methods, these writers exhibited a certain disaffection towards the art of memory that they viewed as often ineffective, pedantic, and sententious.[48] In a parallel line of thought, Francisco Cervantes de Salazar, in his *Colloquia* (titled *Academia Mexicana*), "proclama su tristeza y desolación tras comprobar que en la Universidad de Salamanca, de donde salió bachiller, no se aspira tanto a desarrollar el pensamiento como a engrosar la memoria,"[49] words that, without a doubt, are reminiscent of the Cousin's "engrosada" memory. In fact, Sánchez de las

Brozas refuses to explain this complicated system of learning to his students in the Colegio Trilingüe[50] and forcefully concludes the section on memory in his rhetoric manual: "Por último, nunca memorices nada que no hayas comprendido perfectamente."[51] These words no doubt recall the attitude of Erasmus, also shared by Vives, who emphasized understanding of what was learned over memorization. Vives reacted against memorization systems, arguing that their application should not be limited to that of the art of memory: "Mas la despierta y morbosa afición a las historias y a las fábulas especialmente cuando se llega a aquellas menuderías estultas indignas de saberse, aturden y desconciertan el ingenio, aploman el juicio y embarazan la memoria porque no tenga cabida en ella cosas mejores."[52] Similar advice is found in Ciruelo's work on the art of memory: "amonestamos a todos los estudiosos que no … se dediquen en exceso al arte de la memoria, pues produce tanta utilidad a la memoria como impedimento puede ofrecer al ingenio y a la recta inteligencia de lo que se ha de aprender."[53] Comparable reactions in Spain are also found in *Vida del escudero Marcos de Obregón* (1618), in which the reader encounters the following very pertinent recommendation about the subject at hand: "Tener buena memoria natural es excelentísima cosa; pero gastar el tiempo en buscar dos o tres mil lugares pudiéndolo gastar en actos de entendimiento, no lo tengo por muy acertado."[54]

Despite the rejection of the excesses caused by the art of memory, "the capacity and training of the memory remained a matter for consideration, for treasure-house minds had their uses and the libraries were filling with more and more books."[55] Faced with the tireless search for answers and methods that would facilitate learning, Erasmus approached the subject not in terms of the information explosion and what this overload meant for the scholar's mind, but rather by focusing on what the scholar should know in relation to the outside world, a pragmatic knowledge that did matter to memory and understanding. Don Quixote echoes this perspective himself during his conversations with the Cousin. Given the immense amount of information that the Cousin provides to Sancho to answer his questions, the squire decides not to continue making queries because "para preguntar necedades y responder disparates no he menester yo andar buscando ayuda de vecinos."[56] Don Quixote, who had been attentive to the conversation between the squire and the Cousin, sarcastically acknowledges Sancho's judgment: "Más has dicho, Sancho, de lo que sabes … que hay algunos que se cansan en saber y averiguar cosas que después de sabidas y averiguadas no importan un ardite al entendimiento ni a la memoria."[57] With these words, the writer indeed seemed to be following Erasmus's perspective on memory's place in education. In this sense, memorizing to learn insignificant information is clearly differentiated from the meaningful acquisition of relevant knowledge that was a key characteristic of the intellectual. Like Erasmus, he favoured pedagogical programs that advocated intimate detailed engagement for the sake of long-term learning. Likewise, his reflection reiterates, albeit with parodic and satirical overtones, the scholar's anxiety to memorize and acquire knowledge, reflected once again in Don Quixote's words: "para componer historias y libros, de cualquier suerte que sean, es menester un gran juicio y un maduro entendimiento."[58] As I explore in the next section, the Cousin fails to understand Erasmus's proposition for learning, which elevates the well-being of the student by providing the appropriate tools to master a particular knowledge base without saturating his memory with irrelevant information.

The Cousin: Student and Humanist

It is within this environment that "el primo" emerges, product of a need to store in memory massive amounts of data in the face of an explosion of information. The Cousin is a character who, although secondary, has greater relevance in the novel than it first seems.[59] Like many other characters, such as the duke and the duchess, for example, his name is never known. This anonymity makes him a representative of an entire group of people in society that Cervantes does not favour, mainly, in this case, because of the banal nature of their rote memorization of useless facts simply for the sake of learning something new.[60] The values of the word *primo* and the etymological evolution of the term, analysed by Helena Percas de Ponseti, shed light on the conception of this character. From the Latin *primus, primero,* or first, passing through *rústico, tonto,* or *víctima de un engaño* (rustic, stupid, or victim of a deception), among other meanings, the Cousin is characterized for his empty erudition, which is latent in the genre he cultivates.[61] Memory is an intrinsic part of the Cousin insofar as he continuously tries to delve further into the past, the origins, and the inventions of things. Along these lines, he is driven by the desire to find out who was the first to do most anything. The results of his queries are compiled in books that reveal his eagerness and obsession to know more about the subjects he studies, regardless of the relevance or credibility of the events narrated therein.

The timing of his appearance in the novel is, in itself, strategic: he is introduced when Don Quixote asks for a guide to accompany him to the Montesinos Cave, clearly one of the most emblematic episodes of the novel. His influence will therefore facilitate Don Quixote's dream sequence, where the river and the Ruidera lagoons will be portrayed "en términos ovidianos, como si se tratase de personajes metamorfoseados de la leyenda carolingia,"[62] very much in keeping with the genre of books to which the Cousin dedicates himself. The Cousin is presented as Don Quixote's *alter ego* just as Cardenio was,[63] except this time, like the hidalgo from La Mancha, the Cousin is an avid reader of chivalric novels and another madman intoxicated[64] by books whose effects he obviously suffers:[65] "El licenciado le dijo que le daría a un primo suyo, famoso estudiante y muy aficionado a leer libros de caballerías, el cual con mucha voluntad le pondría a la boca de la mesma cueva y le enseñaría las lagunas de Ruidera, famosas ansimismo en toda la Mancha, y aun en toda España."[66] This "don Quijote de la erudición,"[67] in Riquer's words, will get along wonderfully with the novel's protagonist. As Riley has stated, the Cousin takes Don Quixote very seriously, primarily because he too suffers from the same "ridícula propensión a confundir la fábula poética y el hecho empírico."[68]

The increasingly incipient empirical-scientific atmosphere of the time yielded a negative valuation of individuals like the Cousin, due primarily to the absurdity of their projects and the arrogance they displayed in carrying them out. Whereas the figure of the "humanist" scholar was associated with excellent memory and a strong will to study, he also was deemed dangerously overconfident, as Huarte points out: "los grandes latinos son más arrogantes y presuntuosos"[69] and "los gramáticos son hombres de gran memoria y hacen junta con aquella diferencia de imaginativas, forzosamente son faltos de entender."[70] Similarly, as the educational theorist Pedro López de Montoya emphasizes, the principal weapon the humanist possessed was an uncanny ability to memorize just enough to pass himself off as an expert because he has been able to remember a lot "de coro" – that is, by heart:

> Porque unos llamaban humanistas a los que saben muchos versos de poetas de coro, otros a los que profesan un poco más pulido latín que los demás; otros a los que saben fábulas y historias humanas, otros a los que alcanzan a saber un poco griego y otros a otros que están muy lejos de llegar a saber lo que le obliga el nombre de humanista.[71]

What emerges from the depictions of the humanist above is his portrayal as someone who proclaims himself more knowledgeable and more widely read than others but who likewise knows that no one else is positioned to assess the dubiousness of such claims. Indeed, as Luis Gil Fernández suggests, some humanists' intelligence was so highly suspect that they actually undermined the acquisition of knowledge: "perdido su justificación como 'médico' de la ignorancia y crítico de toda clase de libros. Los avances de la especialización le habían reducido a la categoría de erudito universal, cuyos saberes inconexos y enciclopédicos se revelaban a la postre sólo buenos para amenizar tertulias."[72]

To such evaluations we must also add the ambiguity of the term "humanist"[73] that Cervantes captures in the portrayal of the Cousin. He is the product of the fusion of two tendencies, as described by the narrator in the novel: "su profesión era ser humanista; sus ejercicios y estudios, componer libros para dar a la estampa, todos de gran provecho y no menos entretenimiento para la república."[74] The character thus is a student in addition to being a humanist, and it is very likely that Cervantes's characterization was refined from among the students with whom the author lived and whom he met throughout his life.[75] Thus, for example, many are brought to life in his fiction in *La Cueva de Salamanca, El coloquio de los perros, El Licenciado Vidriera,* in the prologue to *Persiles y Sigismunda,* and in *Don Quixote.* Wardropper has pointed out that Cervantes holds a complex opinion towards the figure of the student – and towards education in general – which is partially revealed by the numerous portraits he paints of them. According to Wardropper, throughout Cervantes's work there is a certain resentment towards all those who have received academic training, the Cousin being one of them, probably because Cervantes was not afforded the same opportunity. In most cases, these students lie constantly, like Carriazo and Avendaño in *La ilustre fregona,* boasting an academic pretense under which falsehood is hidden.[76] Linked to the pedagogical sphere, the figure of the student, as Maxime Chevalier has noted, had a folkloric character related to the genre of "gallos" or university vexations, which had already been cultivated by writers such as Quevedo.[77]

However, in contrast to university graduates, there are those whose lack of resources disallowed formal study, yet they acquire knowledge in the school of life, especially women like Marcela in *Don Quixote* or Preciosa, the protagonist of *La gitanilla* or those who see education as the only way to move up the social ladder, like Tomás Rodaja from *El licenciado vidriera.* It is not surprising that in the absence of academic qualifications such as bachelor's, graduate, or law degrees, the writer considered himself an *ingenio lego,* an autodidact who valued above all the experience, as reflected in *La gitanilla*: "No hay muchacha de doce que no sepa lo que de veinte y cinco, porque tienen por maestros y preceptores al diablo y al uso, que les enseña en una hora lo que habían de aprender en un año."[78] Cervantes, without university training himself but well acquainted with life's lesson through personal study and hard experience, satirizes the figure of the scholar through the "humanist"[79] Cousin. Cervantes mocks his pedantry to the point of placing the sly Sancho above the extravagant character and by questioning and making fun of what he writes. Indeed, when Don Quixote emerges from the cave, the Cousin will believe everything he is told, despite the fact that Sancho considers it all a great "disparate," "embeleco," or "mentira."

External Memories

Beyond the Erasmian debates on pedagogy, through the Cousin, Cervantes also seems to be criticizing the sort of intellectual work that scholars undertake. Indeed, the type of books written by the Cousin are not original research studies yielding insight into a particular topic but rather collections designed to organize facts for easier memorization. The diversity of titles chosen in the episode overtly reflects the miscellaneous nature of research as well as the wide diffusion and subject matter of these books during the period: *Polyanthea, Officina, Sylva, Hortus floridus, Thesaurus, Theatrum, Syntaxis, Panopticon, Argumenta.* In Spain, *Poliantea, Teatro, Fábrica, Jardín,* and *Florilogio*[80] were texts that collected information from other books. Books of this sort were considered scholarly tools, and they emerged as technical aids to help learn the material and relieve the pressure to which the intellectuals of the time were subjected. The books depended on aids or paratextual devices such as subject headings, lists of authorities, alphabetical indexing, and tables of contents that facilitated the search for the topics needed.[81] These paratextual devices were not just accessories, "but an integral part of the text itself, in as much as they give expression to a precise cultural project and a way of perceiving and communicating knowledge."[82] Some of the printed works making up this genre, such as bibliographies or reviews, proliferated, and others, such as florilegia, dictionaries, or collections with a marked encyclopedic character, were consolidated.[83] In particular, ancient texts – collected in many of the miscellanies and *polyantheas* – became a constant obsession for humanist educators who saw these works as the most important instruments of erudition. Ancillary works became necessary in humanistic training to structure available knowledge and were already in use in the Middle Ages in the form of *catena* or chain, *Florilegium,* or *thesauri.*[84] To this end, this category of works collected whatever was considered worthy of being remembered and established a series of techniques and devices to do so. Reflecting the cultural sphere where reading and writing have become professional, these works are intended for a more or less cultured audience. All these reference books were initially a compilation of reading notes adapted from medieval models published since the thirteenth century, and they cited other previously written reference books, in much the same way that the Cousin does in his own works. And this is how, even in the sixteenth and seventeenth centuries, numerous humanists dedicated themselves to the creation of a miscellany of humanistic scholarship. The proliferation of this type of compilation during Cervantes's time, which caused that "cada vez se acudiera menos a las fuentes y más a las polyantheas," was also fostered by institutions such as the Council of Trent, which sought to promote the renewal of eloquence in the pulpit and the erudition of preachers, which created on many occasions "espejismos de sabiduría."[85]

The decision by intellectuals to print their compendia as bound books contributed to the proliferation of published manuscripts and simultaneously served to increase the number of works to be consulted. In other words, even more books were created to summarize, organize, and structure the knowledge contained in other books, which is precisely the Cousin's main scholarly focus. In fact, he declares that he has published three books, which highlights the overarching role of the printing press, which made available an immense quantity of information that made assimilation, digestion, and memorization even more difficult tasks.[86] The narrator says that the Cousin was a "mozo que sabía hacer libros para imprimir y para dirigirlos a príncipes,"[87] whose three books are ready for the printing press. He describes them as "de gran provecho y no menos entretenimiento para la república,"[88] underscoring both the opportunism and his belief that they are valuable to society because they are entertaining. It is also apparent that the Cousin's knowledge comes not from original study but from what he has read or heard from other sources, and not always with any particularly helpful benefit. Don Quixote will clearly note this fact after hearing a description of the books. The first of the Cousin's works on *libreas* is described in the following way:

> donde pinta setecientas y tres libreas, con sus colores, motes y cifras, de donde podían sacar y tomar las que quisiesen en tiempo de fiestas y regocijos los caballeros cortesanos, sin andarlas mendigando de nadie, ni lambicando, como dicen, el cerbelo, por sacarlas conformes a sus deseos e intenciones.[89]

According to its description, the book is clearly not a research study but rather a collection of images of uniforms (*libreas*) designed to help courtly gentlemen. Described as "al celoso, al desdeñado, al olvidado y al ausente,"[90] its only purpose is to provide the appropriate attire at festivals. In books of this nature, the colour of each uniform had a symbolic value, and they were represented as allegorical drawings (figures) alongside verses (*motes*). However, as Julio Caro Baroja has suggested, the word *librea* is not used here as uniform dress, but rather with the meaning of emblem or currency,[91] which prompts memory to connect the book's stylized pictures, or hieroglyphs, to their meaning.

In Cervantes's time works featuring emblems were used as a source for *inventio* and a tool for memory. Thus, for example, in his speech "De la docta erudición y de las fuentes que se saca," Baltasar Gracián describes the emblem, along with the hieroglyphs and companies, as "la pedrería preciosa al oro del fino discurrir."[92] The *Emblemas morales* (1604) by Horozco or those by Covarrubias, along with *Memoria, entendimiento y voluntad* (1677) and *Ver, oír, oler, gustar y tocar …* (1687) by Lorenzo Ortiz include erudite quotes, *exempla*, and fables accompanied by their visual image to facilitate their memorization and as an aid to *inventio*. Juan Solórzano Pereira's *Emblemata centum regio-politica* (1653) and Saavedra Fajardo's *Idea de un príncipe politico-cristiano en cien empresas* (1640) were also consulted by writers and preachers as scholarly sources for their works and sermons. A similar evolution took place with the commentaries on the emblem books, another genre equally esteemed by humanists during the time of Cervantes. Sánchez de las Brozas's commentary to the *Emblemas de Alciato* (1573), for example, served as a source of invention for both writers and painters to develop the concept of *mutuo auxilio* by which "cada uno da rienda suelta a su talante y forma de concebir el epigrama moral produciendo composiciones que teniendo un germen idéntico, dan como resultado frutos diversos en el ejercicio de la *imitación compuesta*."[93]

The Cousin's second book, *Metamorfóseos*, or *Ovidio español*, is basically an imitation of Ovid's masterwork, which he calls "invención nueva y rara," and he admits its parodic intention, "imitando a Ovidio a lo burlesco" (II.22, 812). The Cousin takes advantage of Ovid's legendary themes involving natural and architectural elements as transmutations of human beings:

> [E]n él, imitando a Ovidio a lo burlesco, pinto quién fue la Giralda de Sevilla y el Ángel de la Madalena, quién el Caño de Vecinguerra de Córdoba, quiénes los Toros de Guisando, la Sierra Morena, las fuentes de Leganitos y Lavapiés en Madrid, no olvidándome de la del Piojo, de la del Caño Dorado y de la Priora; y esto, con sus alegorías, metáforas y translaciones.[94]

There is little doubt that the inclusion of the work follows Cervantes's overall strategy to parody previous literary forms or genres. The third and final work, entitled *Suplemento a Virgilio Polidoro*, is similarly parodic. The Cousin's version supposedly builds upon *De inventoribus rerum* (1499) by the Italian humanist Polidoro Virgili, which was widely read in Spain after its 1550 translation to Spanish. According to the Cousin, his supplement deals with the invention of things that Polidoro left out of his original text, but the reader will quickly note a list of meaningless details: "quién fue el primero que tuvo catarro en el mundo, y el primero que tomó las unciones para curarse del morbo gálico, y yo lo declaro al pie de la letra, y lo autorizo con más de veinte y cinco autores, porque vea vuesa merced si he trabajado bien y si ha de ser útil el tal libro a todo el mundo."[95] The Cousin proudly boasts that his supplement is significant and scholarly: "de grande erudición y estudio, a causa que las cosas que se dejó de decir Polidoro de gran sustancia las averiguo yo y las declaro por gentil estilo."[96] However, the reader would quickly recognize the ridiculousness of the subject matter and the overconfidence of its author. Adding new information to existing books was a common practice during the period due to a latent obsession with expanding on existing knowledge sets. For example, Jerónimo de Huerta, the Spanish translator of Pliny's *Natural History*, adds to his translation contemporary inventions such as the printing press, the needle, and the famous "artificio" designed by the Spanish-Italian engineer Juanelo Turriano to lift the water from the Tagus River in Toledo. Something very similar happened with Polidoro's *De inventoribus rerum*. Originally composed of three books, by 1521 five more books were added, and more than fifty editions were published over two centuries while being translated into English, German, Spanish, and Italian. Given the acclaim of Polidoro's work in Spain and the constant additions it had, it is not surprising that the Cousin latches on to its popularity.

The constant growth of works like Polidoro's certainly led to the problem of reconciling conflicting authorities or of determining fact from fiction within the labyrinth of letters. As any serious scholar knows, the obvious dilemma that emerged from this sort of process was that many books put forth information based on dubious claims made in previous publications, yielding studies that lacked credibility or veracity. As the Cousin shows, it was far easier to write a supplement to already-published books than to create original research, particularly when the printed word of previously published books is accepted as factual. The action of publishing dubious research set up a number of issues and contradictions, as Blair states: "the problem of overabundance involved not only too many books, but books ferrying too many different, new, and conflicting authorities, opinions and experiences,"[97] which motivated a number of satirical portrayals of the learned. It is important to underscore that the Cousin's understanding of what is scholarship is suspect; he believes that consulting twenty-five authors will provide the veracity, and therefore importance, of his work, but this may be Cervantes's own commentary on the number of authorities on a single topic, most of whom would not agree on the same information. The Cousin also fails to recognize that the very topics he is studying are in no way important, nor are they really expanding the knowledge base. The entire scenario underscores the burlesque nature of the episode while also providing a space to mock how trivial academic scholarship can be if left to a faux erudite.

The Mimetic Memory of the Cousin

The overwhelming but suspect erudition featured in the Cousin's books reflects the reality of a genre that was still very much in force at the time *Don Quixote* was written and that Cervantes satirizes as only he knows how. As Egido and Montero Reguera have stated, the Cousin's appearance is a criticism focused not only on the student-humanist but also on the genre associated with a character type that was very fashionable at the time and from which Cervantes "realiza un nuevo ejercicio de crítica literaria."[98] In the Cousin's works, like so many others that make up the genre, the past to which these works refers appears repeatedly distorted by the inability to discern between the real and the fictitious and the ease with which it uses unverified sources. Arguably the best example is the Cousin's intent to capture all that happened to Don Quixote in the Montesinos Cave. When, upon leaving the cave, Don Quixote recounts everything that has happened in it, the Cousin, obsessed with obtaining more knowledge, is pleased to be able to add additional information to his *Ovidio español* and *Suplemento de Virgilio Polidoro*:

> Yo, señor Don Quijote de la Mancha, doy por bien empleadísima la jornada que con vuesa merced he hecho, porque en ella he granjeado cuatro cosas. La primera, haber conocido a vuestra merced, que lo tengo a gran felicidad. La segunda, haber sabido lo que se encierra en esta cueva de Montesinos, con las mutaciones de Guadiana y de las lagunas de Ruidera, que me servirán para el Ovidio español que traigo entre manos. La tercera, entender la antigüedad de los naipes, que, por lo menos, ya se usaban en tiempo del emperador Carlo Magno, según puede colegirse de las palabras que vuesa merced dice que dijo Durandarte, cuando al cabo de

aquel grande espacio que estuvo hablando con él Montesinos, él despertó diciendo; 'Paciencia y barajar.' Y esta razón y modo de hablar no la pudo aprender encantado, sino cuando no lo estaba, en Francia y en tiempo del referido emperador Carlo Magno. Y esta averiguación me viene pintiparada para el otro libro que voy componiendo, que es Suplemento de Virgilio Polidoro, en la invención de las antigüedades; y creo que en el suyo no se acordó de poner la de los naipes, como la pondré yo ahora, que será de mucha importancia, y más alegando autor tan grave y tan verdadero como es el señor Durandarte. La cuarta es haber sabido con certidumbre el nacimiento del río Guadiana, hasta ahora ignorado de las gentes.[99]

The publication of such nonsense reveals the great paradox regarding the genre. Books like the Cousin's published verified certainties alongside information that lacked veracity, thus giving equal status to fanciful facts, supernatural phenomena, astrological prediction, and all kinds of wonders. In this instance, the Cousin has no intention of verifying Don Quixote's account – he accepts it at face value.

Works like those of the Cousin were disdained in some circles due to the publication of errors that led some to believe – even repeat to the letter – many incomplete and non-verified details. After all, thanks to their dissemination, one had access to a whole range of information related to classical and modern culture in a relatively fast and accessible way. However, because so many books were printed espousing suspect information, prominent figures in pedagogy such as Erasmus and Vives wrote that it was incumbent upon the individual to determine the veracity of information. As Baltasar Gracián reminds us, readers must examine everything "con seso": that is, by using care and intellect:

Tiene la memoria una como despensa, llena de este erudito pasto, para sustentar el ánimo, y de enriquecer y fecundar los convites que suele hacer a los entendimientos. Es una magacén rebatido, un vestuario curioso, un guardajoyas de sabiduría. Sin la erudición no tienen gusto ni sustancia los discursos, ni las conversaciones ni los libros. Con ella ilustra y adorna el varón sabio lo que enseña, porque así sirve para el gusto como para el provecho ... pero no ha de ser uniforme, ni homogénea, ni toda sacra, ni toda profana, ya la antigua, ya la moderna, una vez un dicho, otra un hecho de la historia, de la poesía, que la hermosa variedad es punto de providencia. Especialmente se ha de atender a la ocasión y a las circunstancias de la materia, del lugar, de los oyentes, que la mayor prenda del que habla o escribe, del orador o historiador, es decir, con seso.[100]

And that's where the Cousin's problem lays. His useless knowledge and his accumulation of uncorroborated or unverified data place him at the height of the false scholars. These "sabios-tontos," so common at the time, were criticized by Erasmus in chapter 50 of *In Praise of Folly*, where the humanist, quoting Homer, points out that "even the fool is wise after the event"[101] and criticizes "those who court immortal fame by writing books."[102] The reproach continues when "they're on show in the bookshops, every title-page displaying their three names, which are mostly foreign and evidently intended to be spellbinding ... Then too those names are invented more often than not, or borrowed from the works of ancients."[103] Therefore, many of these miscellanies and repertoires were sometimes considered a sign of empty erudition – of useless knowledge – and they became very unpopular and a target of satire.

In the end, reference books were only sometimes put to good use. Other times, as literary works attest, they were the base for mockery that led to the creation of negative portrayals of intellectuals, as Saavedra Fajardo states in *República literaria* (1616):

> Otros juntaban, a favor de los perezosos, ramilletes de flores y sentencias de varios autores, en que antes merecían pena que premio, pues deslustraban aquellas sentencias, que fuera de su lugar son como piedras sacadas de su edificio, donde hacen labor, o como moneda de vellón fuera de los reinos donde se acuña y corre. Algunos muy aprisa se paseaban encomendando a la memoria aforismos y brocárdicos para parecer doctos, y otros, con la misma ambición se aplicaban a saber los títulos de los libros y tener ciertas noticias generales de sus materias, con que en todas las conversaciones hacían una vana ostentación de las ciencias.

The most explicit paradigm of this rejection of the excessive use of the pedantic quotation, without utility or profit, to which authors such as Lope de Vega[104] were accustomed, is found in the Prologue to the first part of *Don Quixote*, where the narrator alludes to his

> falta de toda erudición y doctrina, sin acotaciones en las márgenes y sin anotaciones en el fin del libro, como veo que están otros libros, aunque sean fabulosos y profanos, tan llenos de sentencias de Aristóteles, de Platón y de toda la caterva de filósofos, que admiran a los leyentes y tienen a sus autores por hombres leídos, eruditos y elocuentes.[105]

In this Prologue, the author's friend enters the scene to give advice on how to write a prologue. Cervantes laments that his work does not have the typical paratextual devices such as "acotaciones en las márgenes," "anotaciones en el fin del libro," and "sentencias" by authors in alphabetical order, "comenzando en Aristóteles y acabando en Xenofonte y en Zoílo." The procedure the friend recommends is a faithful reflection of the system followed by many intellectuals of the time. In this instance, fond of using erudite quotations, the friend suggests the use of reference books "que os cuesten poco trabajo el buscalle" to find those that best suited the nature and themes of the work. It makes sense, therefore, to think that this taste for scholarly quotations contributed to the massive proliferation of compilations that served as memory aids to adorn all kinds of writings. But Cervantes is not fooled. He denounces the excessive use of citations by contemporaries, and his Prologue to the first part of *Don Quixote* is a great illustration of how to satirize contemporary writers or (pseudo)writers who depend on reference books:

> En resolución, no hay más sino que vos procuréis nombrar estos nombres, o tocar estas historias en la vuestra, que aquí he dicho, y dejadme a mí el cargo de poner las anotaciones y acotaciones; que yo os voto a tal de llenaros las márgenes y de gastar cuatro pliegos en el fin del libro. Vengamos ahora a la citación de los autores que los otros libros tienen, que en el vuestro os faltan. El remedio que esto tiene es muy fácil, porque no habéis de hacer otra cosa que buscar un libro que los acote todos, desde la A hasta la Z, como vos decís.[106]

The advice of the friend follows to the letter the most common practices of many writers who, fans of the erudite citation, resorted to this type of book to find the ones that best suited the nature and themes of their work. The procedure recommended is a faithful reflection of the system followed by many of the intellectuals of the time. Cervantes ironically made good use of the same strategies he criticized, and reference works often make their way into his text. According to Daniel Eisenberg, the writer owned copies of Mejía's *Silva de varia lección* and Pliny's *Natural History*, and there are references found to them in his narrative although he does not specifically cite the source. As Victor Infantes states: "Estas polyantheas circularon, se consultaban, se compraban y se ocultaba (habitualmente) la cita de su conocimiento."[107] The fact that such reference books are used but not cited indicates why Infantes calls them the secret dictionaries of the time.

These books were known as ancillary *tesoros* (treasures or thesauri) of scholarship of invention, or *inventio*, usually consisting of compilations that speakers, writers, scholars, poets, and preachers used as memory aids. The word *inventio* comes from the Latin word *invenire*, whose meaning was none other than "acudir a la memoria (o a los instrumentos de ayuda) en busca de los *loci, topoi* o lugares comunes tipificados."[108] These compilations were not completely devoid of purpose or scholarship. They also served as "auxiliares de la invención"[109] for professional writers like Cervantes and also for preachers and artists to carry out their works, either to adorn them with erudition, endowing them with *auctoritas* through citations, or as a source of *imitatio* and *inventio*. These professionals widely hailed the *polyantheas* as a significant source that could be utilized to adorn their own artistic and erudite creations with helpful facts. Like Cervantes, their livelihood depended on such critical resources as they sought to provide *auctoritas* through citations or as a source of erudition and help to the *inventio*. In fact, other reputable writers often consulted these works. For example, when Francisco de Quevedo was imprisoned in San Marcos de León, friends loaned him their books, including Joseph Lange's *Polyanthea,* which he used to write some of his own works during his incarceration. Similarly, Lope de Vega used the *Dictionarium historicum, geographicum, poeticum* (1603) by Carlos Stephanus to clarify data and historical and geographical terms in the composition of his *Arcadia* (1598).[110] One of the first encyclopedic works in Ancient Rome was that of Pliny the Elder, whose *Natural History* is known to have been used by Cervantes, since the author had a copy in his private library. Among the many miscellanies, in addition to Mejía's *Silva,* that Cervantes mentions or cites in his literary works is Antonio de Torquemada's *Jardín de flores curiosas* (1570), which mixed all kinds of subjects and enjoyed great editorial success. For his part, Mejía took material from Polidoro's famous *De inventoribus rerum* (1499) – the same work that the "humanist" Cousin claims to be improving.

Unlike the Cousin, Cervantes and other authors turned to his sources to create his own narrative rather than to embellish upon others, which is where the main difference lies. It was no longer a question of repeating mimetics but of promoting invention, starting from what was stored in memory. As a matter of fact, the obsession with the past and the importance given to memory are also observed within the literary creation itself, as seen in the studies by Bolzoni, Raphael Lyne, and Terence Cave. Bolzoni in *The Gallery of Memory* shows that at a time when the past and the imitation and reappropriation of classical models were so much in vogue, the action of writing depended on memory:

> In a world so obsessed with giving itself norms and establishing models, memory plays an essential role. If, in fact, imitation of the old is a stage in the production of something new, and if a writer's individuality cannot be expressed without appropriating "other" texts, then *writing means above all*

> *remembering*. The whole game depends on the relationship between imitation and variation. It is essential, therefore, for an author – and his ideal reader as well – to recall easily the text used as a model.[111]

The recollection of these authors and their texts was extremely important for the humanist project and the scholars who participated in it.[112] As an illustration, Cervantes is the representation of the cognitive competence of the humanist of his time as an act of memory in action where he is able to invent and create within a literary mimetic frame.

Memory therefore plays an important role in the composition of the novel through the appropriation of other literary genres that involve constantly remembering and imitating a whole corpus of texts that serve as a starting point for the creative process. From the *Entremés of the Romances* to the most famous predecessors of the genre of chivalry such as Ariosto, Pulci, and Boiardo, Cervantes employs a variety of source material in order to write, as Ramón Menéndez Pidal once put it, "the last of the romances of chivalry, the definitive and most perfect one."[113] As a result, imitation becomes a game in which both the author and the reader of *Don Quixote* participate, where codes of interpretation are constantly activated, and where the role of memory is fundamental.[114] While the positive attributes of imitation were numerous, the *imitatio*, itself an act of memory, also posed a problem that obsessed writers and artists:

> [T]he adopting of prototypes from among best writers, not in servile copywork, but in creative elaboration, which could only be achieved ... by selection, reinterpretation, and improvement. This is both an act of memory and a natural process of memory insofar as perfect recall is plagiarism, while recollection is reconstructive, enhanced by altered circumstances, personal application, improved logic, and a personalization of the style and manner.[115]

This act of memory is part of a Renaissance method of education known as the process of *melification*, an exercise in intertextuality by which what is read is memorized, assimilated, and remembered throughout the humanist movement. For example, in Castiglione's *The Book of the Courtier* (1528), the character Bembo expounds how the courtier's learning and teaching process should be, always with good judgment and understanding:

> [A]nd governing himself with that good judgement which must be his guide, to go about selecting now this thing from one and that thing from

> another. And as the bee in the green meadows is ever wont to rob the flowers among the grass, so our Courtier must steal this grace from all who seem to possess it, taking from each that part which shall most be worthy praise.[116]

Michel de Montaigne, like Erasmus, questions some of the pedagogical assumptions that equated memory and knowledge and recommends taking from the past what is needed to turn it into his own work: "So of matter borrowed of others, one may lawfully alter, transform, and blend it to compile a perfect piece of work altogether his own."[117]

The Cousin's abundance of knowledge should be a guarantee of his success; nevertheless, according to Erasmus's paradigm, it is not. On the contrary, it is a reflection of his intellectual failure. There is a disconnect between what he knows and how he puts it to use, between the quantitative appropriation of knowledge and qualitative selection. Knowing everything – that is to say, remembering everything – is impossible: "Erasmus and the other advocates of the well trained memory realized from the outset that their epistemology of memory placed an enormous burden on the mental stability of the individual student."[118] Cervantes seems to be referencing this debate with the figure of the Cousin. The character is driven by the constant desire to remain faithful to the models, to the principle of authority, and there is no better way to achieve that than with a genre faithful to repetitive memory, faithful to the past such as that of the *polyanthea*. The Cousin, who keeps information in his memory without making the most of what is stored there, is, in Huarte's words, like "la mujer que se empreña y pare un hijo a la luz, la cabeza donde han de estar los pies y los ojos en el colodrillo."[119] Unlike Don Quixote, the Cousin uses his memory without putting too much emphasis on the constructive power of the *reminiscentia*. It seems to be a serious problem, as indicated by Covarrubias in his *Emblemas morales* (1610):

> No son pocos los confiados en su memoria se atreven a subir en las cátedras, y aún en los púlpitos, leyendo y predicando, con gran desemboltura, y donayre lo que otro ha trabajado; y aunque él lo recita, son estos semejantes a los papagayos, y a las demás aves vocales que aprenden lo que les enseñan, y no tienen más que el sonido.[120]

With the inherent risk of being lost among the increasingly abundant number of bibliographic sources, both the character and his works represent the magnitude of a serious problem that beset intellectuals. In short, the Cousin is the product of a culture in which methods of cataloguing, diversification, and memorization of knowledge have become increasingly necessary in the face of a growing number of books and other textual resources. With the rising number of bibliographic sources came an inherent risk of losing information, and textual aids and tools assisted one in remembering. Through the Cousin, we can see both the necessity of these reference works and their impact on the attitudes towards scholarship in Cervantes's time. His inability to forget and the high price he must pay for remembering exhaustively transform him into a victim of an anxiety provoked by the constant learning to which the intellectual submits himself and the havoc caused by his already saturated memory. On the one hand, the eagerness for erudition and admiration for memory made memorization techniques, partly associated with the art of memory, reach their greatest moment of splendor, "convirtiéndose en parte de la compleja búsqueda de una llave universal de acceso al saber, recogido y ordenado en las refundadas enciclopedias,"[121] whose prominence serves as the context for the works by the Cousin. On the other hand, there was a general feeling in learned circles that the importance given to memory led to the weakening of intellectual capacity and, consequently, the inability to think for oneself. This, in turn, led to slavish memory of an *imitatio* without *inventio*, of "los que nada ponen de su casa, refiriendo autoridades agenas por ostentar su memoria, [desluciendo] su entendimiento,"[122] in the words of Francisco Bances Candamo.

Cervantes portrays in this character – satirized and criticized during his short intervention – the inconvenience of remembering everything and the devastating effects on the individual's personality. This leads me back to Borges's *Funes el Memorioso*[123] and another famous memoirist – the mnemonist Solomon Shereshevsky.[124] Their case was studied by the psychologist Alexander Luria and Daniel Schacter, the latter highlighting the crowded memory of both, full of useless memories and trivial and unnecessary information and lacking the adaptive memory function: "Overwhelmed by detailed memories of every page from our past, we would be left out without a coherent story to tell."[125] Similarly, due to the constant memories and knowledge that abound in his memory, the Cousin has no history of his own, overwhelmed by all useless knowledge. Unlike other characters who parade through the novel, the Cousin does not talk about himself or his personal experiences, nor does he tell us "his" story, only those of others found in his books. His memory is referential and mimetic and lacks a creative component, a condition denounced by Cervantes and other representative figures of the time. His memory, like that of Funes, is a dump for things that, in the words of Don Quixote himself, "no importan un ardite al entendimiento ni a la memoria."[126]

Chapter 5

Disputes over Memory: Sancho and the Artful Manipulation of Memory

Hamlet: Do you see yonder cloud that's almost in shape of a camel?
Polonius: By the mass, and 'tis like a camel, indeed.
Hamlet: Methinks it is like a weasel.
Polonius: It is backed like a weasel.
Hamlet: Or like a whale?
Polonius: Very like a whale.
– William Shakespeare
Hamlet[1]

"O Sancho miente o Sancho sueña"

In Part Two of *Don Quixote*, the knight and squire are made the victims of an elaborate hoax in which they are blindfolded and told to mount a wooden horse named Clavileño which, they are told, will fly them to the heavens. The adventure comes to an end when fireworks packed into the pegged horse explode, throwing the riders to the ground, which causes the uproarious laughter of the spectators. The subsequent descriptions of what Don Quixote and Sancho experienced, however, are vastly different. For his part, Sancho convincingly argues that they flew near the constellation Pleiades, what he and others during the time would refer to as "las siete cabrillas":[2]

> – Yo, señora, sentí que íbamos, según mi señor me dijo, volando por la región del fuego, y quise descubrirme un poco los ojos, pero mi amo, a quien pedí licencia para descubrirme, no la consintió; mas yo, que tengo no sé qué briznas de curioso y de desear saber lo que se me estorba y impide, bonitamente y sin que nadie lo viese, por junto a las narices aparté tanto cuanto el pañizuelo que me tapaba los ojos y por allí miré hacia la

> tierra, y parecióme que toda ella no era mayor que un grano de mostaza, y los hombres que andaban sobre ella, poco mayores que avellanas: porque se vea cuán altos debíamos de ir.[3]

The witnesses gathered around do not ask the squire more about his version of the dubious voyage, but a sceptical Don Quixote aptly summarizes their perspective when he says, "o Sancho miente o Sancho sueña."[4] Nevertheless, as the narrator poignantly tells us, Don Quixote proposes a deal. The knight leans into Sancho to speak in his ear: "Sancho pues vos queréis que se os crea lo que habéis visto en el cielo, yo quiero que vos me creáis a mí lo que vi en la cueva de Montesinos. Y no os digo más."[5] The moment has often been cited as the definitive pact between knight and squire, profoundly cementing their personal friendship and destroying any previous socio-hierarchical relationship.

The entire passage also embodies a fundamental idea about memory related to the difference in time between the experienced moment and its later reexamination that accommodates a multitude of perspectives and interpretations. This double apprehension of things remembered is described by Hiscock and Lina Perkins Wilder in the following way:

> as having and not having, examining what is past and therefore not available for direct examination ... To remember is to examine something that was once available to the senses but is no longer available and can be understood only as a mental process ... The apprehension of memory is always "double": the event is experienced, and then, after a gap of time, it is examined again.[6]

Confronted with the impossibility of reliving the experience, the characters only have its memory, knowing that this is not a lived occurrence but rather only the remnants of a mental process. For both Don Quixote and Sancho, that which was remembered, that which one moment was present and was perceived by the senses, is no longer present as such, existing only as a mental splinter in each of their individual memories. As a result, the instability of sensory perception that permeates this episode is similarly relational for the entire novel, which is compounded by the instability of memory. These increasingly persistent discrepancies between that which the two characters remember individually accentuates the gap between their objectivity and subjectivity, conditioned in turn by the multiplicity of perspectives from which the same past experience is approached.

If there is a character in *Don Quixote* who, more than anyone else in the novel, manipulates the retelling of the past and whose memories are subject to the double apprehension of memory, it is Sancho. As the novel unfolds, the squire takes advantage of the dissonance between past and present with greater and greater frequency and with increasing sophistication. In a staggered way, and fundamentally in the second part, the role of memory takes on greater relevance and complexity for the squire. Relative to his character development in the first part of the novel, once he masters the art of manipulation of memories, he realizes the full extent of his power over others, including Don Quixote.[7] In Sancho's recurrent retelling of his past experience, the reader observes the muddy terrain of memory where all types of mental processes occur, such as his revision of memories, the transformation of them into something new, or their outright suppression. These tactics intensify the discontinuity in the novel between the perceived and the remembered. Sancho's ability to successfully evoke memoristic discordances not only reveals how memory processes can function but also, as a consequence of the character's difficulties in remembering accurately, provokes comical situations such as the famous (mis)memorization of the letter to Dulcinea, his specific narration of the story of the shepherdess Torralba, and his increasingly habitual skill at implanting false memories in the mind of Don Quixote, such as the one triggered by Dulcinea's enchantment.

On the other hand, Sancho's manner of manipulating memory says a lot about his character and his objectives. In a society where Sancho's social and economic status would not normally provide him many opportunities to advance, his resolute manipulation of his own past is a way of establishing himself as a character, challenging authority, and asserting a certain position of superiority over others, especially Don Quixote. His flaws and distortions help compensate for the shortcomings of past experiences, transforming them into something else. As will be seen in the pages that follow, as part of his character's evolution, Sancho's memoristic acrobatics serve to obtain authority before his master and upend the initial position of power and autonomy in his otherwise hierarchical relationship with Don Quixote.

The careful analysis of the successive reconfigurations and misalignments of what Sancho remembers reflects not only the malleability of memory at the service of a specific purpose and personal interests, but also the way in which external agents alter the nature of memory. In this regard, in their book *Social Memory: New Perspectives on the Past*, anthropologist James Fentress and medievalist historian Chris Wickham emphasize that personal and individual memories are conditioned by the remembrances of those around us as well as by the culture in which we remember. Similarly, Elizabeth Loftus, an expert in studies on the manipulation of memory, stresses that, together with the reconstructive nature of memory, society is an indispensable and decisive participant in affecting the susceptibility of memory and the implantation of false memories, especially in the judicial field.[8] In short, human memory is vulnerable to society's mobilizations, cultural beliefs and mores, and other similar influences, and the social impact can be inherent, overt, or both – depending on what is being recalled and when. This malleability of memory is highlighted by John Sutton, who explains the influence of external elements, especially social elements, as determining factors in the (re)construction of memories.[9] As Paul Ricoeur states in *Memory, History and Forgetting*, personal memory is always attached to the collective since no one ever can remember alone.[10]

This phenomenon is equally important in Cervantes's era, and Sancho's memory is a good example of social conditioning. In reference to Cervantes's epoch, Pollmann declares in *Memory in Early Modern Europe, 1500–1800* that people's memories were shaped by existing cultural scripts, which is essential to consider when analysing how individual memory is structured, presented, and practised in relation to social and cultural expectations:

> memory is also something that people practice. Memories of a real or imagined past are shared through storytelling, performing, parading, decorating, singing, cooking, eating as much as through the writing of memories, histories, and the collecting and archiving of memorable texts and memorabilia, objects that help us remember.[11]

Memory is, therefore, a practice nurtured by the same culture in which it is practised. In this regard, Pollmann and Erika Kuijpers, in their analysis and interpretation of texts dealing with the individual memory of the time, highlight three related variables that help explain how personal memories are defined:

> When interpreting such texts, we see three interrelated variables at work that determine the content of personal memories: first, the author's frame of reference such as his or her knowledge, presuppositions, concepts, etc.; second, the cultural practices or the way people "do memory" (i.e., rules of genre, narrative templates, topoi, rituals, language, expression etc.); and third, their functionality, that is, the psychological, social, political aims and needs for which memory is instrumental.[12]

The three variables or factors can be applied to how Sancho remembers, explaining in part his constant predisposition to modify and manipulate his memory in specific circumstances. When he organizes, interprets, and narrates what happened in the past, his recall is determined by the time frame, the culture to which he belongs, and the needs and aims he hopes to achieve. First among these circumstances is the point of departure from which he remembers: that is, what the squire already knows from his upbringing that affects his future remembering. Along these lines, he is subject to presuppositions and attitudes that shape his personality, such as what has been instilled in him since he was a child, what he learned growing up, and what he has heard from others. With respect to the latter, we cannot underestimate the influence of important religious figures such as the curate of his village or of members of the lower nobility like Don Quixote, as well as his membership in the Panzas clan or his status as an old Christian. Second, the cultural practices present in the way he remembers plays an enormous role in reconstructing his past, such as his narrative schemas, customs, and the spoken language and body language representative of oral culture. Lastly, the function and purpose of what is remembered in relation to its psychological, social, and religious objectives and needs also plays a role, particularly as Sancho seeks to advance himself financially with a governorship or as he attempts to improve his standing with Don Quixote. In this chapter, I will develop how and why memory is of importance to Sancho's evolution as a character, from the way he is asked and forced to remember through the ways in which he himself has to remember his words and actions to the ways in which Don Quixote remembers what the squire has said and done.

"A fe que no os falta memoria cuando vos queréis tenerla": Sancho's Selective Memory

Memory plays a determining role in the construction of subjectivity in the novel and particularly in the evolution of the squire's personality.[13] The fact that Sancho remembers in a specific manner is due to a series of presuppositions and attitudes that fit his personality, developed according to certain canons and beliefs used by Cervantes in the design of his characters. We have already seen the importance of humoural theory for understanding the mental and emotional changes that affect the physical disposition of Don Quixote. In Sancho's case, the influence of the faculties of the soul – intellect, memory, and will – partially dictate his psychological configuration and help explain why he behaves in certain ways. For Weiger, antecedents such as the faculties of the soul are key to understanding how Cervantes is consistent in his construction of characters.[14] As Weiger notes, Sancho's memory functions according to the characteristics that one would naturally associate with a character of his age, status, and educational level, and memory is pivotal in his evolution in the novel, which more or less begins when the squire sets off with Don Quixote: "It seems clear that both Don Quixote and Sancho are endowed with good memorative faculties and that their limitations are governed by their respective intellects or entendimientos as well as the matters that they believe to be of vital interest to them, which is to say that voluntad also plays a role."[15] All this will be decisive in the design of the character acting according to specific marked characteristics[16] and determined in part by the precepts governing the triad of faculties.

Social, economic, religious, and educational factors also play an important role in how Sancho remembers his past and how he uses memories to improve his lot. In this sense, Sancho epitomizes, perhaps better than any other character the ecological approach, following Tribble and Sutton's idea, to the question of memory and culture, in which remembering is also a "co-constructed" activity for the squire.[17] He is one of the few characters in *Don Quixote* who talks at length about his past, including the influence of his family lineage populated by his "pasados los Panzas."[18] In other moments, he stresses his social and economic position as a "labrador … pobre."[19] He is likewise quite aware that his self-identification as an old Christian with "cuatro dedos de enjundia de cristianos viejos"[20] legitimizes his social status. Such boasting about being an old Christian was common among peasants and people of the lower class, given society's rejection of those who were believed to be tainted by Jewish or Muslim blood. Likewise, his illiteracy, a characteristic emphasized over and over, links him closely with the oral tradition and underscores a necessary dependence on memory for most tasks. It is his memory that serves as a bridge to knowledge but which also decisively influences how he will prioritize information.[21] Consequently, his memory is thus a palimpsest of what he has heard from others, such as through his conversations with Don Quixote or by listening to the village curate, whose sermons he brings up frequently. Additionally, Sancho is dependent on his close relationship with others in the village – some of whom he mentions by name – and on the traditional wisdom of stories, sayings, and riddles that circulated among the townsfolk.[22] His illiteracy also determines the process by which he remembers since he would not have seen in written form many of the words he hears, which also explains why he tends to modify them, basing these changes on what he remembers hearing. Consider, for example, the squire's comical reaction to Don Quixote's navigational and astronomical diatribe regarding "el cómputo de Ptolomeo" during the enchanted boat episode: "Por Dios – dijo Sancho – que vuesa merced me trae por testigo de lo que dice a una gentil persona, puto y gafo, con la añadidura de meón, o meo, o no sé cómo."[23] Sancho's recall is consistent with the phonetic (re)construction of memory based on what one hears, and his accounts are therefore not exact copies of what happened. In other moments he adds new information in order to fill the gaps between what was actually said and what he understood was said, such as in his story of the flight on Clavileño, which I cited at the outset. In still other moments, he adds new descriptions, puns, or linguistic nonsense like "feo Blas" for "Fierabrás,"[24] "Berenjena" for "Benengeli,"[25] and "leña" for "línea;"[26] he also exaggerates and modifies facts as when he speaks of his time in the service of Don Quixote "debe de haber más de veinte años, tres días más o menos."[27]

Paradoxically, Sancho's scant memory in these cases is excellent in others, especially in the constant use of his own formulas derived from the oral tradition, such as the use of proverbs that he constantly "ensarta" or "enhila": "y en lo que él se mostraba más elegante y *memorioso* era en traer refranes, viniesen o no viniesen a pelo de lo que trataba, como se habrá visto y se habrá notado en el discurso de esta historia."[28] There is no doubt that Sancho has an extraordinary memory, with a great associative capacity that allows him to bring appropriate sayings to each situation, as Don Quixote reproaches him at a specific moment: "con todo eso, querría saber qué cuatro refranes te ocurrían ahora a la memoria, que venían aquí a propósito, que yo ando recorriendo la mía, que la tengo buena, y ninguno se me ofrece."[29]

Many times over in the novel, the reader is reminded of Sancho's excellent memory. The duke, for example, declares "Con tan buena memoria … no podrá Sancho errar en nada" and he surprises the reader when he takes "muy bien en la memoria" what he hears.[30] Nonetheless, at other times, such as in the examples above, the squire seems unable to remember even the most essential details. Moreover, Sancho himself admits to having a bad memory, as he points out when trying to memorize the letter to Dulcinea: "pensar que yo [he de tomar] la carta en la memoria es disparate; que la tengo tan mala, que muchas veces se me olvida cómo me llamo."[31] Given Sancho's ability to remember the most minute detail at some points while completely misremembering others, there is no doubt that Sancho's memory is therefore quite selective; he enjoys good memory capacity at times, but not so much at others. Don Quixote himself will begin to realize the apparent selective memory of his squire, whom he reproaches and accuses of remembering only what he wants: " – Socarrón sois, Sancho … *A fe que no os falta memoria cuando vos queréis tenerla.*"[32]

This naturally raises the question of whether he purposefully forgets or alters memory or if the selectivity can be blamed on other factors. The narrator blames his memory loss on the simplicity of his character – "de muy poca sal en la mollera"[33] – or on the fact that his experience over time changes him: "aunque de ingenio bruto, muchas veces despunta de agudo."[34] Thanks to this constant tension between accurately remembering and strategically forgetting, Sancho is acquiring a sense of continuity interwoven with experience, increasingly relevant in his evolution: "Selo yo de experiencia, porque de algunas he salido manteado y de otras molido; pero, con todo eso, es linda cosa esperar los sucesos atravesando montes, escudriñando selvas, pisando peñas, visitando castillos, alojando en ventas a toda discreción."[35] Indeed, given the foolishness that characterizes Sancho, the moments in which he is successful in his trials cannot be overlooked, as Don Quixote indicates: "cada día, Sancho ... te vas haciendo más simple y más discreto."[36] The duke and the duchess, faced with Sancho's "tantos donaires y tantas malicias" also perceive this, which "[los] dejaron de nuevo admirados ... así con su simplicidad como con su agudeza."[37] The constant back-and-forth with respect to how and when Sancho correctly recalls is a hallmark of the squire's characterization and provides important depth to the character's evolution.

Memory is therefore an active element and a significant factor and defining role in the squire's personality. It is also true that Sancho knows how to use it to achieve his purpose: "yo osaré jurar que en cuantas historias vuesa merced ha leído que tratan de la andante caballería no ha visto algún desencantado por azotes."[38] Like so many other characteristics in the novel, Sancho's memory cannot, therefore, be fully understood without understanding the influence of Don Quixote. The impact one has on the other and the resultant changes in character are undeniable. The "quixotization" and "sanchification"[39] of both characters is partly due to what they remember of each other as a result of coexistence and shared experience. Sancho effects this through memory, first imitating the code of chivalric novels and emulating the ideas observed in the behaviour of his master. According to Edwin Williamson, Sancho: "Mal que bien, imita los conceptos y formas que ha podido observar en su amo; hasta consigue remedar el lenguaje arcaizante de los libros de caballerías."[40] As proof of his embrace of his master's tendencies, Sancho will increasingly call on the verbal forms and actions used by a country gentleman, as his wife, Teresa, reproaches him on one occasion: "después que os hicisteis miembro de caballero andante, habláis de tan rodeada manera, que no hay quien os entienda."[41]

"Como ya pasó, no es"

One of the most outstanding aspects in the study of memory is the verification that memories are not exact copies of lived experiences. This was the conclusion reached in the pioneering work of the prominent psychologist Frederick Bartlett, who, in *Remembering* (1932), concluded that memory was the result of a constructive process and not an exact copy of the past: "The first notion to get rid of is that memory is primarily or literally reduplicative, or reproductive. In a world of constantly changing environment, literal recall is extraordinarily unimportant."[42] Since that time, scholars have further confirmed Bartlett's findings and use his studies as the embarkation point for understanding the reconstruction of memories. As Bartlett and others have concluded, memories are therefore reconfigurations resulting from what the brain creates and invents to give meaning to our past from the perspective of the present. As part of the construction of an identity, memory's main objective is to grant reliability and plausibility and, in doing so, to strengthen the reconstructive process by adding new meanings.

In Cervantes's time there was already evidence of the reconfigurations and fluctuations to which memory was constantly subjected. The fluidity and reconfiguration of what was remembered is explicitly manifested on more than one occasion in the novel and in many other situations in Cervantes' work. During a conversation with his wife, Teresa, for example, Sancho reflects on this fragile reconstruction of the past when he recalls the words of a preacher during Lent: "todo lo que pienso decir son sentencias del padre predicador que la Cuaresma pasada predicó en este pueblo, el cual, si mal no me acuerdo, dijo que todas las cosas presentes que los ojos están mirando se presentan, están y asisten en nuestra memoria mucho mejor y con más vehemencia que las cosas pasadas."[43] The squire's unusual wisdom even causes the Translator to suspect that the chapter is apocryphal because it exceeds Sancho's typical abilities: "Todas estas razones que aquí va diciendo Sancho son las segundas por quien dice el tradutor que tiene por apócrifo este capítulo, que exceden a la capacidad de Sancho."[44] However, I believe that this moment illustrates how Sancho makes use of the past in his evolution as a character. Indeed, the squire seems to be referring here to the volatility of memory caused by the lack of vehemence with which one presents "las cosas pasadas." In this regard, the squire later continues:

> – De donde nace que cuando vemos alguna persona bien aderezada y con ricos vestidos compuesta y con pompa de criados, parece que por fuerza

> nos mueve y convida a que la tengamos respeto, puesto que *la memoria* en aquel instante nos represente alguna bajeza en que vimos a la tal persona; la cual ignominia, ahora sea de pobreza o de linaje, *como ya pasó, no es, y sólo es lo que vemos presente ... que no habrá quien se acuerde de lo que fue, sino que reverencien lo que es.*[45]

Sancho adeptly points out that remembering is a process that focuses on that which once was but is no longer accessible, a gap that I alluded to in the opening pages "as having and not having." In other words, for the squire, "las cosas presentes" – what we would call lived experience – supersedes what has passed, which transforms everything that "ya pasó" into a "no es."

Sancho's reflections echo, once again, Aristotle's ideas in *De memoria et reminiscentia*, in which the philosopher established one of the key differences between the act of memory and that of perception – understood here as the reconstruction of memory after the fact. For Aristotle, memory was a condition resulting from an alteration after the passage of time: "Therefore memory is not perception or conception, but a state or affection connected with one of these, when time has elapsed ... And this is why all memory involves time."[46] In this way, it is precisely the fundamental element of elapsed time that converts perception into memory, a fact Sancho will use to take advantage of Don Quixote, who, as is known, has difficulties in differentiating between the past and the present:[47] that is, between the memory and the perception of what is happening around him. Sancho already seemed to have realized the difference between the perception of the moment lived and the memory accentuated by the time elapsed between the two, which he will take advantage of to confer authority on the person of Don Quixote.

Sancho is increasingly aware of the double apprehension of memory that turns what "ya pasó" into a "no es" and will advance Dulcinea's enchantment in three key episodes in the novel by systematically accentuating the gap between what happened and what is perceived to have happened: the adventure of the Batanes, in which Sancho narrates the tale of the shepherdess Torralba (I.20), and his forgetfulness of the contents of Don Quixote's letter to Dulcinea, which Sancho is told to get someone to write down at his first opportunity (I.26), that will culminate with her enchantment in the second part (II.10). The linking of the episodes is achieved when Sancho improvises and manipulates what happened by supplanting facts with false memories in order to create an entirely new fiction that will culminate with the enchantment of Dulcinea. As will be seen in the pages that follow, memory and its many oversights and absurdities accentuate the discontinuities that form the narrative progression of Dulcinea's enchantment thanks to Sancho's memory (and imagination).

The Story of Torralba and the Performative Dimension of Memory

It is in the episode of the fulling mills when the reader may become aware that Sancho has figured out, perhaps for the first time, how to influence Don Quixote and where a change of attitude can be observed in his relationship towards the knight. In this episode, knight and squire decide to spend the night in the open air, but it is not until daylight that they realize that the unknown and fearful pounding noises they hear in the distance are emanating from some fulling mills along the river. In the interim, to take his mind off his own fright, Sancho tells a story about the shepherdess Torralba. According to Sancho, a shepherd tried to cross a river with a herd of goats – one at a time – and he asks Don Quixote to keep track of the number that has safely made it to the other side. Sidetracked by the knight's questions, when he returns to the tale, Sancho asks Don Quixote how many goats had crossed thus far in the story, but the knight cannot remember. Rather than start over, Sancho simply refuses to continue the story, and Don Quixote cannot persuade him otherwise. The entire event is comical due to Sancho's frustration in tracking every detail, but it also reveals another aspect of Sancho's growing personality: he demonstrates his skill at adjusting the details of the story to serve his own interests, a technique that highlights his ability to mislead others, most notably Don Quixote. As Williamson has pointed out, it is precisely in the course of this adventure that the squire deceives Don Quixote for the first time and even mocks him: "Este engaño crea las posibilidades de otros engaños más graves, sobre todo los relacionados con Dulcinea (I.31; II.10) que tendrán importantes consecuencias para el desarrollo de la novela entera."[48]

The entire narration of the story of the shepherdess Torralba is emblematic of an oral tradition that continued to pervade early seventeenth-century Spain even as the printed word was becoming increasingly prominent. As extraordinarily studied by Frenk, Sancho is in many ways the prototypical street narrator who puts distinct strategies to use that were prevalent in a culture in which most things were done orally and which depended on memory to correctly tell them. I do not wish to dwell on the characteristics of orality already analysed by Frenk and other critics;[49] rather, I seek to explore the connections between orality and memory as a determining factor in the way Sancho relates the story of Torralba. Throughout the novel, there are various notable strategies for memorization that were typical of an oral culture. Many of these techniques involved simple rote memorization while others were embedded cultural cues from previous historical and literary sources. In the case of Torralba, the tale is clearly repeated based on what Sancho has heard from others. Other episodes in the novel similarly draw on previous source material, such as the popular stories that featured braying, the Carolingian *romancero* of Maese Pedro "sacado al pie de la letra de las corónicas francesas y de los romances españoles que andan en boca de las gentes y de los muchachos por esas calles,"[50] as well as folkloric stories from collections of medieval tales, such as the *acertijos* that Sancho successfully solves as a governor of his *ínsula*.[51] Sancho's broad experience and deep-seated knowledge of previous source materials are clear exponents in an oral culture of what Walter Ong calls a mnemonically intellectualized experience.[52]

In Cervantes's time, despite a proliferation of the written word thanks to the advent of the printing press, orality still dominated in the majority of society's dealings. But as is often the case with oral stories, even written texts were passed along and repeated, making them as susceptible to constant change as oral texts were. As Frenk notes, texts of all sorts were, in short, "una entidad que podía ser fluida, maleable, capaz de transformarse en sucesivas repeticiones,"[53] owing in part to the residual orality that persisted in the literary culture of the era. Thus, for example, the way in which Sancho tells the Torralba story exemplifies the fact that vocalized literature is in a continual movement that avoids the existence of a fixed text, and, as a consequence, it changes with infinite variants attributable to the oral transmission.[54] In short, even written texts experience transformations when spoken aloud and disseminated across cultures, only to be then written down anew, albeit quite differently from the original. The volatility of the text is an example of what Frenk alludes to when she writes, "si no importaba que el texto leído, dicho, hablado, recitado, contado, narrado o referido estuviera registrado en un papel o en la memoria, no era tampoco importante la reproducción exacta de ese texto."[55] The lack of precision when reproducing a text would partly explain why Sancho freely creates yet one more variant of the Torralba's story, one that has been adapted to his circumstances and his audience, as Don Quixote points out at the end of the story: "– Dígote de verdad – respondió don Quijote – que tú has contado una de las más nuevas consejas, cuento o historia que nadie pudo pensar en el mundo, y que tal modo de contarla ni dejarla jamás se podrá ver ni habrá visto en toda la vida."[56] This facet of Sancho's character emerges repeatedly on other occasions throughout the novel and is due in part to what David Rubin, when speaking of memory processes, sees as stories told "with" memory and not "from" memory.[57] Similarly, for Elizabeth Minchin, stories are always modified for the purpose for which they are used:

> Storytellers, in telling a story, inevitably have a purpose in mind; they may be doing so in order to entertain, to boast, to win sympathy, to persuade, or as a token of intimacy. To fulfill their goals storytellers will plan and shape their stories so that they will catch and hold the attention of their audiences and convey unambiguously the point of their tale. For they are aware that their display will be judged for skill and, without doubt, for effectiveness.[58]

We know that Sancho has a specific purpose in telling his version of Torralba: to deceive Don Quixote so that the pair can spend the night where they are, rather than continue their journey towards the fearful noises ahead. To persuade him, Sancho modifies the story according to what he knows his audience – Don Quixote – will want to hear. In the oral storytelling tradition, Ong speaks of the social pressure that storytellers are subjected to, a fact that, as in the case of Sancho, inevitably influences variations of the story: "Oral memorization is subject to variation from direct social pressures. Narrators narrate what audiences call for or will tolerate."[59]

With the aim of entertaining Don Quixote as long as possible, Sancho is considering his audience by opting for a story from the so-called "never-ending stories" or "undefined action stories" categories. Narrators of these sorts of stories know that the memory of the listener plays a crucial role in the development of the tale, and they also understand that the story is structured to not have a conclusion. Maurice Molho calls this "contracuento," whose sole purpose is to frustrate the receptor: "contracuento que tiene por finalidad frustrar al destinatario del relato prometido, y que finalmente resulta vacío de todo lo que no sea esa misma frustración."[60] In this case, frustration is closely associated with how Don Quixote's memory operates. Despite constant calls that the knight pay close attention, Sancho knows that Don Quixote will be unable to remember everything asked of him. Given that frustration and a false ending are the goals of this sort of story, Sancho also understands that he must insist that if the knight loses count of even a single goat passing to the other side of the river, the story will end: "Tenga vuestra merced cuenta en las cabras que el pescador va pasando, porque si se pierde una de la memoria, se acabará el cuento, y no será posible contar más palabra de él."[61] Faced with this dilemma, Don Quixote, stupefied, asks him,

"¿Tan de esencia de la historia es saber las cabras que han pasado por extenso, que si se yerra una del número no puedes seguir adelante con la historia?"[62] Sancho's answer reaffirms the importance of memory, essential but fleeting, both for listeners and the storyteller: "No, señor ... porque así como yo pregunté a vuestra merced que me dijese cuántas cabras habían pasado, y me respondió que no sabía, en aquel mismo instante se me fue a mí de la memoria cuanto me quedaba por decir, y a fe que era de mucha virtud y contento."[63] This same formula will be repeated later when Cardenio demands that no one interrupt him as he tells his story, which will make Don Quixote *recall* the story of Torralba again, thus linking the two episodes as acts of memory within the oral tradition.[64]

The story of the shepherdess Torralba is an example of how storytelling connects the individual with the collective memory of a group to which the squire belongs.[65] Oral culture and memory practice were expressed in everyday customs and habits, rituals, and festivities and verbally manifested in many varieties of oral literature, both profane and religious.[66] As Rubin points out, "oral traditions depend on human memory for their preservation. If a tradition is to survive, it must be stored in one's person's memory and be passed to another person who is also capable of storing and retelling it."[67] The squire's memory works not only at the individual level but in the collective sphere where memory practices belong to a particular group: "– De la misma manera que yo lo cuento – respondió Sancho – se cuentan en mi tierra todas las consejas, y yo no sé contarlo de otra, ni es bien que vuestra merced me pida que haga usos nuevos."[68] Thanks to memory, Sancho tells the story that he has made his own, and that is also part of the tradition of a collective memory, by telling it in the way it is told in his land. In the Torralba story, memory exemplifies what Carruthers has called the "textualization process" through which a literary work is institutionalized or internalized in the popular imagination:

> In the process of textualizing, the original work acquires commentary and gloss; this activity is not regarded as something other than the text, but it is the mark of textualization itself. *Textus* also means "texture," the layers of meaning that attach as a text is woven into and through the historical and institutional fabric of a society. Such "socializing" of literature is the work of *memoria*, and this is as true of a literate as of an oral society. Whether the words come through the sensory gateway of the eyes or the ears, they must be processed and transformed in memory – they are made our own.[69]

Through the textualization process, Sancho modifies the story, adding its interpretive layers as part of the process of the socialization of literature in which collective memory has an inescapably important role. Sancho has therefore codified the social expectations of storytelling and is able to amply demonstrate his skill and agility at deceptive narration at the individual level.

"Alta y sobajada señora …"

From the perspective of cognitive psychology and linguistics, Minchin, in her study about the resources of memory in the composition and recitation in poems such as *The Iliad* and *The Odyssey,* ties what she calls "'ordinary,' everyday storytellings" – like those of Sancho – to "the 'special' storytelling of Homer."[70] Minchin takes as her point of departure Bartlett's aforementioned *Remembering*, one of the most important works about the reconstructive processes of memory, which I will also use to analyse the squire's memory processes. Bartlett describes the reconstructive (not reproductive) character of memory and the influence that past individual experiences exert over memory, which Bartlett calls "mental schemas":

> Remembering is not the re-excitation of innumerable fixed, lifeless and fragmentary traces. It is an imaginative reconstruction or construction, built out of the relation of our attitude towards a whole active mass of organised past reactions or experience, and to a little outstanding detail which commonly appears in image or in language form.[71]

To test his theory on the influence of the schema in the reconstructive nature of memory, Bartlett carried out an experiment in which a series of British participants with little knowledge of Native American culture had to read the traditional Native American story "War of Ghosts." Participants then were asked to recall and retell the story multiple times over different time intervals. Bartlett discovered that the greater the time interval between reading and the memory of it, the more changes occurred in the recounting of the story. He also observed that when the participants had to remember something that they did not know and that did not adapt to their mental schemes, they simply omitted it or transformed it using terms they knew, a process of making something familiar:

> A special case is where that which is unfamiliar in itself is rendered familiar by its content. It is then frequently preserved, but transformed. Thus in

> my reproductions, "boats" invariably sooner or later replaced "canoes," and "rowing" replaced "paddling"; a "bush-cat" became an ordinary "cat" and "pea-nut" was transformed into "acorn."[72]

Bartlett observed that when participants were asked to tell what they remembered from the story, they did not duplicate the story but rather introduced distortions and errors through a complex mental process. He concluded that in the process of remembering, humans rely on existing summaries or individual "schemas" of the past, from which memories are reconstructed.

The phenomenon Bartlett describes is exhibited over and again in the novel by Sancho. When he must retell or summarize an unfamiliar story, he takes as his point of departure particular schemas from which he reconstructs what he remembers – in a way very similar to the individuals who participate in the experiment of "War of Ghosts."

This phenomenon is especially obvious whenever Sancho reports on what happens to others. In these instances, Cervantes is pointing out memory in the making to the reader, a metamorphic exercise that reaches its peak in the famous mis-memorization of the letter to Dulcinea. Specifically, the memory of the letter, its contents, and its language is subject to the ups and downs of its operation, in which the remnants of oral tradition and the squire's interests and personal objectives coalesce to render familiar essential details. The episode begins when Don Quixote and Sancho head to the Sierra Morena so that the knight can undertake a mock penance in imitation of his chivalric heroes. At this point, he asks Sancho to write down some thoughts in the form of a letter that the squire is to take to Don Quixote's beloved Dulcinea. However, Sancho does not know how to read or write and instead urges Don Quixote to write it in Cardenio's *librillo de memoria*:[73] "Escríbala vuestra merced dos o tres veces ahí en el libro, y démele, que yo le llevaré bien guardado; porque pensar que yo la he de tomar en la memoria es disparate, que la tengo tan mala, que muchas veces se me olvida cómo me llamo." Don Quixote is so thrilled that his words will reach Dulcinea that he lauds Sancho and implores him to "ten memoria" when he finally sees her: "– Anda, hijo – replicó don Quijote –, y no te turbes cuando te vieres ante la luz del sol de hermosura que vas a buscar. ¡Dichoso tú sobre todos los escuderos del mundo! Ten memoria, y no se te pase de ella cómo te recibe."[74] As it turns out, Sancho forgets the notebook and will later be forced to recreate the letter from memory, thus making him a transactional vehicle of Don Quixote's memory, an idea already insinuated when he demanded that Sancho "tenga memoria." Along the way to deliver the message, Sancho meets up with the barber and the priest, who ask him to repeat the letter. Realizing that he has forgotten it, Sancho attempts to remedy his error by noting that he was not very concerned about the loss of the letter because he knew it almost by heart: "que no le daba mucha pena la pérdida de la carta de Dulcinea, porque él la sabía casi de memoria, de la cual se podría trasladar donde y cuando quisiesen."[75] This moment features Sancho in one of the most hilarious moments in the novel as he attempts to recall literally what he had previously heard Don Quixote say aloud. The squire is aware of the powerful role he has acquired by having become the transactive memory[76] of his master, which will unleash an entirely new plot twist that will culminate in Dulcinea's later enchantment.

The fact that Sancho was encouraged to recite a letter that he supposedly "sabía casi de memoria"[77] was not really such a crazy idea in Cervantes's time; it certainly was not outrageous to the priest and the barber, who ask Sancho to repeat the letter "para que ellos asimismo la tomasen de memoria para trasladalla a su tiempo."[78] This is not the only instance of a character having to remember a letter – it happens rather frequently. For example, Cardenio memorizes Luscinda's letter and can recite it verbatim, and Ruy Pérez de Viedma, the Captive, clearly remembers the letter he wrote to Lela Marién through a renegade. In this instance, however, Cervantes puts the lost record in the squire's mouth and creates a completely parodic situation, similar to the earlier deformation of the word Ptolemy in "Meón":

> Por Dios, señor licenciado, que los diablos lleven la cosa que de la carta se me acuerda, aunque en el principio decía: "Alta y sobajada señora."
>
> – No diría – dijo el barbero – sobajada, sino sobrehumana o soberana señora.
>
> – Así es – dijo Sancho. Luego, si mal no me acuerdo, proseguía, si mal no me acuerdo: "el llego y falto de sueño, y el ferido besa a vuestra merced las manos, ingrata y muy desconocida hermosa," y no sé qué decía de salud y de enfermedad que le enviaba, y por aquí iba escurriendo, hasta que acababa en "Vuestro hasta la muerte, el Caballero de la Triste Figura."
>
> No poco gustaron los dos de ver la buena memoria de Sancho Panza, y alabáronsela mucho y le pidieron que dijese la carta otras dos veces, para que ellos asimismo la tomasen de memoria para trasladalla a su tiempo. Tornola a decir Sancho otras tres veces, y otras tantas volvió a decir otros tres mil disparates.[79]

Just as in the adventure aboard the Enchanted Boat, Sancho does not actually remember the specifics of the letter, but instead resorts to his faulty memory of it. And so, in his typical improvisatory manner, every time he is asked to remember the contents, new versions emerge, each different or more elaborate than the previous. This comical transformation of Don Quixote's letter to Dulcinea not only recalls the phenomenon analysed by Bartlett but also summarizes in part the foundations of the memorization process in the oral tradition, which already occurred in the story with the tale of the shepherdess Torralba. Sancho's errors in recalling the details of the letter are partly the result of variations in the oral tradition and the impossibility of memorizing anything literally, as well as the ignorance of words that, due to Sancho's illiteracy, he has likely never seen before in writing and therefore phonetically distorts.

It is nearly impossible to separate orality from the role of memory, since the latter is essential for the transmission and reception of texts within what Ong has characterized as "the psychodynamics of orality": that is, the forms of expression and thought processes found in the oral tradition. "How do people in an oral culture recall?"[80] is the question that Ong asks himself. Ong contrasts the power that the literate person possesses since he or she has access to written knowledge, compared to individuals with no such access, as exemplified over and over in Sancho's case: "Oral folk have no sense of a name as a tag, for they have no idea of a name as something that can be seen. Written or printed representations of words can be labels; real, spoken words cannot be."[81] Like the lyric and other oral genres, the letter that Sancho memorizes seems predestined not to have a fixed text for a number of reasons: variations ("sobajada" vs "soberana", "vuestro hasta la muerte" vs "tuyo hasta la muerte"), passages that are omitted ("no sé qué decía de salud y enfermedad"), the manipulation of the text ("por aquí iba escurriendo, hasta que acababa"), and word inversions ("alta y sobajada" vs. "Soberana y alta"), along with other lexicographic, morphological changes and, above all, the phonic similarity of words (*llego* vs *llagado*), in addition to other common, intentional, and accidental errors resulting from memorization.[82] Each of these are a form of manipulation – some accidental, some intentional – that are clearly representative of an oral culture and perhaps typical of an illiterate man. But Sancho is not as innocent in this deceit as one might think. Later, he confesses to deliberately manipulating what he remembered: "Y en medio de estas dos cosas le puse más de trescientas almas y vidas y ojos míos." As the reader becomes aware, Sancho is fully capable of controlling others.

Rubin, in his outstanding book *Memory in Oral Traditions*, stresses that the oral tradition does not require memorization of exact words but rather of their meaning and form: "What is being transmitted is the theme of the song, its imagery, its poetics, and some specific details."[83]

In this context, the studies of Milman Parry and Albert Lord on the composition of the Greek epic are essential. Parry specifically underscores the necessity and use of metric formulas that could be used over and over and that the poet always had memorized as part of his verbal repertoire.[84] For his part, Lord focused on the illiterate poets of the Slavic tradition and discovered that if they were literate, the process would not have been the same, since the written text would not only have completely controlled their narration but would have interfered with the process of oral composition.[85] Likewise, Minchin has highlighted the uniqueness of these poems, composed and represented without the help of writing,[86] a feat that the author partly attributes to the use of a formulary language and to the use of "typical scenes" or "the theme" – concepts of Parry and Lord, respectively – on which the recitation is built in situ: "Like the formula, each typical scene was learned by an apprentice singer so that he might reproduce an action sequence in song with relative ease."[87] In this respect, Ong insisted that what the poet remembers is not a written text but the memory he has of a poem that has been heard previously:

> An oral poet is not working with texts or in a textual framework … In recalling and retelling the story, he has not in any literate sense "memorized" its metrical rendition from the version of the other singer … The fixed materials in the bard's memory are a float of themes and formulas out of which *all stories are variously built*.[88]

In reality, it was not expected that one would remember everything in detail. This distinction recalls in the same way the necessary talents that one must have to successfully transmit something that was remembered, particularly since remembering a text to the letter was an almost impossible task, as Frenk points out:

> Por hábil que fuera, el memorizador de un poema no podía – ni le importaba – retener un texto en todos sus detalles; invertía palabras y las sustituía por otras equivalentes, quitaba y ponía partículas, cambiaba de lugar versos y secuencias de versos, en un proceso que recuerda, en miniatura, las transformaciones de la poesía de transmisión oral.[89]

As another contemporary of Cervantes, the great playwright Lope de Vega, said, "no se obliga a la memoria a percibir las mismas palabras, sino a las mismas sentencias."[90] Put another way, for Lope, the main ideas of the text rather than the concrete words were memorized. Lope's words undoubtedly recall the distinction between two types of memory to which the ancient classical rhetoric alluded and which were widely known in the time of Cervantes: *memoria rerum* (memory for things) and *memoria verborum* (memory for words): that is, the memory of the content of the discourse versus memory of the language. There is no doubt that the *memoria rerum* is the one used by Sancho in his version of the letter, in which he certainly remembers the main idea but clearly forgets the specific vocabulary since he is mostly ignorant of its meaning and usage. Evoked over and over with a "si mal no me acuerdo," Sancho's memory parodically submits itself not to the exact word but rather to the *sentencia* that Lope de Vega spoke of.

In Sancho's tremendous effort to remember what the letter said, the psychosomatic relationship between memory and the body is quite significant because body language was typical of oral memorization:

> Parose Sancho Panza a rascar la cabeza para traer a la memoria la carta, y ya se ponía sobre un pie y ya sobre otro, unas veces miraba al suelo, otras al cielo, y al cabo de haberse roído la mitad de la yema de un dedo, teniendo suspensos a los que esperaban que ya la dijese, dijo al cabo de grandísimo rato.[91]

Just as minstrels and other street performers played, danced, and used strong gestures to relate their stories, Sancho's form of performance requires similar techniques. It would therefore be the somatic component of oral memorization that, according to Ong, lacks textual memory: "Spoken words are always modifications of a total, existential situation, *which always engages the body*."[92] In this respect, the anonymous author of a *Tratado médico sobre patología general*, written in 1500, affirmed that "Si algo se olvidare ... *rasquese la cabeça detrás en el colodrillo*: en donde está la virtud de la memoria: y entonces pluguiendo a dios: el se recordará fácilmente."[93] The emphasis placed on corporeal performance was therefore typical and necessary in oral cultures like Sancho's.

The process of memorizing the letter culminates with Sancho's "appropriation" of it and the consequent manipulation of remembering it again and again. Through this process, Sancho has made it his own, adapting it to his reality.[94] From here, Dulcinea's enchantment will develop from the constant recall of that false memory that has originated in the false delivery of the letter:

> no la hubiera yo tomado en la memoria cuando vuestra merced me la leyó, de manera que se la dije a un sacristán, que me la trasladó del entendimiento tan punto por punto, que dijo que en todos los días de su

> vida, aunque había leído muchas cartas de descomunión, no había visto ni leído tan linda carta como aquélla.
>
> – Y ¿tiénesla todavía en la memoria, Sancho? – dijo don Quixote.
>
> – No, señor – respondió Sancho – porque después que la di, como vi que no había de ser de más provecho, di en olvidalla, y si algo se me acuerda, es aquello del "sobajada," digo del "soberana señora," y lo último: "Vuestro hasta la muerte, el Caballero de la Triste Figura." Y en medio de estas dos cosas le puse más de trescientas almas y vidas y ojos míos.[95]

With Don Quixote's question "¿tiénesla todavía en la memoria?" one returns again to the idea of memory "as having or not having" and the double apprehension of memory with which the chapter began. Additionally, this brings to mind the question of the usefulness of memory parodied in the Primo episode, in which the character preposterously wants to memorize all facts currently known (a story echoed in Borges's *Funes*). In Sancho's case, however, memory can be manipulated for personal gain, but he also sees that his deception has its limits. The notoriety of the lost letter and Don Quixote's constant questioning about it leads him to want to "forget" it: "como vi que no había de ser de más provecho, di en olvidalla." As Sancho advises, what is interesting and useful endures, but what does not is undone. Once again, as master of the manipulation, Sancho chooses what shall continue and what is to be discarded, such as when he adds his own impressions to the letter: "Y en medio de estas dos cosas le puse más de trescientas almas y vidas y ojos míos."

The False Memory Embedded in Imagination

We have seen how Sancho has gradually become an expert in recounting what happened; however, it will not be until chapter 10 of the second part that he begins to exert full control over his tactic of memory manipulation. Only five chapters after the conversation with Teresa alluded to earlier, the episode begins "donde se cuenta la industria que Sancho tuvo para encantar a la señora Dulcinea." In this episode, Don Quixote asks the squire to go to Toboso so that he can speak to his lady Dulcinea, "pidiéndola fuese servida de dejarse ver de su cautivo caballero, y se dignase de echarle su bendición."[96] Sancho agrees, and by doing so, he once again becomes the agent of the knight's transactive memory. He sets off "confuso y pensativo," giving way to his prominent monologue in which he reflects on what he has done and realizes something that will be key from that moment on and that will mark a before and after with respect to his relationship with Don Quixote.[97]

Sancho's walk alone to Toboso is significant in his character development since he spends a good deal of time in increasingly frequent exercises in retrospection and introspection. The episode will also be key to understanding not only the mechanisms of memory manipulation but also his determination to go further by implanting false memories in the mind of Don Quixote:

> Siendo, pues, loco, como lo es, y de locura que las más veces toma unas cosas por otras y juzga lo blanco por negro y lo negro por blanco, como se pareció cuando dijo que los molinos de viento eran gigantes, y las mulas de los religiosos dromedarios, y las manadas de carneros ejércitos de enemigos, y otras muchas cosas a este tono, no será muy difícil hacerle creer que una labradora, la primera que me topare por aquí, es la señora Dulcinea; y cuando él no lo crea, juraré yo, y si él jurare, tornaré yo a jurar, y si porfiare, porfiaré yo más, y *de manera que tengo de tener la mía siempre sobre el hito, venga lo que viniere*.[98]

This moment is crucial to understanding Sancho's position with respect to the past, since here he will be reminded of the power he wields over Don Quixote as long as he is prepared to manipulate his memory of the events. Sancho will realize that as long as he insists on his version of things, he can "tener la [suya] siempre sobre el hito," thus clearing the way to superimpose his version of the things in Don Quixote's mind, a way of implanting false memories. Julio Rodríguez-Luis has interpreted the end of the soliloquy as the culmination of the new image of Sancho in the second part: "la de un personaje consciente de sus propias motivaciones y del poder de su inteligencia, especialmente en cuanto a controlar a Don Quixote."[99] In addition to intelligence, I would argue that memory holds equal importance since the squire knows that his master will always react according to what he remembers from his own sources: chivalry books, poems, and the like. Faced with the more than obvious malfunction of Don Quixote's perception, Sancho knows that he can transform the experience of what he has lived by adjusting it to his needs. He knows that he can manipulate Don Quixote's perceptions of the past by supplanting them with new or different ones. Although Sancho anticipates that disputes that will arise from what is remembered, he knows that he will be able to negotiate as long as he sticks with his plans "venga lo que viniere."

In this episode, Sancho exploits memory's lack of stability to implant false memory, which serves as the first step in planning Dulcinea's enchantment, what Anthony Close describes as the greatest deceit towards his master. But the notion of misleading his master had already been subtly suggested in the first part, just after Don Quixote left the Montesinos Cave. After recounting what happened in the cave, Sancho suspects that Merlin may have implanted false memories in Don Quixote:

> – Creo – respondió Sancho – que aquel Merlín o aquellos encantadores que encantaron a toda la chusma que vuestra merced dice que ha visto y comunicado allá bajo *le encajaron en el magín o la memoria* toda esa máquina que nos ha contado y todo aquello que por contar le queda.
>
> – Todo eso pudiera ser, Sancho – replicó don Quixote – pero no es así, porque lo que he contado lo vi por mis propios ojos y lo toqué con mis mismas manos.[100]

The fact that Merlin and other enchanters can fit "en el magín o la memoria" all kinds of fabrications opens up a whole range of possibilities for the squire who will take advantage of paramnesia: that is, the phenomenon through which events that did not happen are recalled or the original experience is distorted by remembering it. The term, coined by the German psychiatrist Emil Kraepelin, refers to a type of fantasy or collusion – such as that experienced by those who believe they have been abducted by aliens – based on the recollection of lived experience when the impossibility of distinguishing between true memories and imagined memories prevails.[101]

The idea immediately brings to mind the famous summary of Sancho's flight on Clavileño with which this chapter began. From the moment Sancho draws up the plan to implant false memories in "el magín o la memoria" of his master, Sancho stages what cognitive psychologists, especially Loftus, have referred to as the "misinformation effect": that is, "the distorting effects of misleading post-event information on memory for words, faces, and details of witnessed events."[102] Sancho uses information that he already has as a weapon to shape Don Quixote's memory, which causes multiple discrepancies in what happened. Deception with memory destabilizes the memory process and the relationship between the two. From this moment on, the memory Don Quixote has formed around Dulcinea based on a wide array of images that other characters have offered becomes somewhat contradictory. As a result, Don Quixote can keep Sancho in check because of the squire's carelessness:

> [H]e caído, Sancho, en una cosa, y es que me pintaste mal su hermosura, porque, *si mal no me acuerdo*, dijiste que tenía los ojos de perlas, y los ojos que parecen de perlas antes son de besugo que de dama; y, a lo que yo

> creo, los de Dulcinea deben ser de verdes esmeraldas, rasgados, con dos celestiales arcos que les sirven de cejas; y esas perlas, quítalas de los ojos y pásalas a los dientes, que sin duda te trocaste, Sancho, tomando los ojos por los dientes.[103]

As in so many other instances, the characters's attempts to grasp memory, and the resulting remembrances, are always accompanied by the aforementioned "si mal no me acuerdo." Like a defendant under cross examination, Sancho will seek to stake claims of innocence on the fragility of memory, using it in his defence; he knows that it is delicate and malleable and subject to the double apprehension referred to at the beginning of this chapter. Whether or not his relationship with Don Quixote can endure now depends on the knight's skill at differentiating his own memories from those of others and his ability to identify memory stunts. For his part, Sancho acquires a sense of continuity that interweaves with experience but that he does not always manage to carry out successfully. He is aware of the impossibility of fully apprehending memory, and for this he will hide behind the words "si mal no me acuerdo" – a crutch that he resorts to endlessly to justify his version of events or to reduce the risk of being caught in the lie that he falsely presents as a memory. At the time this style, called "hablar con bordón" – what today would be called *coletillas* and *muletillas* – was avoided in diction by those who were said to have excellent memory. Lucas Gracián Dantisco speaks of this phenomenon in *Galateo español* (1593):

> *[P]ara ello es menester tener bien en la memoria* el caso, cuento o historia, y las palabras promptas, y aparejadas *para no hablar con bordón*, como hazen algunos, diziendo: – Assí señores, que como digo, y en fin que aquel tal, o el otro, como se llama, ayudadme a dezillo, acordadme el nombre, etc. que todas éstas son malas mañas, y que molestan al cuerdo oyente.[104]

Sancho's behaviour illustrates Gracián's warning to speak concisely and clearly. In fact, Sancho constantly alludes to the cognitive process by which something is remembered; before starting a speech, he repeatedly alludes to memory: "Todo pudo ser – respondió Sancho – pero a mí bardas me parecieron, si no es que soy falto de memoria."[105] The "todo pudo ser" with which Sancho responds is only the possibility that what they both remember is therefore valid. His use of the previously cited expression "si mal no me acuerdo" is habitual, and the irony lies in his necessary concern for not getting caught in his lie. Cervantes could be referring here to the debate at the time regarding the intentionally faulty memory of the liar like Sancho who deceives with some difficulty. It could be perhaps that the writer had in mind once again Gracián, who advises that "el que miente debe tener gran memoria, y acordarse, porque luego es cogido."[106] The advice is repeated in *Elocuencia española en arte* (1604), in which Jiménez Patón insists on the importance of memory for those who tell lies: "Si dijéremos mentiras, las ordenaremos de suerte que parezcan verdades, como lo advierte Horacio, y seguiremos el consejo del refrán: que el mentiroso ha de tener memoria."[107] Sancho's deliberate deceit in the encounter with Dulcinea is presented as the culmination of the evolution of his ability to play with memory's malleability.

Thus, Sancho does have a good memory, and he knows how to implement it, in most cases, for his own benefit or personal aggrandizement through improvisation and manipulation. Sancho discovers that the past disintegrates and vanishes and, therefore, can be transformed. The character is increasingly aware of the power of memory and of his ability to shape the past for his own benefit. Likewise, the squire's personal memory appears constantly modified by external agents. His status as a farmer, his social and economic situation, his illiteracy, his status as an old Christian, his constant desire to govern, and the influence of other characters, as well as his intrinsic relationship with oral culture are determining factors in how the squire narrates his experiences. Motivated by his ambitions and the aspiration to govern the promised island, as well as by the economic benefit that he could obtain from the service to Don Quixote, he will selectively remember what is important for personal gain. At the same time, his actions also provide a glimpse of his desires to leave behind or forget his own past. One could almost speak of an evolutionary process that parallels the overall development of his character and that is reflected in the attitude towards his relationship with Don Quixote. As the novel progresses, the squire is increasingly aware of the power of memory to create false memories and to (re)invent the past. Sancho's *auctoritas* not only gives him power over his audience – that is, Don Quixote – but also forces him to create memories to further his ambitions.

Memory helps Sancho create other alternatives to his existence. He discovers that he can construct another reality from his memories just as Don Quixote has done. In short, he is no more limited by his past than is his master. In fact, he is perhaps better positioned to exploit his past since he realizes that his memories can be shaped and manipulated for personal gain and to acquire social status. For Sancho, memories can embrace the past or completely oppose it, thus leading to the creation of his own version of the present while still nodding to the origins of the deceit. Through this process of memory creation, incorporation, and revision, Sancho increasingly customizes the past with a specific purpose. His memories are used and manipulated for personal reasons and modified to acquire status, but he also acts according to the acquired status as the character he became in the first part.

Epilogue

Lethe and the Laws of Oblivion: Sites of Forgetting in *Don Quixote*

[L]o que habemos dicho de la memoria muestra quién es el olvido.[1]
– Juan Velázquez de Azevedo
El Fénix de Minerva y Arte de Memoria (1626)

In *El Coloquio de los perros* (1613), the sorceress Cañizares, reflecting on her dubious wanderings and past life, stresses very aptly the already-referred-to ephemeral nature of memory with these words: "Pero esto ya pasó, todas las cosas se pasan; las memorias se acaban, las vidas no vuelven, las lenguas se cansan, los sucesos nuevos hacen olvidar los pasados."[2] A similar deliberation had already appeared in the first part of *Don Quixote*, uttered as a wise piece of advice by the protagonist to Sancho: "que no hay memoria a quien el tiempo no acabe, ni dolor que muerte no le consuma."[3] While much of this study has dealt with the physiological and psychological function of memory and its value to early modern Spanish society, it is equally imperative to consider that Cervantes ingeniously breaks with the traditional strategies for mastering memory by weaving forgetfulness and forgetting into his characterization of memory.

At a time when the human capacity of memory confronted massive information overload caused by the global upheaval of the Renaissance, multiple social anxieties surfaced as citizens of this new social paradigm attempted to come to terms with the sheer quantity of information that was accelerating the change in social, political, and economic structures. As part of dealing with this revolution, processes such as memory and its counterpart, oblivion, became subject to reexamination, particularly memory's fragility when faced with cultural demands. The general concern among the learned class about managing new knowledge sets is highlighted in *Don Quixote* by the Cousin, whose desperate attempts at capturing data as it is revealed exposes both the aforementioned social anxiety and the futility of coming to grips with a changing early modern culture. Within this social paradigm, in a culture in which remembering the past becomes an obsession, forgetting and memory avoidance likewise will have an important purpose.

It is reasonable to think that Miguel de Cervantes felt this very same anxiety in his own life, and he responded in many ways. He tried several times to secure a better standing through dedicated service to the Crown and by formally petitioning for sounder employment. Among these the most well-known example is Cervantes's careful acquisition of written letters of recommendation from major royal figures such as John of Austria, who highlighted the scope of his extensive experience and heroic service in the famous battle of Lepanto in 1571. Later, he would make several requests to the Crown for different positions in the government, as well as ask permission to move to the New World. But Cervantes's efforts at improving his lot were fruitless. Indeed, the Greek renegade Dali Mamí used John's letter of commendation as justification to ransom Cervantes for a significantly higher price than other Spaniards. The written word, treasured by all sectors of society, will have no major positive impact for Cervantes since the letters he prudently amassed are lost, and along with their erasure went the author's military standing and his past glories. Unfortunately for the author, an entire life built on military service was forgotten, as evidenced by the official of the Council of the Indies who wrote on the back of Cervantes's memorial of June 6, 1590: "Let him look on this side of the water for some favor that may be granted him."[4] In a culture in which remembering the past becomes an obsession, Cervantes ironically falls victim to a different social paradigm, one that values oblivion, forgetting, and the avoidance of remembering.

From the very beginning of *Don Quixote*, oblivion becomes that still yet abiding presence that permeates the narrative. Time and again, the novel unfolds permanently against the shadow of oblivion that slithers silently across the novel, almost as if becoming an invisible character itself. I began the pages of this book alluding to the importance of memory throughout Cervantes's work and his insistence on reminding readers to reflect on memory's traps, ellipses, and fragility, in a way parallel to the ongoing debate regarding the partial nature of memory during early modern period. I finalize this book by accentuating the fact that the fragility of memory is reinforced by the presence of oblivion and that, in fact, one faculty cannot exist without the other. By weaving forgetting into memory, Cervantes breaks with the traditional formulations that delineate both practices. Oblivion becomes a decisive force in the novel and has its own uses and practices. Besides being a physiological necessity for the correct functioning of memory, Cervantes turns oblivion into one of the many effects that literature has on readers, an illustration of the anxiety of the early modern self and the fragility of the social order.

As this book has shown, in *Don Quixote*, perhaps more than in any other literary work by Cervantes, the anxiety over memory's failures, ploys, and instability is omnipresent. As a result, memory, it would seem, is used in the novel as a force for maintaining present certain acts. However, there is a startingly obvious flip side to memory: the persistent concern over being forgotten. In fact, the novel constantly captures this obsession and apprehension of being "entregad[o] a las leyes del olvido,"[5] as appropriately expressed at the end of chapter 8 by the so-called second author, who fears that the history of Don Quixote would be subjected to the laws of oblivion. The main protagonist himself is undoubtedly the most representative of these fixations. His constant tenacity to fight against the notion of losing his story to oblivion leads him to incessantly seek "aventuras memorables." Yet his almost persistent fear of being forgotten is not unfounded since oblivion awaits in silence, paradoxically, in the very same sites commonly inhabited by memory: satchels, archives, flea markets, and desks, where the written word gets buried, lost, or discarded. The characters themselves repeatedly offer further proof of the fragility of memory when they either intentionally or accidentally forget when they are granted the opportunity to remember. As they are forgetful beings (*animal obliviscens*), obliviousness surely exercises a certain power in their lives. When evoking a myriad of thoughts and feelings, characters forget words, names, and plots. When this happens, Cervantes often freezes these scenes to capture the precise moment when forgetting occurs as if to underscore the fluidity of their memory. By shaping their cognitive processes, their memory lapses also become an aesthetic resource for Cervantes. Take the case of Dorotea performing as Princess Micomicona as part of a cunning plan to bring Don Quixote home. Unable to remember the character's name given to her by the priest, Cervantes carefully portrays a gap in memory that exposes the very human tendency to forget – even at the most pivotal moments – which is then further emphasized by the intruding narrator: "'vuestras mercedes sepan, señores míos, que a mí me llaman' … Y detúvose aquí un poco, porque se le olvidó el nombre que el cura le había puesto."[6] Such lapses, where the early modern reader contemplates the process of forgetting in action, are also part of Cervantes's techniques to humour readers as the story evolves, as in the case of Sancho trying to remember the letter from Don Quixote to

Dulcinea. However, the issues involving forgetting are not relegated to character actions alone. Besides characters' omissions, Cervantes himself will be accused of forgetting details in the first part of the novel and even of having a bad memory as a writer. In the opening pages of the second part of *Don Quixote*, Sansón Carrasco enumerates some of the complaints held by the readers of the 1605 first part, and chief among these were the author's own ellipses:

> y algunos han puesto falta y dolo en la memoria del autor, pues se le olvida de contar quién fue el ladrón que hurtó el rucio a Sancho, que allí no se declara, y sólo se infiere de lo escrito que se le hurtaron, y de allí a poco le vemos a caballo sobre el mesmo jumento, sin haber parecido. También dicen que se le olvidó poner lo que Sancho hizo de aquellos cien escudos que halló en la maleta en Sierra Morena, que nunca más los nombra, y hay muchos que desean saber qué hizo dellos, o en qué los gastó.[7]

Quite ingeniously, Cervantes will not try to hide such lapses; on the contrary, they become an aesthetic source in the development of the narration. Within the Pirandellian-like gaps caused by the effects of metafiction, even the characters will urge the author not to forget, reminding him of certain disremembered details that should be included in future editions: "Yo tendré cuidado – dijo Carrasco – de acusar al autor de la historia que si otra vez la imprimiere, no se le olvide esto que el buen Sancho ha dicho, que será realzarla un buen coto más de lo que ella se está."[8] However, as we saw in the introduction, Sansón's accusation is not necessarily accurate, considering the sheer number of sources the writer uses in the composition of the narrative and the abundance of details from history and mythology – all without having the original source material at hand.[9]

Characters also persistently remind each other not to forget, almost as a mandate, and they do so with the help of different artefacts and written records that function as external memory aids, such as letters. One example is when Teresa anxiously begs Sancho not to forget her during his absence: "No se le olvide a vuestra pomposidad de escribirme, que yo tendré cuidado de la respuesta, avisando de mi salud y de todo lo que hubiere que avisar deste lugar, donde quedo rogando a Nuestro Señor guarde a vuestra grandeza, y a mí no olvide."[10] For his own part, Sancho will experience the persistent anxiety of forgetfulness as he incessantly pesters Don Quixote not to ignore the pledged *ínsula*. Sancho becomes obsessed with the island governorship which becomes his own fight against oblivion throughout the rest of the novel: "– Mire vuestra merced, señor caballero andante, que no se le olvide lo que de la ínsula me tiene prometido; que yo la sabré gobernar, por grande que sea."[11] Just as Sancho reminds Don Quixote over and over about this well-deserved award for his skills and deeds as a good squire, the knight constantly reminds his squire of the significance of the lashes needed to disenchant Dulcinea, a trepidation reinforced by Altisidora: "Todas estas malandanzas te suceden, empedernido caballero, por el pecado de tu dureza y pertinacia; y plega a Dios que se le olvide a Sancho tu escudero el azotarse, porque nunca salga de su encanto esta tan amada tuya Dulcinea."[12]

One should not consider oblivion the opposite of memory but rather an intricate part of the faculty which appears because memory is by nature flawed and faulty. Memory cannot exist without oblivion; they go hand in hand as counterparts. Saint Augustine, in his reflections on memory in his *Confessions*, clearly understood the close dialectic between these cognitive functions. For Saint Augustine, forgetting is the absence of memory but also something in need of remembrance.[13] In this regard, Carruthers has observed a change in perception between how we see oblivion today and how it was perceived by classical and medieval writers who, like Saint Augustine, considered human memories imperfect by nature, and consequently, forgetting things was a necessary condition to remember others.[14] Engel has acknowledged this dialectical relation – allegorically as well as ontologically – between memory and oblivion during the Renaissance period by aptly emphasizing that "even though each depends on the other to be recognized fully for what it is, the allegorical presence of the one does not cancel out the meaning or identity of the other ... [I]n acts of forgetting, something always remains."[15] As already seen in the examples above, the paradox is also present in Cervantes's work and in the early modern Spanish culture in general. This is implicit in Covarrubias's definition of *olvido* as a memory defect – *"latine oblivio, nis, memoriae defectus sive imbecillitas"*[16] – accentuating that the etymology of the verb denotes the dual nature of forgetting. Furthermore, *olvidar* in Spanish comes from the Latin *oblivisci*, a verb which, as Harald Weinrich rightfully has noted, is deponent: that is, a passive form with an active connotation, which fits with the psychic meaning of forgetting, situated halfway between activity and passivity.[17] Thus, *olvidar* evolved from Latin forms that carry out lexical negations of memory whereby one can implicitly assume its presence by absence.

A decade after the appearance of the second part of *Don Quixote* in 1615, Velázquez de Azevedo in *El Fénix de Minerva y Arte de Memoria* (1626) included a lesson under the title "Del olvido" that declared the importance of forgetting for the correct functioning of memory. The author confirmed the inherent paradox between the practices: "lo que habemos dicho de la memoria muestra quién es el olvido, pues como dicen los filósofos y juristas: *Oppositorum eadem est disciplina*."[18] By including in his art of memory such a section, Azevedo clearly states the need for an art of oblivion within the art of memory: "Y si bien parece que el tratar dél no era necesario para el arte de la memoria, se hallará ser preciso si se advierte bien."[19] The idea of an art of forgetting – *ars oblivionis, ars oblivionalis*[20] – was not new in Cervantes's times. It was born to the politician and military leader Themistocles (ca. 524–459 BC), who paradoxically was known for his extensive capacity to remember. According to Plutarch, Themistocles was able to remember the names of all Athenians and learn new languages in just one year. When Simonides of Ceos, the inventor of the art of memory, offered to teach him some of the techniques, Themistocles replied that he did not need an art to remember but rather one that would help him forget the information he already possessed. It followed, then, that the art of memory led inevitably to an art of forgetfulness.[21] It should not surprise us that the *ars memorativa* included sections on how to remove and erase images. In order to create and store powerful new images, it was important to empty memory places and erase the old images inhabiting them, "del todo borradas porque no causen confusión."[22] Not only was oblivion present in some treatises of the art of memory, but its presence was also seen in other aspects of the early modern culture. To give an illustration of its importance, in his *Diálogos de la pintura* (1633), in painting, Carducho considers oblivion equally as important as memory. Constantly learning from sources and acquiring new skills are both very important for the artist; otherwise "ese día olvidará lo que alcanzó cuando los tuvo empleados en la contemplación."[23]

This same paradox – that is, the simultaneous presence and absence of memory – is likewise inherent in the pages of *Don Quixote*. By becoming memorable through his feats and endeavours, the protagonist will pursue glory as a legendary knight while also actively seeking to "erase" the deeds of other famous adventurers: "Yo soy, digo otra vez, quien ha de resucitar los de la Tabla Redonda, los Doce de Francia y los Nueve de la Fama, *y el que ha de poner en olvido* los Platires, los Tablantes, Olivantes y Tirantes, los Febos y Belianises, con toda la caterva de los famosos caballeros andantes del pasado tiempo."[24] In chivalric novels, memory is, as Beecher suggests, "at the heart of it all,"[25] and therefore oblivion, its counterpart, is always present as one of the knight's biggest fears. To counteract the possibility of being forgotten, the knight declares an active approach to supplanting the authority of the very knights he emulates. Thanks to his attempts at reviving the past chivalric orders and raising up their deeds, *Don Quixote* becomes a sort of *mnemon* of chivalric novels, a "resucitador insigne de la ya puesta en olvido andante caballería."[26] The *mnemon*, according to Jacques Le Goff, maintains the memory of the past as an official and living memory in the present.[27] The protagonist, as a *mnemon*, acts against its very nature. Cervantes's condemns the chivalric novels by creating one so that "todo él es una invectiva contra las novelas de caballerías,"[28] a sort of early modern exercise of a *damnatio memoriae*.[29] This legal concept is especially significant in the cultural history of remembering and forgetting.[30] After all, the novel is born from the expressed desire to condemn chivalric novels to oblivion once and for all.[31] In this way, forced oblivion as condemnation is a tool of defence, such as when Cervantes's similarly uses *damnatio memoriae* against Avellaneda, the author of the apocryphal *Quixote*, as a form of condemnation of memory and punishment to discredit the author and his work.

Like memory, oblivion has metaphorical qualities and can occupy physical space, although such places tend to possess added negative connotations. Consider as an illustration the references to the regions of oblivion mentioned by Lotario in one of the poems that appear in the interpolated tale "El curioso impertinente": "podré yo verme en la región de olvido."[32] Lotario reveals a tendency to express oblivion as a "region" or an encompassing space – just as other authors have described memory.[33] This is also seen when Don Quixote talks about the bottomless "abismo del olvido" that he views as a constant threat and the ultimate goal of the enchanters: "Perseguido me han encantadores, encantadores me persiguen y encantadores me perseguirán hasta dar conmigo y con mis altas caballerías en el profundo abismo del olvido."[34] These type of *loci* must have been present in the protagonist's mind as a sort of continuous menace opposed to the desired eternal fame as a knight. However, oblivion is not viewed in *Don Quixote* as only a place or location. There is also an enduring sense that the very writing of the story is subject to constant loss. Hence, as some scholars have pointed out, oblivion is generally represented as "desert wastes, sandy areas in which what is to be forgotten is gone with the wind. Thus, it amounts to almost the same thing as writing on sand or on the wind."[35] This idea simulates the fleetness of the written word in the novel, as Roger Chartier states:

> En *Don Quijote*, las palabras jamás están protegidas de los riesgos de la desaparición: los manuscritos se interrumpen, como el que cuenta las aventuras del caballero andante, los poemas escritos sobre los árboles se pierden, las páginas de los libros de memoria pueden borrarse, y la misma

> memoria falla. Al igual que *Hamlet*, la historia narrada por Cide Hamete Benengeli está obsesionada por el olvido, como si todos los objetos, todas las técnicas encargadas de conjurarlo nada pudieran contra él.[36]

As Chartier notes, it is not just the human faculty of forgetting that is omnipresent in the novel; it is the artefacts contained within the text that also are lost to oblivion.

Classical mythology lays the foundation for the treatment of oblivion in Cervantes's novel. In chapter 69 of the second part, to commemorate Altisidora's funeral, Don Quixote and Sancho are part of a theatrical presentation in which a young man dressed in Roman fashion sings:

> Y aun no se me figura que me toca
> aqueste oficio solamente en vida;
> mas, con la lengua muerta y fría en la boca,
> pienso mover la voz a ti debida.
> Libre mi alma de su estrecha roca,
> por el estigio lago conducida,
> celebrándote irá, y aquel sonido
> hará parar las aguas del olvido.

The stanza, taken from Garcilaso de la Vega's third *Eclogue*, represents the common understanding of oblivion in the collective memory during Cervantes's time. The "estigio lago" refers to the dark Styx, one of the five rivers between Earth and Underworld, along with the river Lethe, as referenced in the poem as the waters of oblivion ("aguas del olvido"). According to mythology, all who drank from these waters experienced forgetfulness. Along with the duke and the duchess, the two protagonists are sitting on the stage with two other people wearing crowns on their heads. Two kings represent the brothers Minos and Rhadamanthus, guardians in the realm of Hades later described as "cavernas lóbregas de Dite."[37] Dite, like Hades, is another word for Pluto, the god of the Underworld. The fact that Cervantes included these references in the novel reveals how such concepts and figures were part of the iconographical memory of the time often employed to represent Oblivion, although with many adaptations.[38] For example, the painting "Charon Crossing the Styx" (1520–4) by Joachim Patinir immortalized Charon transporting the souls of the dead on his boat to the gates of Hades guarded by the dog Cerberus. Besides Greek writings, Patinir also draws from biblical sources such as the figure of the angel on the promontory as well as the depiction of Heaven and Hell as the ultimate destination when Death arrives. Symbolically, the river served as a threshold to another life: either to be reincarnated or to enter into eternity in heaven by forgetting earthly sins. These ideas would explain why death is described as the eternal oblivion in Grisóstomo's funeral: "en memoria de tantas desdichas, quiso él que le depositasen en las entrañas del eterno olvido."[39]

Lethe, as the allegorical representation of oblivion so beautifully portrayed in the verses above, was also associated with other concepts such as silence, sleep, subjectivity, and transformation. These were captured eloquently by Erasmus of Rotterdam in *The Praise of Folly*, in which the humanist presents Lethe as a lethargic female figure: "She that looks as if she were half asleep is Lethe, Oblivion."[40] This correlation between forgetfulness, sleep, and silence is also found in the Prologue of *Don Quixote*, written by an author who has no significant public face and has consequently been forgotten:

> Porque, ¿cómo queréis vos que no me tenga confuso el qué dirá el antiguo legislador que llaman vulgo cuando vea que, *al cabo de tantos años como ha que duermo en el silencio del olvido*, salgo ahora, con todos mis años a cuestas, con una leyenda seca como un esparto, ajena de invención, menguada de estilo, pobre de concetos y falta de toda erudición y doctrina?[41]

Old age accompanies Cervantes as the metaphor of erasure, and *Don Quixote* is the author's seeming last chance to be remembered. A fifty-eight-year-old Cervantes, who had enjoyed only moderate success in his literary career to date, emerges from the darkness and silence to "gamble it all with this bold and original book."[42] Oblivion, messenger of the passage of time, becomes the "death of the mental work performed"[43] or, stated another way, the remains of what was once stored in memory and that now resembles the ruins and the effects of time's passage. From Cervantes's own words in the Prologue, it follows that Oblivion is associated with darkness and ruthlessly appears as something hidden and occult, much like the old trade of the errant chivalry and the old armor that rests in the dark corner of Alonso Quijano's house: "Y lo primero que hizo fue limpiar unas armas que habían sido de sus bisabuelos, que, tomadas de orín y llenas de moho, luengos siglos había que estaban puestas y olvidadas en un rincón" (I.1, 41). There is an inevitable comparison in Cervantes's words since he and Don Quixote can easily be viewed as victims whose final actions seek to halt time and reverse of laws of oblivion. Both of their stories are presented as a hole or gap within the receptacle or treasure chest that is memory. In *Lethe: The Art and Critique of Forgetting*, Weinrich aptly states that "forgetting appears as a gap in the text, which must be filled in by means of efforts of writing and thinking but which perhaps also makes the text really enigmatic and interesting in the first place."[44] One could say that Cervantes's project in *Don Quixote* is precisely to fill those gaps by offering an alternate narrative on authorship and literature from multiple perspectives.

Forgetting, from a physiological point of view, was believed to be the result of an imbalance of bodily humours. Velázquez de Azevedo asserts that "la demasiada humidad, particularmente si procede del agua, causa olvido, como retención de la sequedad; también el exceso y demasiada intención de las demás calidades debilita y pierde la memoria."[45] It should come as no surprise, then, as stated by Christopher Ivic and Grant Williams in *Forgetting in Early Modern English Literature and Cultures*, that a culture "whose hegemonic order exhibited anxieties over the decay of memory should pathologize forgetting" and that "part of this pathologization is generated by medical discourse."[46] Along these lines, care of the body and concurrent avoidance of forgetting were believed to be somatic and not just cognitive activities converting the "forgetful body as an idle and unregulated one."[47] Linked to natural philosophy, medical manuals played an important role in the first attempts to explain the psychological aspects of memory and how to avoid forgetting. In Álvarez Miraval's *Libro intitulado la conservación de la salud del cuerpo y del alma … agora nuevamente impreso con un singular tratado de la firme y tenaz memoria y del bueno y claro entendimiento* (1599), the doctor offers common dietetic remedies for memory loss as well as advice on the proper treatment of the body to prevent forgetfulness. Contrary to these dietetic precepts, there were also drugs that had the opposite effect. Known aliments that were believed to help included the fruit of lotus, as described in Homer's epic, as well as homemade potions, love, the plant *nepenthe*, and, of course, wine. As Sancho knows very well, the latter makes one forget all his troubles.

Cervantes was living in a society in which the acts of remembering (and forgetting) became institutionalized or politicized by the bureaucratic and administrative apparatus of the monarchy. In a society obsessed with documenting its past, citizens across the realm went to great lengths to prove their noble lineage by constructing elaborate family trees in the hopes of securing royal favour. Those who did not possess enough proof to boast nobility could still confirm their allegiance to Christian values and reject any semblance of Jewish or Muslim bloodlines. Just think how many times Sancho reminds us that he is a "cristiano viejo." But, while some worked feverishly to construct their past and some to dubiously claim a particular status, still others sought to forget their past. Ivic and Williams argue that "forgetting may be seen to operate as a force in its own right, exposing the fragility of the social order in early modern literature"[48] that can also be seen in *Don Quixote*. Peter Burke's concept of "social amnesia"[49] becomes very useful to this reasoning since it provides insight into the ways in which the past is censored for Don Quixote by those around him. In this context, forgetting is attached to culture, and, just like memory, it possesses its own discourses and practices. By social amnesia, Burke means the official and unofficial erasure of memories and acts of censoring the past in the interest of cohesion: "To understand the workings of the social memory it may be worth investigating the social organization of forgetting, the rules of exclusion, suppression or repression, and the question of who wants whom to forget what, and why."[50] The "exclusion, suppression, or repression" of memories relates to the ideological uses of forgetting as a form of social control through disciplinary procedures.[51] An example of this type of corrective practice is clearly seen in the burning of the books and erasing by covering that "gap" in the protagonist's library.

Forgetting is therefore affected by the environment and social conditions that surround the individual. In his study on Renaissance drama, Sullivan makes the point that memory and forgetting are closely related to larger social and cultural functions – not just to individual practical questions of remembering.[52] Sullivan enumerates the many cultural expectations that were connected with with exhortations to recall: "questions of doctrine and filial piety, norms for sexual behavior, or gender norms. Forgetting by contrast introduces a state of bodily indiscipline that challenges all of these cultural expectations … thus presenting forgetting not just as a lapse or a failure but as 'action.'"[53] Thus, following Sullivan, forgetting does not equal memory failure, but rather it is a deviation from social and cultural norms. Sullivan perceives forgetting as a form of subjectivity and as a representation of selfhood in early modern literature in that:[54] "forgetfulness, like subjectivity, appears at those moments that threaten to destabilize – or even to shatter identity ...[55] [I]t is both a condition of being and a pattern of behavior."[56] This form of forgetting about one's own identity, deemed self-forgetting by scholars today, was not viewed positively. For medical and psychological theorists during the early modern period, self-forgetting was seen as physically and mentally abnormal and unhealthy and as a socially subversive transgression. As Jonas Barish has noted, "forgetfulness of self seems to spell, or to threaten, a loss of identity, transforming the self-forgetter into something unpredictable, unrecognizable and therefore frightening."[57] This is clearly the case of Alonso Quijano's transformation into Don Quixote. Cervantes begins the novel, not with the birth of

Alonso Quijano, but when the protagonist was already at the threshold of reinventing himself as Don Quixote.[58] Cervantes dramatizes self-forgetting in the figure of Alonso Quijano for whom his books are not only the trigger of his selective forgetting but also the emblematic forces that underlie his self-forgetting. Equally important are the ways in which Alonso Quijano's bookish memories are censored by other characters, mainly his niece, the house servant, the Priest and the Barber – all of whom act as guardians of his old selfhood (the Priest in charge of soul and the Barber of the body, respectively).[59] Contrary to expectations, their methods do not go far towards making Alonso Quijano forget Don Quixote or making Don Quixote remember Alonso Quijano. In fact, these manipulators of memory impose forgetting by paradoxically forcing him to remember. Ultimately, by reenacting his chivalric memories before his eyes, they are unsuccessful in erasing his other self.

And yet it is important to consider that in this complex and dialectical interplay between forgetting and remembering, his identity as Don Quixote continuously evolves such that forgetting is not absolute. Hence, to the question of whether Alonso Quijano completely loses his memory, the answer is that he does not. He forgets the routine tasks that, not by chance, happen to be those he is not fond of, which he refuses to continue doing. The only sentence that the narrator utters in this regard is that Alonso Quijano "olvidó casi de todo punto el ejercicio de la caza y aun la administración de su hacienda."[60] To put it in other words, he forgets just that portion of his life that he cannot stand anymore, that which is driving him crazy in a different way. And so he conceives, as Carroll Johnson puts it, "a project that will give meaning to his life."[61] This project will imply a new identity carried out in multiple forms with the transformation of Alonso Quijano being just one of them. That act of oblivion is in itself an act of rebellion, and although he loses touch with reality, he actually becomes more real to his true self. To put it bluntly, literature makes Alonso Quijano slowly forget himself by inducing new mental patterns from his chivalric books that subsequently convert him into Don Quixote. And by extension, these books come to be the script of this new identity, with his scenarios (*loci*) and images fashioned according to the expectations set forth in the *ars memoriae*.

Self-forgetting is not a minor theme in Cervantes's literary works but rather one that surfaces on multiple occasions. Further support for this claim can also be found in *El licenciado Vidriera*, in which the protagonist undergoes a similar transformation that evolves into forgetting of himself. Tomás Rodaja claims to have a poor memory, and therefore he forgets the names of his parents and his home village. On the contrary, the narrator will later say that he had "tan felice memoria, que era cosa de espanto." According to Wardropper,[62] Rodaja's lapse of memory has been deliberate since later he will reveal his family name and that of his village. Equivalent to Rodaja's temporary memory loss, Isabela, the protagonist of *La española inglesa*, shows selective recall that erases memories from her past. In these two cases, as in *Don Quixote*, forgetfulness is not so much a loss a memory as a transformation of the self. The knight's forgetfulness is associated with a resistance to social conduct and codes that establish normative models of behaviour. His forgetfulness is an act of rebellion and a way to stress his new identity.

In early modern narratives of identity formation, the idea of forgetting relates to a transformation rather than an annihilation,[63] a sort of amnesia according to Benedict Anderson: "All profound changes in consciousness, by their very nature, bring with them characteristic amnesias. Out of such oblivions, in specific historical circumstances, spring narratives."[64] Ivic and Williams similarly argue that in order for new narratives and identities to be posited, older narratives and identities must be erased or rewritten.[65] The scholars view the act of forgetting as a sociocultural performance: "To forget oneself is not simply a lapse of memory; it often signals a slide from one social category to another."[66] For Alonso Quijano, leaving aside his identity as a lesser noble in place of a meaningful vocation as a knight-errant affords him the opportunity to play a role in history by reviving and living a noble and heroic code that has seemingly fallen out of favour. By doing so, Don Quixote fulfils "the universal desire to become another close to one's dreams and aspirations."[67] But, paradoxically, as the pages of the book are filled with his life as a knight, each turn of the page furthers the act of erasure, of self-oblivion, of Alonso Quijano. To put it differently, through his practice of memory, Don Quixote's oblivion sharpens as he detaches himself from Alonso Quijano.[68]

I end this book where I began – where Cervantes began – with the opening words from his novel, wrought with tendencies from the rhetorical tradition of the locus in the *ars memorativa*:[69] "En un lugar de la Mancha, de cuyo nombre no quiero acordarme." As I stated at the outset and developed through this study, the opening words mark a narrative bent on highlighting the need to remember while also revealing memory's fragility. In the end, however, we see that the opening words paradoxically and perhaps subversively also hide a tendency to elevate forgetfulness. The syntactic construction "(no) querer acordarse de" was well known and used during Cervantes's time[70] and uncovers the tension between forgetting and remembering which is the heart of the novel and which is actively at work in Cervantes's own life. Oblivion, ellipsis, and silence will therefore become key elements in the construction of the narration. As in the opening sentence, where there is a voluntary and conscious act of memory, the author determines what to include or not, what is considered worth of remembering or forgetting. What he could not have known – and what is blatantly obvious to any reader of *Don Quixote* – is that the novel would become one of the most memorable works of fiction in history.

Notes

Introduction: Obsessions with Remembering

1 Emphasis added, cited in Yates, *Art of Memory*, 29.
2 Emphasis added, *Silva*, III, 7, 48.
3 By establishing a place and control over what the author chooses to remember at the outset, memory responds to an intention. As Joaquín Casalduero explains, the novel begins with that sentence with the goal of opposing the techniques of chivalric books and to disobey the tradition of honouring the hero's origins: "Si siempre se nos dice donde nacieron, ignoraremos siempre el lugar donde D. Quijote vino al mundo" ("Explicando," 148). The author establishes control over why and how the narrator remembers, an act of rebellion that promotes disobedience towards the servile *imitatio* of previous models during the Renaissance.
4 As Américo Castro has observed, Fernando de Rojas was one of the first to put into practice the technique of literary perspectivism, which is also closely linked to memory and equally attributable to Cervantes's novel: "Sus figuras humanas saben unas de otras, se representan unas a otras en varias formas; no se afectan unas a otras sólo por lo que hacen sino a través de cómo son vividas por las otras; están relativizadas, es decir, humanizadas" (150–1).
5 Lathrop, "Introduction," xvii.
6 The extent of Cervantes's memory is astonishing considering that, as Richard L. Predmore states, "young Cervantes cannot have enjoyed much more than six years of formal schooling. In most men this amount of study could not have created a sufficient base for the very considerable literary culture visible in Miguel's later writings, which reveal a good knowledge of the outstanding Latin authors, a smattering of Greek literature, a close familiarity with some of the great writers of the Italian renaissance and the kind of acquaintance with his own literature that one might expect a

boy with strong literary inclinations to possess. What he knew of the Latin language and literature was certainly grounded in his schooling; the rest *must have been the product of his own reading*. The five years he was soon to spend in Italy contributed decisively to his continued education and account for his extensive reading in Italian literature" (emphasis added, 49).

7 Hiscock, *Reading*, 3.

8 These recent studies on early modern memory and literature also show a shift in the scholarship from groundbreaking studies on the significance of memory in the Middle Ages and early modern period by Frances Yates in *The Art of Memory* (1966), Paolo Rossi's *Logic and the Art of Memory* (1983), Mary Carruthers's *The Book of Memory: A Study of Medieval Culture* (1990), *The Craft of Thought: Meditation, Rhetoric, and the Making of Images* (1998), and Lina Bolzoni's *The Gallery of Memory: Literary and Iconographic Models in the Age of Printing Press* (1995). The area of early modern memory studies was built on the foundational works by Yates and Rossi and their emphasis on the art of memory. In her pivotal study, Yates described the development of the art of memory from classical antiquity, particularly Roman rhetoric, to the Renaissance, where it was radically transformed. Yates's stature as the first scholar to examine the art of memory in Europe laid the groundwork for subsequent scholarship. Rossi traced the art of memory towards the logic and the new scientific discourses of the time. Additionally, and as a result of the memorial practices inherited from the arts of memory, Bolzoni stressed the importance of their representation through iconographic models in early modern Italy. For her part, Carruthers developed the importance of trained memory in medieval studies and its presence in literature, music, architecture, and manuscripts.

9 See Nikulin, *Memory: A History.*

10 See Rebeca Helfer for a complete and updated list of publications on the subject.

11 As an illustration, Yates's foundational work in *The Art of Memory* included an examination of the cultures of most European countries, but inexplicably left out Spain, a country that arguably elevated the importance of memory above the status it enjoyed in other countries. As a result, scholars who have followed Yates's path or depended greatly on her work have likewise not sufficiently considered Spain's important role in the expansion of memory studies and the techniques they espoused.

12 "Cervantes, al configurarse a su héroe, no parece sino que tuviera en cuenta la concepción aristotélico-platónica recogida en el *Examen de ingenios* que concebía la memoria 'como el papel en blanco y liso en el que ha de escribir.' Así tuvo el héroe siempre a punto ese libro que su imaginativa había grabado en la memoria y que imponía constantemente a la realidad, por encima de toda percepción sensorial inmediata. Con la ayuda de la

imaginativa, Aristóteles y Galeno, ya preveían esa constante relectura que cada uno podía hacer en el libro de su propia memoria. Ésta, a solas, era como papel exento, espacio en el que escribir y nada en definitiva, sin los auxilios de la imaginativa" (Egido, "Memoria *Quijote*," 42).

13 Egido initiated the study of memory and Cervantes. Besides her studies on memory in *Don Quixote, Los trabajos de Persiles y Sigismunda*, and the exemplary novels *El casamiento engañoso* and *El coloquio de los perros*, she has examined the application of the *ars memoriae* in literature and art (see complete bibliography). Although these studies are important for my analysis and my book clearly engages with all of them, I expand on Egido's approach by focusing more on the adaptation of memory practices as a response to the demands of Renaissance culture and by inserting Cervantes's works in the midst of the debates on memory during his time. In sum, I place the theme of memory within the larger context of memory debates of the early modern Spain.

14 Accessed in June 2020.

15 In his *Libro de albeitería* (1564) Francisco de la Reina speaks of the importance of memory in the theory of shoeing: "Theórica en herrar se entiende que todo aquello que el entendimiento entiende del arte y memoria retiene encerrado en sí es theórica."

16 Memory is also crucial for engineers and professors of military architecture. Cristóbal Lechuga defines it thusly in *Discurso en que trata de la artillería con un tratado de fortificación* (1611): "y esto por la mucha experiencia y por el uso padre de la sabiduría, como la memoria madre, tomando de ellos el pareçer, sin aguardar medidas ni proporciones, por ser cosa que no la entienden todos y propias de los ingenieros, profesores de la architectura militar" (243).

17 The subject is discussed in Juan de Yciar's *Arte breve y provechoso de cuenta castellana y arithmetica donde se muestran las cinco reglas de guarismo por la cuenta castellana y reglas de memoria* (1559).

18 *Silva*, III, 7, 48.

19 "Etymologically, 'Muses' are 'those who think.' They know everything and remember everything because of their origin from their mother Memory (Mnēmosinē) and their father Zeus who in later Platonic interpretations, becomes the embodiment of reason and nous" (Nikulin, "Memory," 37).

20 See Egido, "Literatura efímera."

21 I borrow the term from Ann M. Blair. See her book *Too Much to Know*.

22 Greenblatt, *Renaissance Self-Fashioning*, 2.

23 "As a sequence of recent early modern studies has indicated (e.g., Engel, 1995; Engel et al., 2016; Hiscock, 2011; Karremann, 2015; Lyne, 2016; Pivetti, 2015), the narrative drive in successive early modern texts sought to render human experience legible in terms of recovery and retrieval,

embedding the faculty to remember in a range of widely available and established intellectual discourses of enquiry – Platonic, Aristotelian, rhetorical, anatomical, architectural, historiographical, chorographical, and scientific" (Hiscock, "Debating," 70). In this respect, Kurt Danziger speaks of "an outburst of writings devoted to memory" during XVI and XVII.

24 Beecher, "Recollection," 367.

25 Hiscock, *Reading*, 8.

26 Beecher, "Introduction," 17.

27 Danziger, *Marking the Mind*, 7.

28 Hiscock, *Reading*, 3.

29 In *Meno* 81c–e and *Phaedo* 73c, Nikulin, "Memory," 46.

30 As Egido has indicated, Don Quixote himself "expresará las ideas del Filebo platónico sobre la impresión imborrable de la amada en la tabla rasa del alma, lo que equivale a la afirmación de su imperecedero recuerdo" ("Memoria *Quijote*," 36).

31 Huarte, *Examen*, 191c, d.

32 The notion of "anamnēsis" is, according to Dmitri Nikulin, Plato's original contribution to philosophy: "The discussion of *anamnēsis* occurs in the *Meno* 80d–6c and *Phaedo* 72e–4a and is centered on the discussion of the problem of whether we can learn something about the things that are" (Nikulin, "Memory," 45).

33 Nikulin, "Introduction," 7.

34 Aristotle also compares the process of recollection to "a logical syllogism that moves from premises to a conclusion. In this respect, recollection has features of narrative, insofar as it needs to reproduce a movement of reasoning by telling a story in order to obtain that for which it searches" (Nikulin, "Introduction," 7).

35 Schacter, *Searching*, 308.

36 "Remembering is not like playing back a tape or looking at a picture; it is more like telling a story. The consistency and accuracy of memory is therefore an achievement, not a mechanical production. Stories have lives of their own. Some memory stories do achieve a kind of stability – especially if they have been frequently repeated – but their accuracy cannot be presumed simply because they are vivid and clear. With this in mind, it's always a good idea to take memory with a grain of salt" (88).

37 Cervantes, *Comedias y tragedias* I, 484–6.

38 Libro I, 230–1.

39 Magnus, *De memoria et reminiscentia*, 450a22.

40 I will be citing from Francisco Rico's edition in the following order: part one or two, chapter, and page number. Emphasis added, I.1, 42.

41 See Domínguez's "The 'Janus Hypothesis' in *Don Quixote*."

42 I use Richard Sorabji's edition of *De memoria et reminiscentia*, 450a25, 48.

43 *De memoria et reminiscentia*, 450a25, 48.
44 Huarte, *Examen*, 363.
45 Pollmann, *Early Modern Memory*, 29.
46 Cervantes, *Don Quixote*, I.27, 311.
47 Cervantes, *Don Quixote*, I.28, 156.
48 Cervantes, *Don Quixote*, I.43, 501.
49 This refers to the powers of the soul, although the meaning is the same: "Estas cavernas son las potencias del alma" (De la Cruz, *Llama de amor viva*, 239).
50 Cervantes, *Don Quixote*, I.52, 583.
51 de Vega, *El cuerdo loco*, II, 1643–5.
52 Cervantes, *El rufián*, 134.
53 Gracián, *Agudeza y arte*, 212.
54 See Carruthers, *Book*, 31–55. See also Draaisma.
55 His text, the sole treatise during the period about memory written from a medical perspective, serves as a guide to explore the knowledge circulating in Cervantes's era. Of course, there had been references to the maintenance and conservation of memory before Alvarez de Miraval's, but until then no one in Spain had written a manual dedicated exclusively to this topic. In his pages emerge ideas about memory from a physiological point of view as well as the high esteem in which the faculty of memory was held. The maintenance and care of natural memory appears in other treatises, but generally these references were rhetorical in nature.
56 Campuzano, *Coloquio*, 294. See Domínguez's "Cervantes and the Mother of the Muses."
57 *Silva*, III, 7, 49.
58 Engel, *The Memory Arts*, 11. Engel, *Mapping Mortality*, 3, 11.
59 Egido, "Memoria y *Don Quijote*," 44. As Egido has observed, through the traditional technique of *ab initiis inicipendum*, as dictated by the arts of memory, to begin a story from the very beginning is a constant feature in the *ars memorativa*, as Juan Velázquez de Azevedo states in *El Fénix de Minerva y el arte de memoria*: "La mejor disposición para referir un suceso, o historia, es el progreso de cómo sucedió començando siempre en todo, desde el principio, que esta guía, además de escusar la perturbación, causa que no se olvide nada." Quoted in Egido, "Persiles," 622, n2.
60 See also Taylor's *El arte de la memoria en el Nuevo Mundo*.
61 Bolzoni, *Gallery*, xxi.
62 Gutiérrez de los Riós, *Noticia general*, 167–8.
63 Engel et al., "Introduction," 25.
64 Gutiérrez de los Riós, *Noticia general*, 167.
65 Besides heraldry, one must take into consideration medieval symbolism in bestiaries, lapidaries, and allegories as the source of the emblematic.

An interesting case in point when talking especially about the mnemonic values of artefacts in Spain is the relic. These were popular objects during Cervantes's time thanks to Philip II's collection of 7,500 of them: "literal objects, symbolically representational objects, and potentially poetic objects through the simple transfer of the saints' powers as miracle workers to their material remains" (Beecher, "Recollection," 398).

66 Vicente Espinel offers a similar critique in the *Vida del escudero Marcos de Obregón*, which demonstrates the criticisms that existed in society towards these systems of artificial memory: "Tener buena memoria natural es excelentísima cosa; pero gastar el tiempo en buscar dos o tres mil lugares pudiéndolo gastar en actos de entendimiento, no lo tengo por muy acertado, porque para la memoria sirve la estampa, las imágenes, los colosos, estatuas, escrituras, edificios, piedras, señales de peñascos, ríos, fuentes, árboles, y otras cosas sin número; y para el entendimiento sola la naturaleza lo da y lo enriquece con la lección de los autores graves y comunicación de amigos doctos" (II, 210).

67 Cervantes, *Novelas ejemplares II*, 293–4.

68 Hiscock, *Reading*, 25.

69 Cervantes, I. Prólogo, 12.

70 For Aristotle, knowledge is converted into experience and memory is responsible for converting that information into ideas, or, using Aristotle's words, "experience is formed of many memories" (*Metaphysics* I, I, cited in Carruthers, *Book*, 54).

71 Pliny. Translation by Jerónimo de Huerta, Fol. 57V.

72 Pliny. Translation by Jerónimo de Huerta, Fol. 58.

73 Cited in Yates, *Art of Memory*, 20.

74 Ágreda, *Cartas*, 184. Letter of March 6, 1654 [Cartas entre Felipe IV y Sor María Jesús de Ágreda] (1654).

75 Jesús, *Obras*, 223.

76 Quevedo, Cap. 2, Fol.11v.

77 On memory as part of the triad of the soul, see Otis Green, *España y tradición occidental*, Madrid: Gredos 1. 68–73 and 2. 182, and John G. Weiger. *The Substance of Cervantes*. Cambridge: Cambridge University Press, 1985.

78 Weiger, *Substance*, 139.

79 Cervantes, *La Galatea*, Libro II, 292.

80 Carruthers, *Book*, 14.

81 Carruthers, *Book*, 1.

82 Carruthers, *Book*, 11.

83 Pliny. Translation of Jerónimo de Huerta, Capítulo XXIIII. Fol. 57 R.

84 Cervantes, *Novelas ejemplares* II, 44.

85 Furió Ceriol, *El concejo*, 16.

86 Aristocratic ethos were shared by Philip II, who was passionate about the rituals of knighthood: "Todavía a mediados del siglo XVII está muy presente en la construcción de un ethos aristocrático que hacía de la memoria caballeresca de la centuria anterior uno de sus signos distintivos y una referencia inexcusable en su pedagogía" (Bouza, *Corre manuscrito*, 217).
87 "Todos los personajes son memoria y se nutren de la memoria" (Egido, "Memoria *Quijote*," 31).
88 Egido, "Memoria *Quijote*," 28.
89 Cervantes, *La Galatea*, Libro I, 226.
90 Cervantes, *Novelas ejemplares I*, 117.
91 Cervantes, *Entremeses*, 103.
92 Cervantes, *Novelas ejemplares II*, 154.
93 Cervantes, *Comedias y tragedias*, 550.
94 Cervantes, *Don Quixote*, II.68, 1181.
95 Cervantes, *Don Quixote*, I.5, 73. See Chad M. Gasta's "'Señora, donde hay música no puede haber cosa mala:' Music, Poetry, and Orality in *Don Quijote*" and "Writing to Be Heard: Performing Music in *Don Quixote*."
96 For more information on the polysemy of verbs – in some cases quasi-synonymous – see Frenk, *Entre la voz*, 100, who calls these "reliquias léxicas" (43).
97 Frenk, *Entre la voz*, 104.
98 Cervantes, *Don Quixote*, II.66, 1167.
99 "Muchas veces, *leer* significaba, de hecho, un hacer vivir, en voz alta un texto más o menos memorizado. Es evidente el parentesco con el rezar." Schön, 35. Cited in Frenk, *Entre la voz*, 104.
100 Carruthers has also seen a very similar meaning in the ancient Greek: "Ancient Greek had no verb meaning 'to read' as such: the verb they used, *amagignōsko*, means 'to know again,' to recollect" (*Book*, 30). This refers to a memory procedure.
101 de Vega, Lupe. Prólogo. *Trecena parte de las comedias de Lope de Vega Carpio*. Madrid: Viuda de Alonso Martín, 1620.
102 Frenk, *Entre la voz*, 146. For other examples of the presence of memorization in everyday life, see Frenk, *Entre la voz*, 144.
103 Frenk, *Entre la voz*, 61.
104 Quoted in Frenk, *Entre la voz*, 27.
105 Quoted in Frenk, *Entre la voz*, 61.
106 de Vega, *Novelas a Marcia Leonarda*, 1.
107 Alan Deyermond has also noted how orality – and therefore memorization – "influye en casi todos los géneros literarios" in which, for example, "un género culto se moraliza como la transmisión oral-memorial de los *Proverbios morales* de Sem Tob, o la composición oral de los libros de caballerías" (32). See also Harvey, "Oral Composition," 84–100.

108 Cervantes, *Don Quixote*, II.31, 881.
109 "Yet whereas the need to organise, interpret and narrate memories seems universal, the way people do this – the when, where, what and how – is socially, culturally and thus historically determined" (Pollmann and Kuijpers, "Introduction," 16).
110 Azevedo, *El Fénix*, 125v.

1 The Anatomy of Early Modern Memory

1 Arnold's story can be found in the chapter "Remembering Pannonian Dragons" in *Phantoms of Remembrance: Memory and Oblivion at the End of the First Millennium* by Patrick Geary.
2 Emphasis added, Schacter, *Searching*, 105.
3 Schacter, *Searching*, 105.
4 Cervantes, *Don Quixote*, I.16, 173.
5 Emphasis added, Cervantes, *Don Quixote*, I.1, 42.
6 These are some of the terms used by Schacter to refer to the nature of memories in *Searching for Memory*.
7 Sacks, *River*, 121. Similarly Sacks also talks about imaginative reconstructions (and not reproductions of reality) and offers numerous examples in daily life in *The Man Who Mistook His Wife for a Hat* (175–7).
8 Howard Mancing introduced the field of cognitive literary studies and its application to early modern Spain and Cervantes, see his co-edited *Theory of Mind and Literature*, and particularly his essay "Sancho Panza's Theory of Mind" in this collection. Also, on Cervantes and cognitive literary studies, see the special cluster *Cognitive Cervantes* for the journal *Cervantes* edited by Julien Simon, Barbara Simerka, and Howard Mancing. See also Isabel Jaén and Julien Simon, *Cognitive Approaches to Early Modern Spanish Literature* and *Cervantes and the Early Modern Mind*.
9 Beecher, "Introduction," 23.
10 The attempt at defining the vague line between the corporeal and non-corporeal was carried out by what might seem like two very different groups: doctors and philosophers. The latter focused on the perspective of the soul while the former concentrated on the causes of affliction of the body. As E. Ruth Harvey has suggested in *The Inward Wits*, the line between the corporeal and the non-corporeal was difficult to define and therefore "both medicine and philosophy contributed to the final formulation of the idea of the inward wits … but the idea developed differently in the two disciplines" (5). On early modern memory studies and historical cognition, see particularly John Sutton and Evelyn Tribble. See also Rico.
11 For more information on this relationship, see Lina Bolzoni's *The Gallery of Memory*.

12 See Domínguez's "Cervantes and the Mother of the Muses: Views of Memory in Early Modern Spain."

13 On early modern medicine in Spain, see José María López Piñero; Luis Granjel; and more recently *Medical Cultures of the Early Modern Spanish Empire*, edited by John Slater, Marialuz López-Terrada, and José Pardo-Tomás, and *Health and Medicine in Hapsburg Spain: Agents, Practices, Representations*, edited by Teresa Huguet-Termes, Jon Arrizabalaga, and Harold J. Cook.

14 The practice of medicine in Spain produced printed materials by renowned doctors. The majority of these were collected in the work of the bibliographer Nicolás Antonio *Bibliotheca Hispana Nova* (1696) between the years 1500 and 1674, such as Andrés Laguna; the Divino Vallés Francisco Vallés, also known as the Spanish Galen; Cristóbal Pérez de Herrera; and Matías de Llera – respectively, doctors of Charles I, Philip II, Philip III, and Charles II. It is also worth highlighting the studies of Michael Servetus on the pulmonary circulation in his *Christianismi Restitutio* (1533) and the work of Bernardino Montaña de Monserrate, which distinguished between the arterial blood circulation of the veins in his *Libro de anathomia del hombre. En el qual se trata de la fabrica y compostura del hombre, y de la manera como se engendra y nasce y de las causas porque necesariamente muere* (1551). Other doctors of importance are Luis Mercado, physician and anatomist Juan Valverde de Amusco, Juan Huarte de San Juan, Miguel de Sabuco, and surgeons such as Juan Calvo, Dionisio Daza Chacón, Francisco Díaz, and Juan Fragoso. There is little doubt that Spanish medicine in the early modern period was extremely important. The field of psychology itself centred on the physiology of the brain, its representation, its functions, its disorders, and its interpretation. With this interest in the brain's physical disposition came also an emphasis on the inner senses and, subsequently, memory. As a consequence, memory is repeatedly associated with different facets of the physical body in Cervantes's time. Following the foundational figures mentioned above, thinkers, doctors, and natural philosophers, such as Juan Luis Vives, Juan Huarte de San Juan, Antonio Gómez Pereira, Francisco Vallés de Covarrubias, and Miguel de Sabuco y Álvarez, contributed to the advancement of the study of psychology in Spain. See the work of Josep Lluís Barona *Sobre medicina y filosofía natural en el Renacimiento* for more details on the evolution of medicine and natural philosophy in early modern Spain. See also Carpintero and Jaén and Simon.

15 See Bailón Blancas; Barreiro González et al.; García Barreno; López Méndez; López-Muñoz et al.; Heiple; Palma; and Palma, Peset, and Soufas.

16 As Stephen Gilman has stated, "The presence of no less than five physicians in Cervantes's immediate family will seem highly significant to those familiar with the social history of the time" (*The Spain of Fernando de Rojas*, 20).

17 *Hippocratis prognosticum*, 1596.

18 Huarte exercised great influence during the time; for example, Pinciano echoes his naturalistic explanation of the interior faculties: "y como quiera que para las obras del sentido común baste un moderado calor, a las de la memoria es necesario sea fuerte, como lo vemos en las cosas exteriores … y de aquí nace que los niños por mucha humidad, y los viejos por defecto de calor, tengan esa potencia flaca;' por su parte, la tercera potencia, la imaginación, y siguiendo a Huarte; no atiende la imaginación a las especies verdaderas, mas finge otras nuevas, y acerca de ellas obra de mil maneras: unas veces las finge simples, otras las compone … porque abraza las especies pasadas, presentes y futuras" (*Philosophia antigua poética*, 47–9).

19 In fact, it is very likely that Daza Chacón, named chief surgeon at the Battle of Lepanto, helped Cervantes with his wounds during the battle, although he could have been helped by another well-known doctor, Gregorio López. See Eisenberg's "La biblioteca de Cervantes."

20 Anselmo, one of the protagonists of the tale of "El curioso impertinente," uses this example to describe how asking a friend to tempt his wife has made him sick: "Prosupuesto esto, has de considerar que yo padezco ahora la enfermedad que suelen tener algunas mujeres que se les antoja comer tierra, yeso, carbón y otras cosas peores, aun asquerosas para mirarse, cuanto más para comerse" (Cervantes, I.33, 388).

21 Huarte was one of the most well-known doctors in early modern Europe. The popularity of his *Examen* is demonstrated by its eighty-two editions and its translations to seven languages, becoming one of the best-known and most widely available treatises across the continent regarding the psychophysiology of the time. On the relationship between Huarte and Cervantes, see the works by scholars and scientists such as Iriarte, Jaén, Salillas y Panzano, and López-Muñoz et al.

22 This topic is discussed in depth in Domínguez's "The Internal Senses in *Don Quixote* and the Anatomy of Memory."

23 Carruthers explains that "diagrammatic" refers to drawings that were not anatomical; the sole purpose of such images was to show just the process that occurs in the brain as it was understood. In Spain, these images became known through their publication in the *Historia de la composición del cuerpo humano* (1556) by the Palencian anatomist Juan Valverde de Amusco. In turn, Amusco's work drew on illustrations by the Spanish painter and sculptor Gaspar Becerra. Amusco's illustrations provided insight into the processes of the brain for many writers and thinkers, such as the doctor Juan Huarte de San Juan. As Serés has suggested, it is very probable that Huarte possessed the images that Gaspar Becerra carried out for the work of Amusco for his *Historia de la composición del cuerpo humano* (1556).

24 Two of the most important scholars in the subject, H.A. Wolfson and Ruth Harvey, have pointed to the variety of approaches, descriptions, and functions that Aristotle's work, Arab commentators, and Galenic humanists have given to these internal faculties throughout centuries. This a very important point because it is quite confusing to see the inconsistencies not only in their translation, enumeration, and definition but also in the different ways these inward wits or faculties were described in the context of the definitions offered by physicians, philosophers, theologians, and rhetoricians; it is very important to keep in mind the cultural context. Each of these interpretations is associated with one or more quality, element, or humour. For example, Avicenna and Gómez Pereira mentioned five but Thomas Aquinas only four.

25 For Aristotle the *sensus comunis* is a faculty that channels the sensations captured by the senses. Huarte accepts Aristotle's theory tacitly, influenced fundamentally by the traditional tripartite division of the three faculties and the cerebral anatomy of the time (Serés, 206 n63). See also Daniel Heller-Roazen's "Common Senses: Greek, Arabic, Latin" and Simon Kemp and Garth Fletcher's "The Medieval Theory of the Inner Senses."

26 Sabuca, *Neuva filosofía*, 314–15. The cognitive process described above was in use until the last decades of the seventeenth century, when discoveries in the human anatomy carried out by the English doctor Thomas Willis unseated the millenary ventricular system. During Cervantes's time, this cognitive system was the most prevalent. It would not be until the end of the sixteenth century when, in Spain, the so-called group novatores broke with this tradition.

27 See Laín Entralgo, *La medicina*.

28 Huarte, *Examen*, 321.

29 Fuentes, *Suma*, Fol. CLVR.

30 Cervantes, *Don Quixote*, I.52, 583.

31 Cervantes, *Don Quixote*, II.7, 678.

32 Cervantes, *Don Quixote*, II.17, 761.

33 Cervantes, *Don Quixote*, II.10, 706.

34 Cervantes, *Don Quixote*, II.62, 1134.

35 Huarte, *Examen*, 421.

36 See Domínguez's "A Window onto the Heart: Cervantes and the Cardiocentric Self."

37 Carruthers, *Book*, 59. This cardiocentric conception had a wide range of followers up until the seventeenth century. For example, William Shakespeare attributed the faculty of reason to the brain but thought the heart generated emotions.

38 Emphasis added, Cervantes, *Don Quixote*, II.1, 625.

39 Cervantes, *Don Quixote*, II.17, 770.

40 The legacy of the Platonic and Aristotelian traditions in Renaissance memory theory is indisputable, and their notions will be "somewhat modified by Averroes, transmitted by Albertus Magnus, Thomas Aquinas, and thence into all kinds of compilations, repeated in the sixteenth century by Vives and others, and easily available in many printed sources" (Rothstein, *Reading in the Renaissance*, 75).
41 Emphasis added, Plato, *Dialogues*, I.269.
42 Plato, *Phaedo*, 75e.
43 As it appears in both *Theaetetus* (194C) and *Philebus*.
44 Plato, *Dialogues*, 4.23.
45 Aristotle, *De anima*, 430a.
46 Carruthers, *Book*, 62.
47 The idea that memory uses images persists today. Richard Sorabji, in his edition of *De memoria et reminiscentia*, describes how Plato also noted the process of memorization and later recollection involved a "seeing of internal pictures" as if they have been imprinted in memory with a wax ring.
48 Aristotle, *De memoria*, 450a25.
49 Emphasis added, Azevedo, *Fénix*, 63.
50 The illustration by Doré was part of the French translation of *Don Quixote* by Louis Viardot, *L´ingénieux hidalgo Don Quichotte de la Manche*. Paris: Hachette and Co., Paris, 1863.
51 "[A]llí le podré dar más de trescientos libros que son el regalo de mi alma y el entretenimiento de mi vida; aunque tengo para mí que ya no tengo ninguno" (Cervantes, *Don Quixote*, I.24, 268).
52 Carruthers, *Book*, 29. "Because they are themselves sort of pictures these representations were thought to be best retained for recollection by marking them in an order that was readable, a process the ancients thought to be most like the act of seeing … [R]eading was considered to be essentially a visual act, despite the fact that most ordinary social reading, at least, was done aloud by someone to a group of listeners, throughout antiquity and until the Renaissance" (Carruthers, *Book*, 20).
53 Cervantes, *Don Quixote*, II.26, 852.
54 Cervantes, *Don Quixote*, I.24, 262.
55 Cervantes, *Don Quixote*, I.27, 311.
56 Aristotle, *De memoria*, 450a25.
57 As Carruthers explains: "Since our knowledge comes to us through our senses, every image impressed in our memories has been filtered and mediated through our senses – it is not merely objective. Our senses produce 'affects' in us, physical changes such as emotions, and one of those 'affects' is the memory itself" (*Book*, 65).

58 Huarte, *Examen*, 363.
59 Aristotle, *De anima*, 430a.
60 Huarte, *Examen*, 280.
61 The tetralogy of a text (structure in four) reflects the forces of nature, especially in the first two chapters of the novel, according to De Armas, where there are many quaterns: four types of food that account for three-quarters of the hacienda del Hidalgo, the four members of the house, the four names of the nobleman, etc. (*Quixotic Frescoes*, 52–70). Heninger says with respect to this Pythagorean cosmology: "All things are born from hot, cold, moist and dry" (160). The four qualities are essential for the composition of the four elements earth, water, air, and fire.
62 "Just as the four basic qualities interact to produce the four elements that comprise the world's body, they similarly produce the four humours that compose the body of man and make him a microcosm" (Heninger, *Touches*, 168).
63 Sabuco, *Nueva filosofía*, 256.
64 Huarte, *Examen*, 357.
65 Huarte, *Examen*, 129.
66 Cervantes, *Don Quixote*, I.1, 39. See Serés , "Introducción," 209, n69.
67 In the novel, the housekeeper makes exactly this point when she squarely puts blame for Alonso Quijano's behaviour on his books – and by association, on his readings: "Encomendados sean a Satanás y a Barrabás tales libros, que así han echado a perder el más delicado entendimiento que había en toda la Mancha" (Cervantes, *Don Quixote*, I.5, 74).
68 Serés, "Introducción," 209, n69.
69 Aristotle, *De anima*, 450.22.
70 Citado en Serés, "Introducción," n46, 363.
71 Emphasis added, Galen, *De motu musculorum*, 363. This is expanded in Domínguez's "The 'Janus Hypothesis' in *Don Quixote*: Memory and Imagination in Cervantes." Similarly, this reciprocal dependency between imagination and memory was noted by Huarte, clearly following the ideas of both Galen and Aristotle: "la imaginativa escribe en la memoria las figuras de las cosas que conocieron los cinco sentidos y el entendimiento y otras que ella misma fabrica. Y cuando quiere acordarse de ellas, dice Aristóteles que las torna a mirar y a contemplar … Esto mismo hace la imaginativa: escribir en la memoria y tornar a leer cuanto se quiere acordar" (363). See also Murray Wright Bundy's *The Theory of Imagination in Classical and Medieval Thought*.
72 Cervantes, *Don Quixote*, I.19, 201.
73 Cervantes, *Don Quixote*, II.23, 825.
74 Iriarte, *El doctor*, 321.

75 During the Renaissance, melancholy was a state of mind considered very conducive to creative activity. One of the experts in melancholy and the consequences of this disorder, which afflicted the Cervantes character, was Alonso de Santa Cruz, whose work was published by his son, the doctor Antonio Ponce de Santa Cruz, a friend of Cervantes during his stay in Valladolid. López-Muñoz et al. have suggested that it is very likely that Antonio personally gave Cervantes this treatise on melancholy, a subject very much in vogue and the epitome of mental insanity in the time of Cervantes as demonstrated in Robert Burton's *The Anatomy of Melancholy* (1621).
76 Only testimonies by Cicero and Plutarch ensure this authorship.
77 Aristotle, *Problemata* XXX section 1, 953. Although this was seen in Plato's *Phaedrus*, it will later be very important for the Neoplatonics, as Marsilio Ficino established the connection between black bile and the poetic furor.
78 de Vega, *La prueba*, 211.
79 de Molina, *El Melancólico*, 71.
80 Melancholy was therefore the temper for a good memory. See R. Klibanskly, E. Panofsky, F. Saxl, *Saturn and Melancholy. Studies in the History of Natural Philosophy, Religion, and Art*, 69, 337.
81 Cited in Yates, *Art of Memory*, 58–9.
82 Cited in Yates, *Art of Memory*, 69.
83 Yates, *Art of Memory*, 69. On another occasion, Albertus Magnus in *De bono* also talks about the good memory of melancholics: "The goodness of memory is in the dry and the cold, wherefore melancholics are called the best for memory" (cited in Yates, *Art of Memory*, n57, 69).
84 Emphasis added, Borgnet IX, 117, cited in Yates, *Art of Memory*, 69.
85 For a complete account of the number of times Huarte cites the works of Hippocrates, Galen, Plato, and Aristotle, among others, see Iriarte, *El doctor*, 136–8.
86 Huarte, *Examen*, 343.
87 Huarte, *Examen*, 352.
88 Cervantes, *Don Quixote*, I.1.
89 Huarte, *Examen*, 226.
90 Aristotle, *De memoria*, 59.
91 Cervantes, *Don Quixote*, II.14, 738.
92 Cervantes, *Don Quixote*, II.28, 867.
93 Carruthers, *Book*, 68.
94 Fuentes, *Suma*, Fol. CLIVV.
95 Schacter, *Searching*, 27.
96 Méndez, *Libro*, Fol. XXXIIIV.
97 Cervantes, *Don Quixote*, I.28, 322.
98 Aristotle, *De memoria*, 451b18.
99 Vives, *Sobre*, II, 1189.

100 Vives, *Sobre*, I, 93.
101 Emphasis added, Bóscan, *Traducción*, 210.
102 Emphasis added, Cervantes, *Don Quixote*, I.5, 71.
103 Egido, "Memoria y *Don Quijote*," 42.
104 Cervantes, *Don Quixote*, I.2, 49.
105 Dudai and Carruthers, "Janus Face," 567. See also Alan Richardson.
106 Cervantes, *Persiles*, 386.

2 Mental Libraries: The Places of Memory

1 Artiga, *Epítome*, 420.
2 Anonymous, *Rhetorica*, 209.
3 Cervantes, *Don Quixote*, I.6, 76.
4 Gesualdo, *Plutosofía*, Lettione XVII, 55r.
5 Cited in Azevedo, *Fénix*, 119v.
6 Azevedo, *Fénix*, 119v.
7 *Gazophylacium artis memoriae*, cited in Bolzoni, *Gallery*, n15, 314.
8 Bolzoni, *Gallery*, 14.
9 Bolzoni, *Gallery*, xvii.
10 Rodríguez de la Flor establishes this interesting type of parallel. See "Estudio introductorio," xxxix. See also Domínguez, "Imaginar mundos."
11 Hiscock, *Reading*, 16.
12 Foer departs from the cultural history of remembering and the art of memory to teach and transform human memory.
13 Augustine, *Confessions*, 173.
14 According to Víctor García de la Concha, the text *Coloquio de la Memoria, la Voluntad y el Entendimiento* would be the first text in romance.
15 Emphasis added, Mejía, *Silva*, vol. 2. 57–8.
16 Cited in Merino, *Retórica*, 195.
17 Merino, *Retórica*, XXVIII.
18 Engel et al., *Memory Arts*, 4.
19 Engel et al., *Memory Arts*, 8.
20 Bolzoni, *Gallery*, xvii.
21 See Lausberg.
22 Riley, *Cervantes*, 7.
23 Pliny the Elder, *Natural History*, Chapter XXIIII, 295. See also chapter XXX, 2 as an example of the transmission of the art.
24 See de Armas, *Quixotic Frescoes*, 17 and ff. De Armas, "Cervantes y Della Porta," 634. De Armas explains the importance of mnemonics and visual representation in *La Numancia*, *La Galatea*, and *Don Quixote*. He has also seen other possible influences in Cervantes's use of mnemonics from Cicero's *De oratore* and the *Ad Herennium*.

25 de Armas, *Quixotic Frescoes*, 15.
26 Cervantes, *Don Quixote*, I.23, 249.
27 Cited in Yates, *Art of Memory*, 2.
28 Beecher, "Recollection," 372.
29 Huarte, *Examen*, 440.
30 de Armas, *Quixotic Frescoes*, 21.
31 "It is necessary in this way to invent similitudes and images because simple and spiritual intentions slip easily from the soul unless they are as it were linked to some corporeal similitudes, because human cognition is stronger in regard to the sensibilia" (cited in Yates, *Art of Memory*, 74).
32 Yates, *Art of Memory*, 21. Cicero's thoughts find their echo in Cervantes's time through Huarte, who similarly relates prudence to the faculties of the rational soul (*Examen*, 574; 587).
33 Carruthers, *Book*, 11.
34 See Genovart on knighthood as a sort of superior pedagogy and its relation to *Don Quixote*.
35 For more information on the two facing illustrations, see Bolzoni, "The Play of Images," 29.
36 Emphasis added, Beecher, "Recollection," 384.
37 Cervantes, *Don Quixote*, I.47, 550.
38 On the relationship between Titian's painting and Camillo's *Theater*, see Yates, *Art of Memory*, 162 and ff.
39 Ceriol, *El concejo*, 16.
40 Funes, *Libro*, Fol. 12R. See also the description by Diego Álava de Viamont in *El perfecto capitán* (1590): "Considerando la prudencia en operación o acción, como todas las virtudes, según dize Séneca, necessariamente a de aver para ella estas tres cosas para las quales, como dize Arquitas Pitagoreo, son necessarias otras tres: agudeza, memoria y inclinación a todo trabajo y la perseverancia en él" (Fol. 20R).
41 See Barbeito Díaz., "El Brocense."
42 Yates, *Art of Memory*, 6.
43 See the extraordinary project "Artificiosa Memoria" carried out at the Universidad de Extremadura under the leadership of Luis Merino: http://www.artificiosamemoria.es/index.php.
44 Yates, *Art of Memory*, 122 and ff.
45 de la Flor, "Estudio," xviii–xix.
46 Somehow, such obelisks, cubes, and other forms remind us of "los ciertos rombos y caracteres" (Cervantes, *Don Quixote*, II.35, 922), with whom Merlin entertains himself in the Montesinos Cave.
47 Lygia Rodrigues Vianna Peres sees a parallel between "la idea del teatro de todo el mundo de Giulio Camillo con sus divisiones espaciales, lugares de memoria [y] la idea del teatro de toda la literatura en *El Quijote*" ("El Quijote,"

540). Similarly, de Armas has seen in *La Numancia* a relationship to Camillo's theatre in that each of the four acts represents one of the four elements of the cosmos ("Della Porta," 12–13).

48 Yates, *Art of Memory*, 254.

49 Bolzoni, *Gallery*, 241.

50 On the role of Hermetic and Neoplatonic thought in Spain through the Florentine writer Marsilio Ficino, see Susan Byrne's *Ficino in Spain*.

51 Egido, *De la mano* 69. See also Ignacio Gómez de Liaño on Giordano Bruno.

52 Bolzoni, *Gallery*, 70.

53 Engel et al., *Memory Arts*, 11.

54 Engel et al., *Memory Arts*, 11.

55 Bolzoni, "The Play of Images," 21.

56 See Egido, "Memoria y *El Quijote*," 7.

57 See Egido, "Ejemplar," 467.

58 Rodríguez de la Flor, "Ars," 50.

59 Bolzoni, *Gallery*, 212.

60 According to Bolzoni, and as stated also by Marshall McLuhan and Walter Ong, printing is not just a tool, "it has a feedback effect upon the subject using it, and it contributes to changes in the perception of the world" (*Gallery*, xviii).

61 Bolzoni, *Gallery*, 191.

62 Sancho illustrates the ease with which he remembers his readings: "no debía haber historia en el mundo ni suceso que no tuviese cifrado en la uña y clavado en la memoria" (Cervantes, *Don Quixote*, II.58, 1097), an indication also of his memory being a product of mnemotecnic trainings since "[sabía] de memoria todas las ordenanzas de la andante caballería" (Cervantes, *Don Quixote*, II.14, 738).

63 "La memoria andante de Don Quijote es tan poderosa que las imágenes que percibe y los lugares por los que transita pasan a identificarse inmediatamente con los lugares e imágenes que guardaban en su mente" (Egido, "Memoria y *El Quijote* Egido," 11).

64 For this, it was necessary to have a witness like Sancho who "tome bien en la memoria" that which he observed: "¡Oh tú, escudero mío, agradable compañero en mis prósperos y adversos sucesos, toma bien en la memoria lo que aquí me verás hacer, para que lo cuentes y recites a la causa total de todo ello!" (Cervantes, *Don Quixote*, I.25, 279).

65 Egido considers the episodes as "el ejemplo más rico de cómo opera la máquina mnemotécnica" ("Memoria y *El Quijote*," 17).

66 The term is borrowed from Hiscock, *Reading*, 17.

67 Several critics have observed the symbolic value of the Sierra. Augustin Redondo grants it a transgressive character where anything can happen. Chiong Rivero defines it as *anti-locus amoenus*. Regarding the idea of Sierra Morena as an emblem of the labyrinth, see Javier Herrero, Salvador Jiménez Fajardo, Joan Ramón Resina, and Chiong Rivero. See also Finello.

68 Cervantes, *Don Quixote*, I.23, 251.

69 In this respect, Quintilian, in his *Institutio oratoria*, speaks of the "eye of the mind," which is fixed "not merely on the pages on which the words were written, but on individual lines, and at times he will speak as though he were reading it aloud" (cited in Yates, *Art of Memory*, 25).

70 Cervantes, *Don Quixote*, I.25, 278.

71 Cervantes, *Don Quixote*, I.25, 278.

72 Jiménez Fajardo, "Sierra Morena," 215.

73 Azevedo, *Fénix*, 98.

74 Anonymous, *Rhetorica ad Herennium*, 209.

75 See Michael Gerli's study "El Castillo interior y el 'Arte de la memoria.'"

76 According to Herrero, Sierra Morena is an emblem of hell that brings to memory the Dantesque places of the *Divina Comedia* linked to the medieval art of memory. In regard to the influence of Dante in Cervantes, see William Avery. As we have seen, Cervantes's references to Dante's *Divina Comedia* through the *loci* of purgatory and hell came from the medieval tradition that in turn proceeded from the Italian tradition of the art of memory, as stated by Yates (*Art of Memory*, 122).

77 Pagán, *Geografía*, 552.

78 Cervantes, *Don Quixote*, I.25, 281.

79 Egido, *Puertas*, 222. Hugues has also observed concomitances between the Platonic theories of memory by San Augustine in his *Confessions* and the cave motif (113). In addition, the protagonist's dream in the Cave of Montesinos goes back to the words in *De insomniis* where Aristotle says that some people have dreams in which they "seem to be arranging the objects before them in accordance with their mnemonic system" (cited in Yates, *Art of Memory* 31). Egido, Avalle-Arce, and Riley have observed similarities between these two symbolic spaces within the novel, Sierra Morena and the cave. Avalle-Arce and Riley, *Don Quijote*, 55. Egido, *Puertas*, 220.

80 Aristotle, *De memoria*, 54.

81 451b18, 54.

82 Emphasis added, Cervantes, *Don Quixote*, I.25, 275.

83 Merino, *Retórica*, 47.

84 Aristotle, *De memoria*, 55.

85 In his analysis of Sierra Morena as a labyrinth, Chiong Rivero sees the uses of these verbs as "un juego literario que refleja el proceso mismo de la creación novelesca" ("A imitación," 288).

86 See Cervantes, *Don Quixote*, I.25, 278–9.

87 Cervantes, *Don Quixote*, I.26, 290–1.

88 Cervantes, *Don Quixote*, I.26, 291.

89 Cervantes, *Don Quixote*, I.26, 293. These images are thus the "formas, símbolos, representaciones" stored in memory, belonging to the eclogues

and mythological fables of his abundant readings inhabited by "rústicos dioses" and "napeas y dríadas" of which he now makes us participants too.

90 Emphasis added, Cervantes, *Don Quixote*, I.25, 275.

91 See Weigner's *The Substance of Cervantes.*

92 de la Flor, *Teatro de la memoria*, 73.

93 Brito Diáz, "Cervantes," 41.

94 Avalle-Arce, "Penitencia," 163. However, Don Quixote's penance, like Amadís's, does not have a strictly religious meaning. Avalle-Arce establishes the connection with the religious context because chivalry in the Middle Ages was considered a religious military order. The chivalric novels adapted penance by endowing it with an entirely secular character.

95 See Avalle-Arce and Riley, "Don Quixote," and Williamson, "Lecturas."

96 Emphasis added, Cervantes, *Don Quixote*, I.26, 291.

97 There are two types of metaphors used to designate memory. On one hand, there are metaphors that link memory to the spatiality where all kinds of metaphorical spaces arise, such as the tree, the field, the labyrinth, the garden, or the jungle – wide and disorderly – and in contrast, a more ordered and confined space, such as the house. On the other hand, there is a second group of metaphors related to writing, including, par excellence, the wax tablet and the book, which are considered technologies of memory.

98 The words that have best exemplified the admiration for the immense capacity of memory are found in the *Confessions* of Augustine of Hippo, who, in book X, describes it as if he were within his own memory – which he considers theological space – contemplating the images present there, both those proceeding from sensory impressions and those produced by the soul, in a Platonic key – in short, all divine creation: "I come to the fields and spacious palaces of memory, where are the treasures of innumerable images, brought into it there from things of all sorts perceived by the senses. There is stored up, whatever besides we think, either by enlarging or demising, or any other way varying those things which the sense hath come to; and whatever else hath been committed and laid up, which forgetfulness hath not yet swelled up and buried.... Behold in the plains, and caves, and caverns if my memory, innumerable and innumerably full of innumerable kinds of things" (cited in Yates, *Art of Memory*, 46–7). Reading these passages, one cannot help but notice similarities between the mental geography that Don Quixote traverses and the spaces of memory that Saint Augustine describes. By Cervantes's time, Benito Arias Montano, in his *Rhetoricum libri quattuor*, addressing the subject of memory, will again describe memory in a Platonic and therefore Augustinian key, as an immeasurable memory that one ranges through.

99 Engel et al. see in Augustine's view of memory "the conversion of the loci system into a theological space, a second creation locked in the subject's interiority. Augustine makes the memory palace private and personal, not just instrumental" (*Memory Arts*, 6). Don Quixote also converts the memory palaces of ancient rhetoric into mental space for private use.
100 Anonymous, *Rhetorica ad Herennium*, 205.
101 Escarramán, *El rufían*, 134.
102 Cervantes, *La Galatea*, 292.
103 Cervantes, *Don Quixote*, II.43, 973.
104 Cervantes, *Don Quixote*, I.5, 71.
105 These expressions are abundant in Cervantes's work. For example, Trampagos, in the *entremés Rufián viudo llamado Trampagos*, "ya se me ha reducido a la memoria la treta de denantes" (119); in *La Galatea* "y al fin hallo en mi memoria" (306); in *El celoso extremeño* "bien se os debe acordar (que no es posible que se os haya caído de la memoria)" (132).
106 Emphasis added, Cervantes, *Don Quixote*, II.60, 1116.
107 Cervantes, *Don Quixote*, I.5, 71.
108 Emphasis added, Cervantes, *Don Quixote*, I.5, 71.
109 Emphasis added, Cervantes, *Don Quixote*, I.2, 45.
110 Emphasis added, Cervantes, *Don Quixote*, I.4, 62.
111 Merino, *Retórica*, 195. Here, El Brocense follows the *Rhetorica ad Herennnium*.
112 Azevedo, *Fénix*, 117.
113 Bolzoni, *Gallery*, 241.
114 Cited in Bolzoni, *Gallery*, 210.

3 *Ut Pictura Memoria*: The Mnemonic Power of Images

1 Yates, *Art of Memory*, 100.
2 "[S]ixteenth-century printing practice frequently reused existing woodcuts so that what is an illustration when it first appears, no longer directly illustrates the text it accompanies in successive appearances" (Rothstein, *Reading in the Renaissance*, 85).
3 "The illustration is therefore a locus of recapitulation, and a large part of the pleasure of examining it must lie in rediscovering the components of the episode it renders, recalling the chapter's events" (Rothstein, *Reading in the Renaissance*, 85).
4 Beecher, "Introduction," 17.
5 Emphasis added, Rothstein, *Reading in the Renaissance*, 86.
6 Báez Rubí speaks of the externalization process of the art of memory: "Paulatinamente la metodología del arte de la memoria iniciará un proceso de externalización y exteriorización similar al que siguen todo diseño mental al pasar de lo interno a lo externo" (*El arte*, 328).

7 Beecher, "Recollection," 383.
8 Engel et al., Memory Arts, 25.
9 Engel et al., Memory Arts, 277.
10 On the evolution of the art of memory, see *The Art of Memory* by Frances Yates.
11 Engel et al., Memory Arts, 9.
12 "The Renaissance's mnemonic episteme fostered a mental ecosystem conducive to cultivating the memory arts" (Engel et al., *Memory Arts*, 11).
13 Bolzoni, *Gallery*, 15.
14 Beecher, "Recollection," 379.
15 Beecher, "Recollection," 380.
16 de la Flor, "Imagen leída," 107.
17 "At the same time, the iterative and replicative powers of print culture enabled such mnemonic images to spread throughout the Renaissance world and, on a competitive basis, seek iconic status, thereby entering into the common consciousness of the age" (Beecher, "Recollection," 380).
18 Engel et al., *Memory Arts*, 4.
19 See chapter 16 in *The Art of Memory* by Yates (342–65).
20 See René Taylor's *Arquitectura y magia*.
21 Chaparro, "Per locos et imagines," 10.
22 Emphasis added, Yates, *Art of Memory*, 91–2.
23 Cicero speaks of the comparison between the formation of images and painting and its relation to rhetoric in *De oratore*.
24 See Mercedes Alcalá-Galán's "La noción de museo en el *Persiles*: las colecciones de arte en la imaginación literaria"; de Armas's *Quixotic Frescoes* and *Cervantes, Raphael and the Classics*, Ana Laguna's *Cervantes and the Pictorial Imagination*; and Helena Percas de Ponseti's *Cervantes the Writer and Painter of Don Quijote*, among others.
25 Cervantes, *Don Quixote*, II.71, 1203.
26 Bolzoni, *Gallery*, xv.
27 Bolzoni, *Gallery*, 182.
28 Bolzoni, "Play of Images," 19.
29 "The theory of the equation of poetry and painting also rests on the supremacy of the visual sense; the poet and the painter both think in visual images which the one expresses in poetry the other in pictures. The elusive relations with other arts which run all through the history of the art of memory are thus already present in the legendary source, in the stories about Simonedes who saw poetry, painting and mnemonics in terms of intensive visualization" (Yates, *Art of Memory*, 28). See also Praz.
30 Bolzoni, "Play of Images," 22–3.
31 Maravall, *Cultura del Barroco*, 501. Fernando Bouza attributes the same power to the period along with writing and the spoken word as expressions to

establish memory, fulfilling the function of communicating and preserving knowledge (*Communication, Knowledge, and Memory in Early Modern Spain*, 3).

32 Ledda, "Los jeroglíficos en los sermones barrocos," 128.

33 There is a constant parallel between painting and memory used in the arts of memory of the time which in itself reflects the confluence and contamination among the arts as illustrated once again by della Porta in regard to the *imaginatio*: "it takes in images of perceptible things and, as if it were an excellent painter, it uses its brush to draw them in the memory, which has been made into a blank canvas for this purpose" (cited in Bolzoni, *Gallery*, 214).

34 Cited in Bolzoni, *Gallery*, 184.

35 de Armas, *Quixotic Frescoes*, 28.

36 See Battista and Battisti, *Le Machine*.

37 Cited in Bolzoni, *Gallery*, 184.

38 Cited in Bolzoni, *Gallery*, 184.

39 Cited in Bolzoni, *Gallery*, 184.

40 "Enriquecida la memoria, i llena la imaginación de las buenas formas que de la imitación a criado, camina adelante el ingenio del pintor" (*Arte de la pintura*, 159).

41 Carducho, *Diálogos*, 51.

42 Rodríguez de la Flor, "Imagen leída," 105.

43 Beecher, "Introduction," 17.

44 Beecher, "Recollection," 369.

45 Beecher, "Recollection," 380.

46 Infantes, "Ludo," 25.

47 See the recent editions by Enrique Suárez Figaredo and Javier Blasco.

48 Infantes, "Ludo," 26.

49 Beecher, "Recollection," 380.

50 "Cual vemos del rosado y rico oriente," *Poesías*, 172.

51 Riley, "*Don Quixote* from Text to Icon," 108.

52 Cervantes, *Don Quixote*, II.3, 653.

53 Cervantes, *Don Quixote*, II.71, 1203.

54 de Armas, *Quixotic Frescoes*, 9 and "Simple Magic," 22.

55 Egido, "Arte Persiles," 633.

56 Cervantes, *Persiles*, III.1, 437–8.

57 Cervantes, *Persiles*, III.1, 439.

58 Cervantes, *Persiles*, IV.8, 680–1.

59 Egido, "Memoria y *El Quijote*," n60.

60 Cervantes, *Don Quixote*, I.8, 104.

61 Cervantes, *Don Quixote*, I.9, 109.

62 In this regard, Julián Gállego speaks of an exercise of mental gymnastics that clearly prepared "el ojo y el cerebro a asociaciones muy interesantes"

and where memory will play an important role in different aspects of culture during Cervantes's time (*Visión y símbolos*, 188).

63 Laguna, *Cervantes*, 30.

64 Aristotle, *De memoria*, 449b30. Sorabji, Aristotle, 48.

65 Cited in Yates, *Art of Memory*, 4.

66 Yates, *Art of Memory*, 9.

67 Cervantes, *Don Quixote*, I.25, 286.

68 Cervantes, *Don Quixote*, I.2, 48.

69 Emphasis added, Cervantes, *Don Quixote*, II.67, 1176.

70 Brito Díaz, "Cervantes al pie de la letra," 40.

71 Cervantes, *Don Quixote*, I.II, 46 n19.

72 Cervantes, *Don Quixote*, I.2, 46–7.

73 Azevedo, *Fénix*, 118. Similar classifications exist that demonstrate a relationship to the referent to which they allude. For example, Jorge de Trebisonda distinguishes between equal images (*similes omnino*), different images (*omnino dissimiles*), or partially equal images (*ex parte similis*) (Merino, *Retórica*, 86).

74 Emphasis added, cited in Muñoz Delgado, "Juan de Aguilera," 184.

75 De Armas, "Simple Magic," 18.

76 The main tenets and outlines of the *Rhetorica ad Herennium* will still be used in the art of memory treatises during Cervantes's time (Yates, *Art of Memory*, 6).

77 Cited in Yates, *Art of Memory*, 10.

78 Cited in Yates, *Art of Memory*, 9.

79 Cited in Merino, *Retórica*, 205.

80 Nebrija, *Retórica*, 155.

81 Juan de Aguilera in his *Ars memorativa* demands movement from images, and El Brocense states the importance of "imágenes de seres vivos en movimiento pues de esta forma excitarán más vigorosamente la memoria" (cited in Merino, *Retórica*, 188). Leporeus also recommended the animated use of gestures (Morcillo Romero, *Ars*, LXXXVII).

82 For the use of the techniques of the art of memory to create powerful mnemonic images in Cervantes's theatre, see Domínguez's "Writing to Rescue from Oblivion: The Phantasms of Captivity in Cervantes's Theatre."

83 "In *De somnis*, Aristotle says that some people have dreams in which they 'seem to be arranging the objects before them in accordance to with their mnemonic system' – rather a warning, one would think, against doing too much artificial memory, though this is not how he is using the allusion. And in the *De anima* there is a similar phrase: 'it is possible to put things before our eyes just as those who invent mnemonics and construct images'" (Yates, *Art of Memory*, 32).

84 Emphasis added, Cervantes, *Don Quixote*, I.50, 569.

85 Cited in Bolzoni, *Gallery*, 177.

86 Emphasis added, Cervantes, *Don Quixote*, I.50, 569–70.

87 Bolzoni, "Espectáculo," 11.

88 Yates, *Art of Memory*, 10.

89 Carruthers, *Book*, 69. "Medieval memory advice stressed synesthesia in making a memory-image. The Aristotelian description of how a memory-image is formed after data from all five external senses is processed in the sensus communis already implies a large degree of synesthesia, and this – while according pride of place to visual factors – is reflected in mnemonic procedure. Memory images must 'speak', they must not be silent. They sing, they play music, they lament, they groan pain. They also often give off odor, whatever sweet or rotten. And they can also have taste or tactile qualities" (Carruthers, *Book*, 97).

90 "Si deseas recordar con rapidez," he insists for the third time in the same passage, "pon jovencitas muy bellas, pues la colocación de muchachas anima admirablemente la memoria" (cited in Merino, *Retórica*, 67).

91 Huarte, *Examen*, 170.

92 De Armas, *Quixotic Frescoes*, 12.

93 Cervantes, *Don Quixote*, I.2, 49.

94 Cervantes, *Don Quixote*, I.45, 525–6.

95 "The reason for recollecting not being under their control is that just as it is no longer in people's power to stop something when they throw it, so also he who is recollecting and hunting moves a bodily thing in which the affection resides" (Aristotle, *On Memory*, 59).

96 Bolzoni, *Gallery*, 130. On the power of images, see David Freedberg, *The Power of Images*, where he talks about the ability of the image to raise passions and provoke fear or pleasure, among many other reactions. Similarly, Hans Belting has studied the impact of sacred images.

97 Emphasis added, Azevedo, *Fénix*, 146.

98 Libro II. Cap. 15. Tít. VII. *De la reformación de la imaginación*.

99 Cited in De la Flor, *Siete ensayos*, 119.

100 "In fact, some people have actually experienced such dreams, e.g. those who judge that they are arranging a given set of items according to the system for memorizing them" (Aristotle, *De somnis*, 87).

101 Bolzoni, *Gallery*, 131.

102 See Massimo Ciavolella and Bolzoni, "Erotic."

103 For this reason, it is important to highlight the predominant role the Catholic Church will grant to the image to spread the faith after the famous XXV session of the Council of Trent. Also relevant is the decisive influence of Saint Ignatius and the so-called *compositio loci*, which were to be used as a method of praying as part of the Exercises through which "se difundió en la conciencia católica la teoría de los lugares e imágenes de la retórica mnemónica de la antigüedad" (Sebastián, *Emblemática*, 53).

104 Particularly on the Augustinian faculties of the soul's intellect, will, and memory.

105 Cited in Bolzoni, *Gallery*, 131. Certainly, Paleotti saw the potential of the images in the art of memory and their externalization and application to sacred images. According to Bolzoni, he was referring to the theory of the *imaginatio* and the power of images as it was also understood by philosophers and doctors at the time: "the various conceptions that our imagination apprehends of things, firm imprints are made in it, and from these imprints are derived substantial alterations and signs in the body" and finalizes saying, "there is clearly no stronger or more effective means that that of realistic images that seem to violate our unwary senses" (cited in Bolzoni, *Gallery*, 141). In sum, he certainly believed in the power of images and considered them a dangerous force that can go out of control. It was also within this religious context that the danger of the image of memory and its heretical propositions – such as the prayer of recollection with its different degrees (vocal, mental, and affective) outlined in the catechesis of *Camino de Perfección* by Saint Teresa or the religious movement of the *alumbrados*. See Antonio Márquez, *Los alumbrados: Orígenes y filosofía* (1525–59).

106 Fray Diego de Estella recommends the extensive use of images "por quedarse más en la memoria de los oyentes su doctrina" (*Modo de predicar*, I, 68).

107 Bolzoni, *Gallery*, 143.

108 Particularly in the session XXV (*La invocación, veneración y reliquias de los santos y de las sagradas imágenes*, 1563), where the use of images for educational purposes was advocated: "the honor that is given to the images, refers to the originals represented in them; of luck, that we adore Christ by means of the images that we kiss, and in whose presence we discover ourselves and kneel; and let us venerate the saints, whose likeness they have." My translation. http://www.intratext.com/IXT/ESL0057/__P1G.HTM.

109 Cervantes, *Don Quixote*, II.58, 1095.

110 Cervantes, *Don Quixote*, II.58, 1095.

111 Cervantes, *Don Quixote*, II.58, 1095.

112 Cervantes, *Don Quixote*, II.58, 1095–6.

113 Cervantes, *Don Quixote*, II.58, 1096.

114 Cervantes, *Don Quixote*, II.58, 1096.

115 Cervantes, *Don Quixote*, II.58, 1096.

116 Cervantes, *Don Quixote*, II.58, 1096.

117 Cervantes, *Don Quixote*, II.58, 1096.

118 Bolzoni, *Gallery*, 185–6. There are many examples in painting where a particular profession was closely linked to social class, such as in popular portraits of *The Jurist* or *The Librarian* by the Italian painter Giuseppe Arcimboldo.

119 López Díez, *Ars Memorativa*, CLII.
120 Gállego, *Visión y símbolos*, 84.
121 Orozco has also linked the *compositio loci* to baroque plasticity. See "Mística y plástica" in *Mística, plástica y Barroco* (9–57).
122 In Córdoba, Cervantes studied at the Jesuit College of Santa Catalina in 1555, and later on in Seville he continued his studies at another Jesuit College (Durán, "Vagabond Life," 24).
123 Egido, "Memoria y *El Quijote*," 18. In his study on ecclesiastical institutions in the work of Cervantes, Celso Bañeza Román recognizes the infinity of practices and manifestations of a religious nature – among them the ascetic penance of Don Quixote, which he associates with "prácticas de mortificaciones, sacrificios voluntarios y flagelaciones en actos públicos o procesiones penitenciales, propias de la vida ascética – aconsejadas por San Ignacio de Loyola en sus *Ejercicios espirituales* y otros autores ascéticos y místicos de España y Europa" (Román, "Instituciones y costumbres," 74).
124 Selig, *Coloquio*, 515.
125 Cervantes, *Don Quixote*, II.5, 669. F.S. Escribano has also pointed out that same reference as a clear influence of the Ignatian composition of place.
126 Ricard, "Los vestigios," 266.
127 Ricard, "Los vestigios," 268. In fact, the rhetorical manuals in early modern Spain include a section on mnemotechniques for use in the *ars praedicandi*, the sacred oratories that recommended the use of emblems and hieroglyphs.
128 Curiously, and as César Chaparro points out, the *exempla* were sometimes taken from chivalric books. See "Retórica y libros de caballerías. La presencia de *exempla* en la *Rhetorica christiana* de Diego Valadés."
129 Cervantes, *Don Quixote*, II.20, 800.
130 Cervantes, *Don Quixote*, I.20, 209.
131 My translation. Ledda, *Contributo*, 32.
132 Engel et al., *Memory Arts*, 27–9.
133 "The emblem book merits its place in memory studies for its calculated exploitation of the materials of the arts of memory, linked to a concerted use of memorably images and the order of the book as a mnemonic device" (Beecher, "Recollection," 382).
134 The popularity of the work is estimated in its more than ninety editions.
135 Bolzoni, *Gallery*, 188.
136 Bolzoni, *Gallery*, 182.
137 Gállego, *Visión y símbolos*, 84.
138 Emphasis added; there is no page number in the original.
139 In this regard, Rosemary Freeman and Frances Yates have seen an overlap between emblems and mnemonics, as have Peter Daly, Michael Bath, and John Manning. The art of memory contributed considerably

to the development of emblematic literature along with Neoplatonism, Hermeticism, *ut pictura poesis*, scholasticism, Trentine politics (Sebastián, *Emblemática*, 11).

140 Juan Horozco y Covarrubias, *Emblemas morales* (1591), Libro III, 241v.

141 Azevedo, *Fénix*, 123. For the practice and memorization of poetry, he will also recommend the use of the emblem. For example, for a sonnet that begins with the word *fuerza*, Azevedo suggests "para símbolo de la fortaleza pone Alciato cinco emblemas y la pintura de cualquiera dellas podía servir aquí de imágenes a la primera palabra de este soneto" (167).

142 See "Motivos emblemáticos en la poesía de Cervantes." As Ignacio Arellano has also indicated with respect to the multiplicity of repertoires and sources, it is impossible to determine "si un motivo se relaciona con el mundo emblemático o es simplemente una referencia (mitológica, erudita, fabulística, zoológica …) que encuentra sus correspondientes en los libros de emblemas sin que haya una relación mutua" ("Cultura" 93). See also Olivares Zorrilla.

143 Pinillos, "Emblemas," 103.

144 Cervantes, *Don Quixote*, II.31, 879.

145 Pfandl, *Cultura y costumbres*, 126.

146 Yates, *Art of Memory*, 126.

147 Aguilera thus collected "la tradición medieval de gran interés para las representaciones plásticas de cosas espirituales y aludiendo a los emblemas de Alciato" (cited in Muñoz Delgado, "Juan de Aguilera," 185).

148 Cited in Flórez Miguel, "Pedro Ciruelo," 293.

149 Cervantes, *Comedias y tragedias*, 12.

150 Cervantes, *Don Quixote*, II.56, 1086.

151 Cervantes, *La Galatea*, 427.

152 Cervantes, *Don Quixote*, II.20, 800.

153 Cervantes, *Don Quixote*, II.20, 800.

154 See Pinillos's essay for a complete analysis of the episode in relation to emblems.

155 Cervantes, *Don Quixote*, II.23, 822.

156 "Porque así como las facciones son imágenes y señales que nos muestran y dan a conocer las personas, eso mismo hacen las imágenes en este arte, que nos muestran aquello de que nos queremos acordar" (Azevedo, *Fénix*, 71v).

157 Cited in Bolzoni, *Gallery*, 164.

158 Cervantes, *Don Quixote*, II.1, 636.

159 Sebastián, *Emblemática*, 17.

160 Cervantes, *Don Quixote*, I.18, 190–1.

161 Equally important within the tradition of the art of memory is the topographical order and the memorization of lineages to which the protagonist resorts again and again as a result of his readings (Egido, "Memoria y *El Quijote*," 26): "¡Válame Dios, y cuántas provincias dijo,

cuántas naciones nombró, dándole a cada una con maravillosa presteza los atributos que le pertenecían, todo absorto y empapado en lo que había leído en sus libros mentirosos!" (Cervantes, *Don Quixote*, I.18, 193). According to Egido, the Canon brings a series of historical heroes, arranged topographically, just as the mnemonic manuals stated and linked to the technique of the heteroclite lineage: "Un Viriato tuvo Lusitania; un César, Roma; un Aníbal, Cartago; un Alejandro, Grecia; un conde Fernán González, Castilla; un Cid, Valencia; un Gonzalo Fernández, Andalucía; un Diego García de Paredes, Estremadura; un Garci Pérez de Vargas, Jérez; un Garcilaso, Toledo; un don Manuel de León, Sevilla" (Cervantes, *Don Quixote*, I.51, 581–2).

162 Cervantes, *Don Quixote*, I.19, 205.
163 Cervantes, *Don Quixote*, I.19, 206.
164 Cervantes, *Don Quixote*, II.27, 857.
165 Azevedo, *Fénix*, 175. Jorge Trebisonda advised, in the case of abundance of mental images, to differentiate them "con adiciones, disminuciones, cambios, formas, colores," (cited in Merino, *Retórica*, 111).
166 These "libreas" were "'uniformes o atavíos propios de las fiestas cortesanas,' de colores con un valor simbólico y que solían llevar dibujos alegóricos (cifras) glosados en versos (motes)" (Cervantes, *Don Quixote*, II.22, 812, n27).
167 Cervantes, *Don Quixote*, II.22, 812.
168 As Bolzoni states: "If we put together the parts that the treatises on memory dedicate to the construction of image, we can see the various pictorial typologies begin to emerge during the sixteenth and seventeenth centuries. They belong to a rich iconological repertory" (*Gallery*, 184).
169 Beecher, "Recollection," 381.
170 Beecher, "Recollection," 380.
171 Bolzoni, *Gallery*, 180.

4 Information Overload: Stocking Memory in the Age of Cervantes

1 Borges, *Funes*, 128.
2 As seen in chapter 24 on memory in Book VII of Pliny's *Natural History*, translated into Spanish by Jerónimo de Huerta in 1599. Cervantes expressly cited it in *Los trabajos de Persiles y Sigismunda* in I.18, 245.
3 Pliny, *Natural History*, 127.
4 "Sospecho, sin embargo, que no era muy capaz de pensar. Pensar es olvidar diferencias, es generalizar, abstraer" (Borges, *Funes*, 131).
5 Borges, *Funes*, 130.
6 See Cervantes, *Don Quixote*, chapters I.22–4.
7 Burton, *Anatomy*, 37.
8 Blair, *Information*, 16.

9 Erasmus, *Collected*, 665.
10 Blair, "Reading Strategies," 11.
11 Cited in Blair, "Reading Strategies," 11.
12 Emphasis added, de Otálora, *Colloquios*, 209.
13 Beecher, "Introduction," 18.
14 Emphasis added, Fajardo, *República*, 71–2.
15 Blair, *Too Much to Know*, 93–102. See also Cevolini and Lerner.
16 Cited in López Poza, "Polianteas y otros," n3 192.
17 Cited in López Poza, "Polianteas y otros," n3 192.
18 Likewise, adages, sentences, fables, anecdotes, phrases, and everything that could not be entrusted to memory was treasured in the most diverse methods, techniques, and artefacts, such as the aforementioned *cartapacios (codex excerptorius)*, index cards (*esquelae*), or tables, to imitate, disclose, or use later as a source of the *inventio*.
19 On the spatialization of knowledge, see chapter 4 in Danziger.
20 "El estudiante de retórica debe leer los textos y anotar en su cuaderno, en el capítulo correspondiente, expresiones significativas, arcaísmos, neologismos, argumentos de sutil invención o de acertada disposición, ornatos elocutivos, y los adagios, ejemplos y sentencias que, junto con todo lo demás, merezca ser memorizado" (cited in Merino, *Retórica*, 38–9).
21 Merino, *Retórica*, 38–9.
22 Merino, *Retórica*, 38–9.
23 Vives, *De trandenis*, 479.
24 Emphasis added, Vives, *De trandenis*, 425.
25 Castillo Gómez "Escritura representada," 316. On the *librillo de memoria*, see Castillo Gómez, Chartier, Chartier and Saborit, Mandigorra Lavata, and Stallybrass et al.
26 See the extraordinary essay by López Poza, "Polianteas y otros."
27 Blair, "Reading Strategies," 19.
28 Erasmus, *Concerning the Aim and Method of Education* 66, *De ratione studii* 522e–3f.
29 Jiménez Patón, *Elocuencia*, 122.
30 Merino, *Retórica*, 37.
31 Merino, *Retórica*, 38.
32 Merino, *Retórica*, 36.
33 Cervantes, *Don Quixote*, II.318.
34 Cervantes, *Don Quixote*, II.318.
35 Beecher, "Introduction," 18.
36 "We have to remember that for Erasmus, confidently emerging into a brave new world of modern humanist scholarship, the art of memory would wear a medieval look. It belonged to the ages of barbarism; its

methods in decay were an example of those cobwebs in monkish minds which new brooms must sweep away" (Yates, *Art of Memory*, 127).

37 Beecher, "Recollection," 419.

38 Emphasis added, Erasmus, *Collected Works*, vol. 1, 134.

39 Cervantes, *Don Quixote*, II.22, 813.

40 Beecher, "Recollection" 418.

41 "Esta misma tensión existe entre los partidarios y los detractores de la memoria artificial se refleja en los tratados de retórica que se mueven entre la sumisa aceptación del método tradicional (Miguel de Salinas) y su explícita condena (Furió Ceriol y Pedro Juan Núñez)" (Merino, "Imagen Montano," 220). Saavedra Fajardo himself in *República Literaria* complains upon his arrival at the homes of the madmen about the presence of Llull's disciples, whom he saw "voltando unas ruedas, conque pretendían en breve tiempo acaudalar todas las ciencias" (117).

42 Beecher, "Recollection," 410.

43 Hiscock, *Reading*, 25.

44 Erasmus, *Collected Works*, vol. 1, 134. These Erasmian reflections are also found in his other works on pedagogy, such as *De ratione studii* (1511) and *De peris static ac liberatiter instituendis* (1528).

45 Cited in Rodríguez de la Flor, "Estudio introductorio," XXXVII.

46 Cited in Beecher, "Recollection," 410.

47 Cited in Beecher, "Recollection," 410.

48 Merino has seen as antecedents of this vision the doctrine of Quintilian and Erasmus's *De ratione studii* (*Retórica*, 185–6).

49 I take the reference from Merino, *Retórica*, 29.

50 See Merino, "Memoria y Retórica en El Brocense."

51 Cited in Merino, *Retórica*, 36.

52 Vives, Libro II *De las disciplinas*, 402.

53 Cited in Flórez Miguel "Pedro Ciruelo," 239.

54 Espinel, *Vida del escudero*, 355.

55 Beecher, "Recollection," 418.

56 Cervantes, *Don Quixote*, II.22, 813.

57 Cervantes, *Don Quixote*, II.22, 814.

58 Cervantes, *Don Quixote*, II.3, 653.

59 The figure of the student was very common in the letters during Cervantes's time, becoming a prototype from sayings and tales of the folklore tradition. See the study by Maxime Chevalier, "Un personaje folklórico de la literatura del Siglo de Oro: el estudiante."

60 See particularly the study "Humanismo, erudición y parodia en Cervantes: del *Quijote* al *Persiles*" by José Montero Reguera.

61 In this sense, Helena Percas de Ponseti adds: "Léase en el diccionario de Corominas la evolución etimológica de la palabra primo, resumida a continuación para aclarar el texto: del latín *primus*, primero de

donde, figurativamente, de *primera calidad*, y de ahí *escrupuloso, sutil, sencillo, rústico, tonto, víctima de un engaño, primitivo, prístino*, todas ellas acepciones que parece tener presentes Cervantes al caracterizar al *Primo*. Conocimiento que del lenguaje picaresco y jergal tiene Cervantes, puede haberle sugerido el nombre del Primo, originado en *primerizo*, que como explica Rafael Salinas, en su libro sobre 'antropología picaresca' del Hampa, significa *manejable y explotable*, de donde viene el *no seas primo* del lenguaje hablado, con el consiguiente sentido de *necio*. En el siglo XVI … el equívoco era un medio de comunicación muy deseable según indicaba Valdés en el *Diálogo de la lengua*" (n27, 439).

62 Avalle-Arce, *Don Quijote*, 226.
63 Avalle-Arce and Riley, "*Don Quijote*," 55.
64 This is how Egido, following Riquer's idea in "*El Quijote* y los libros," describes him (8).
65 Following Leo Spitzer, what Cervantes did in every possible sense was "sentar el problema del libro, y de su influencia sobre la vida" (295).
66 Cervantes, *Don Quixote*, II.22, 811.
67 Riquer, *Aproximación*, 111.
68 Riley, *Introducción*, 158.
69 Huarte, *Examen*, 411.
70 Huarte, *Examen*, 413.
71 López de Montoya, *Libro*, 310.
72 Gil Fernández, *Panorama*, 249.
73 Riquer argues that the word "humanista" was recent in Spanish, since Covarrubias mentions it for the first time in 1613; cited in Montero Reguera, "Humanismo," n9, 90.
74 Cervantes, *Don Quixote*, II.22, 811.
75 Montero Reguera has convincingly traced the student's prototype to several literary models that could have inspired Cervantes's creation of the figure of the Cousin. Among these are *Los inventores de Juan de la Cueva, Fiel desengaño contra la ociosidad y los juegos. Utilísimo a los confesores y penitentes, justicias y los demás, a cuyo cargo está limpiar de vagabundos, tahúres y fulleros de la República Cristiana* (1603) by Francisco Luque Fajardo – whose influence Riquer has already noted – the *Parte Primera de varias aplicaciones y transformaciones, las cuales tractan términos cortesanos, práctica militar, casos de estado, en prosa y verso con nuevos hieroglíficos, y algunos puntos morales* (1613) by Diego Rosel y Fuenllana, and possibly the *Plaza Universal de todas ciencias y artes* (published in 1615 and composed in 1612) by Cristóbal Suárez de Figueroa – translation of the work by the Italian Tomasso Garzoni, *Plaza Universal de todas las profesiones*.
76 See Wardropper, "Cervantes and Education."
77 See Chevalier, "Un personaje" and Egido, "Literatura." As Egido has stated, the character must be analysed as an anti-scholastic invective

collected in the works of the writer Cristóbal de Villalón, *El Crotalón* and in *El Scholástico* "bajo la imitación de los falsos filósofos de Luciano en el *Icaromenipo*" (*Puertas*, 171). Egido also sees in the character's clothing and his appearance on the back of a pregnant donkey a relationship with Erasmus's *The Praise of Folly* (*Puertas*, 172). See also Morreale.

78 Cervantes, *La gitanilla*, 76.

79 Riquer sees the character as a satire of Francisco Luque Fajardo, author of *Fiel desengaño contra la ociosidad y los juegos* (1603). See *Aproximación*, 112.

80 From the Greek *polyanthea* and its corresponding Latin *florilegius*, "muchas flores," has a metaphoric value that linked both voices with the garden sense of knowledge that the writer appropriates and nurtures upon contemplating it: "El espacio del libro se convierte en analógico del espacio que organiza la memoria y las tablas y árboles de significación que preceden a los artículos se consideran como los más importantes y desempeñan el papel de teatro de la memoria" (López Poza, "Poliantea y otros," 197). In this case, there is a certain parallelism between the bibliographic and mnemonic systems; it was therefore about ordering in memory, as in a library, all kinds of works, texts, or authors (Morcillo Romero, *Ars*, LXIII).

81 Search was facilitated through all these techniques, which made knowledge visual. At times, the structure and disposition of these aids simulated the spaces of memory. In fact, the titles found in the corpus of works that make up this genre are closely linked to metaphors of space and writing used to describe memory. With respect to the spatial character, Yates has pointed out similarities with which he shares its spatiality and structure: "There can be no doubt that these *topoi* used by persons with a trained memory must be mnemonic *loci*, and it is indeed probable that the very word 'topics' as used in dialectics arouse through the places of mnemonics" (*Art of Memory*, 31).

82 Bolzoni, *Gallery*, xix.

83 See Blair, "Reading Strategies."

84 On this type of ancillary works during the Middle Ages and the Renaissance, see Carruthers and Blair.

85 López Poza, "*Florilegios* 63–4."

86 Giorgina Dopico Black points out the impact of the printing press in Spain since its arrival, ten years after its invention, and its rapid expansion during the reign of the Catholic monarchs (100). On the other hand, it is important not to leave aside the somewhat paradoxical situation caused by the progressive rise of the press and its relationship to memory: "Techniques of memory reach their greatest development in a world in which their meaning and importance are gradually being stripped away from them by the development of technology, especially the printing press. At the same time, we will see how techniques of memory interact, often productively, with the new possibilities created by the printed word" (Bolzoni, *Gallery*, xviii).

87 Cervantes, *Don Quixote*, II.22, 811.
88 Cervantes, *Don Quixote*, II.22, 812.
89 Cervantes, *Don Quixote*, II.22, 812.
90 Cervantes, *Don Quixote*, II.22, 812.
91 Caro Baroja, "Cervantes," 11. Sebastián de Covarrubias defines the term in his *Tesoro de la lengua castellana o española* as: "Antiguamente solo los reyes daban vestido señalado a sus criados; y oy día en cierta manera se hace así, para ser distinguidos y diferenciados de todos los demás, y porque estos tienen muchos privilegios y libertades, se llamó aquel vestido librea" (523v).
92 Baltasar Gracián. *Agudeza y arte de ingenio*, tratado segundo, discurso LVIII, tomo 2, 217–18.
93 As an example, López Poza gives two sonnets with notable differences by Lope de Vega and Quevedo inspired by the same epigram and its sources; see "Emblemas."
94 Cervantes, *Don Quixote*, II.22, 812.
95 Cervantes, *Don Quixote*, II.22, 813.
96 Cervantes, *Don Quixote*, II.22, 813.
97 Blair, *Too Much*, 75.
98 Montero Reguera, "Humanismo," 101.
99 Cervantes, *Don Quixote*, II.24, 830.
100 Baltasar Gracián, *Agudeza y arte de ingenio*, tratado segundo, discurso LVIII, tomo 2, 217–18.
101 Erasmus, *Folly*, 43.
102 Erasmus, *Folly*, 81.
103 Rubin, *Memory*, 82–3.
104 The criticism in the Prologue is directed mainly at Lope de Vega, who, according to Montero Reguera, "había alardeado y dado muestras de erudición mostrenca y artificial en cuatro libros aparecidos por los años en que se gesta el *Quijote*: *La Arcadia* (1598), *El Isidro* (1599), *La hermosura de Angélica* (1602) y *El peregrino en su patria* (1604)."
105 Despite the criticism carried out by Cervantes, he himself is guilty of doing the same thing, especially in the composition of poems in the preliminaries. See Montero Reguera.
106 Cervantes, *Don Quixote*, I. Prólogo, 16–17.
107 Infantes, "De Officinas," 244.
108 López Poza, "Libros de emblemas," 266.
109 Fernández López, "Retórica," 178.
110 It should be noted, however, that not all writers used these sources of invention in the same way. Authors with less training used the material without contrasting its information or without directly consulting the original sources, while more intellectual authors used the material only as a starting point to later search for the original. See López Poza.

111 Emphasis added, Bolzoni, *Gallery*, XV.

112 The result of this interplay between imitation and variation of these texts is the textual multiplicity, the infinite possibilities that open to both the text and the reader. This very same game of constant imitation, as Bolzoni calls it, requires the mobilization of the memory of all its participants: "the game does not work if the writer cannot find an interlocutor capable of remembering, and hence recognizing the text that is object of imitation and emulation" (Bolzoni, *Gallery*, xx). Terence Cave writes in this regard: "the texts used as models become cornucopian texts: the play of interpretation and imitation transforms them into fountains of infinite wealth" (cited in Bolzoni, *Gallery*, xvi).

113 Ramón Menéndez Pidal, "Genesis," in *Casebook*.

114 Important in this context is the idea of *auctoritates*, which was extensively studied by José Antonio Maravall in *Antiguos y modernos*. The concept of *auctoritates* is still a form of textualization by which reading and writing are united through the work of memory: "an author was not valued because of the text's innovativeness but on the contrary because of its skillful redeployment of already well-known and well-established ideas and thematic material" (Bouza, *Communication*, 50).

115 Beecher, "Recollection," 420.

116 Castiglione, *Book*, 35.

117 De Montaigne, "Of the Education of Children" (I, XXV): 32.

118 Hunter, "Well-Stocked Memory," 178.

119 Huarte, *Examen*, 216.

120 Covarrubius, *Emblemas*, 78v.

121 Chaparro, "Per locos et imagines," 10.

122 Bances Candamo, *Theatro*, 89.

123 "The price of perfect retention is high: Funes' mind is so cluttered with precise memories that is incapable of generalizing from one experience to the another" (Schacter, *Searching*, 81).

124 See *The Mind of a Mnemonist: A Little Book about a Vast Memory*. Schacter describes his case like this: "[He] was plagued by Funes's fictional problem: he was overwhelmed by detailed but useless recollections of trivial information and events. He could recount without error long lists of names, numbers, and just about anything else that Luria presented to him recalled endless details without understanding much of what he read or heard. And like Funes, he had great difficulty grasping abstract concepts" (*Searching*, 81).

125 Schacter, *Searching*, 81.

126 Cervantes, *Don Quixote*, II.22, 811.

5 Disputes over Memory: Sancho and the Artful Manipulation of Memory

1 Shakespeare, *Hamlet*, III.2, 67.
2 Cervantes, *Don Quixote*, II.41, 965.
3 Cervantes, *Don Quixote*, II.41, 964.
4 Cervantes, *Don Quixote*, II.41, 966.
5 Cervantes, *Don Quixote*, II.41, 966.
6 Hiscock and Wilder, *Shakespeare and Memory*, 3.
7 Through memory and awareness of the passage of time, and through what he has learned from living with his master as well as his knowledge of the publication of the first part, Sancho acquires historical awareness as a character through which he governs himself in order to act in the second part: "Y de mí – dijo Sancho –, que también dicen que soy yo uno de los principales presonajes de ella" (Cervantes, *Don Quixote*, II.3, 650).
8 See *Witness for the Defense: The Accused, the Eyewitness, and the Expert Who Puts Memory on Trial*.
9 Sutton, "Spongy Brains," 14.
10 Part I, chapter 3, "Personal Memory, Collective Memory." See also Maurice Halbwachs's *On Collective Memory*.
11 Pollmann, *Memory*, 1.
12 Pollmann and Kuijpers, "Introduction," 17.
13 Important in the characterization is the term "quijotización" by Salvador de Madariaga. Studies devoted to his psychological and spiritual evolution (García, Menéndez y Pelayo, Oelschläger, Douclos) or his lack of it, with an emphasis on his foolishness and lack of judgment consistent with the origin and genesis of the character of the squire in literature and popular folklore (Molho, Close, Urbina), have not analysed the function of memory and the selective use that the squire makes of it as an essential element in his evolution and in the collateral effects in his relationship with Don Quixote. More recently Isabel Jaén has analysed Sancho's psychological development from a cognitive historicist approach that departs from cognitive scientific ideas of the time. See also the aforementioned essay by Mancing, "Sancho Panza's Theory of Mind."
14 "[T]he notion that the human soul comprised memory, will, and intellect was a commonplace of the age … the triad underlines much of Cervantes' portrayal of the human struggle for self-realization" (Weiger, *Substance*, 139). According to Weiger, Cervantes was familiar with the three faculties thanks to the work of the preceptist Alonso López Pinciano who, in his ancient poetic *Philosophía* (1596), wrote about the function of each faculty, following the ideas of Aristotle in his *Ethics*: "Vamos a las que como racional y intellectual tiene, que son otras tres: entendimiento,

memoria y voluntad, cuyos bienes son propríssimamente tales, según el Philósopho, en sus Ethicos, y por quienes es llamado feliz y amigo de los dioses el hombre sabio. Esto mismo significa el mismo Philósopho quando en el lugar mismo dize: que la felicidad no está en las cosas de burlas, sino en las veras" (36). The three faculties were also the subject of a variety of contemporaneous publications such as Damián de Vegas's *entremés, Coloquio entre un alma y sus tres potencias* (1590). This work, part of the *entremés* genre, a fairly popular short theatrical performance piece, inescapably guaranteed that the triad was widely known throughout all sectors of society. The title of the work alone denotes an obvious perceived correlation between the three faculties ("tres potencias") and the configuration of one's personality (Weiger, *Substance*, 138).

15 Weiger, *Substance*, 164.

16 The importance given to the family past was a fairly common practice at the time, as Pollmann and Kuijpers have pointed out: "Almost all early modern claims to rights or authority were also claims about the past, on the whole early modern people believed things to be true or legitimate only if they could also be proven to be old … a knowledge of lineage was highly desirable" ("Introduction," 6) and "In early modern autobiographical sources however, the self is more connected to the body and the bodily experiences and defined in terms of membership of family or community … Individual's life is a function of the religious or civil community to which he or she belongs and part of a greater design that is beyond the own's author control" (8).

17 Tribble and Sutton, *Cognitive Ecology*, 96. On cognitive ecology see also *Cognitive Ecologies and the History of Remembering: Religion, Education, and Memory in Early Modern England*, edited by Evelyn Tribble and Nicholas Keene.

18 Cervantes, *Don Quixote*, II.40, 950.

19 Cervantes, *Don Quixote*, I.4, 62.

20 Cervantes, *Don Quixote*, II.4, 661.

21 See Domínguez's "'Básteme tener el *Christus* en la memoria para ser buen gobernador:' Sancho y las cartillas de instrucción áurea."

22 Faced with this double facet of his memory, I fully agree with Roger Chartier when he sees the squire as someone lacking memory on the one hand, as he declares on more than one occasion, and, on the other, as Sancho the Memorious, "who keeps in his memory a vast repertory of proverbs, tales and sayings" and other manifestations of popular classes (*Author's*, 131).

23 Cervantes, *Don Quixote*, II.29, 870.

24 Cervantes, *Don Quixote*, I.15, 161.

25 Cervantes, *Don Quixote*, II.2, 645.

26 Cervantes, *Don Quixote*, II.29, 870.

27 Cervantes, *Don Quixote*, II.28, 865.

28 Emphasis added, Cervantes, *Don Quixote*, II.12, 720.

29 Cervantes, *Don Quixote*, II.43, 977.
30 Cervantes, *Don Quixote*, I.27, 301.
31 Cervantes, *Don Quixote*, I.25, 286.
32 Cervantes, *Don Quixote*, II.3, 650.
33 Cervantes, *Don Quixote*, I.7, 91.
34 Cervantes, *Don Quixote*, I.25, 284.
35 Cervantes, *Don Quixote*, I.52, 590.
36 Cervantes, *Don Quixote*, II.12, 720.
37 Cervantes, *Don Quixote*, II.70, 1197.
38 Cervantes, *Don Quixote*, II.67, 1174.
39 See Madariaga, *Guía del lector*.
40 Williamson, "Lecturas," 58.
41 Cervantes, *Don Quixote*, II.5, 664.
42 Bartlett, *Remembering*, 204.
43 Cervantes, *Don Quixote*, II.5, 669.
44 Cervantes, *Don Quixote*, II.5, 669.
45 Emphasis added, Cervantes, *Don Quixote*, II.5, 669.
46 Aristotle, *De memoria*, 449b24.
47 This same incapacity to discern between perception of the present and what happened in the past was also pointed out by Egido: "[Don Quixote] no es capaz de discriminar el tiempo, identificando, como apuntamos, el pasado de sus lecturas con las percepciones presentes, pues la memoria tiene como objeto el pasado y don Quixote la proyecta hacia el futuro o la actualiza sin apenas fisuras" ("La memoria y el *Quijote*," 14).
48 Williamson, "Lecturas," 58.
49 Frenk, *Entre la voz*, 50. Likewise, the folk sources and the story's paths of transmission have already been studied by Francisco Rodríguez Marín, Marcelino Menéndez y Pelayo, Maurice Molho, Rosa Lida de Malkiel, and Maxime Chevalier. More specifically, the episode of the story of the shepherdess Torralba has been analysed by Michel Moner, who views the oral tradition as essential in the figure of Sancho and an important feature of Cervantine orality. See also the work of López Martínez (77–8).
50 Cervantes, *Don Quixote*, II.26, 846.
51 "[Y] más que él había oído contar otro caso como aquél al cura de su lugar, y que él tenía tan gran memoria, que a no olvidársele todo aquello de que quería acordarse, no hubiera tal memoria en toda la ínsula" (Cervantes, *Don Quixote*, II.45, 996).
52 Ong, *Orality and Literacy*, 42.
53 Frenk, *Entre la voz*, 70.
54 Frenk, *Entre la voz*, 123. The many variants and modifications of the story produced by the improvisation of memory come by means of what Alan Deyermond has called "la transmisión oral-memorial" through what has been heard (32).

55 Frenk, *Entre la voz*, 61.
56 Cervantes, *Don Quixote*, I.20, 215.
57 Cited in Minchin, *Homer*, 29; see Rubin, *Memory*, 304–7.
58 Minchin, *Homer*, 18.
59 Ong, *Orality and Literacy*, 67.
60 Molho, *Cervantes*, 223.
61 Cervantes, *Don Quixote*, I.20, 214.
62 Cervantes, *Don Quixote*, I.20, 215.
63 Cervantes, *Don Quixote*, I.20, 215.
64 "Si gustáis, señores, que os diga en breves razones la inmensidad de mis desventuras, habeisme de prometer de que con ninguna pregunta ni otra cosa no interromperéis el hilo de mi triste historia; porque en el punto que lo hagáis, en ése se quedará lo que fuere contando. Estas razones del Roto trujeron a la memoria a don Quixote el cuento que le había contado su escudero, cuando no acertó el número de las cabras que habían pasado el río, y se quedó la historia pendiente" (Cervantes, *Don Quixote*, I.24, 262).
65 "Sancho is a being of shared memory, the memory that inhabits all the individuals of a same community and a common patrimony and that provides tales and formulas they have heard, retained and recalled. But that memory, organized within the social frameworks of memory of the village, in no way excludes an individual appropriation that can quote a proverb at the right moment or apply to current circumstances the recitation of a tale" (Chartier, *Author's*, 131).
66 Frenk, *Entre la voz*, 18. Frenk adds an extensive list from epic songs, narrative, and lyrical songs to nursery rhymes, verses, prayers, and incantations, as well as stories and sayings linked to a collective heritage passed from generation to generation. Gasta also analyses sonnets, romances, couplets, and other poetic devices drawn from the oral tradition.
67 Rubin, *Memory*, 9–10.
68 Cervantes, *Don Quixote*, I.20, 213.
69 Carruthers, *Book*, 14.
70 Minchin, *Homer*, 7.
71 Bartlett, *Remembering*, 213.
72 Bartlett, "Experiments," 36.
73 "Soberana y alta señora: El ferido de punta de ausencia y el llagado de las telas del corazón, dulcísima Dulcinea del Toboso, te envía la salud que él no tiene. Si tu fermosura me desprecia, si tu valor no es en mi pro, si tus desdenes son en mi afincamiento, maguer que yo sea asaz de sufrido, mal podré sostenerme en esta cuita, que, además de ser fuerte, es muy duradera. Mi buen escudero Sancho te dará entera relación, ¡oh bella ingrata, amada enemiga mía!, del modo que por tu causa quedo: si gustares de acorrerme, tuyo soy; y si no, haz lo que te viniere en gusto, que con

acabar mi vida habré satisfecho a tu crueldad y a mi deseo. Tuyo hasta la muerte, El Caballero de la Triste Figura" (Cervantes, *Don Quixote*, I.25, 286).

74 Cervantes, *Don Quixote*, II.10, 700.

75 Cervantes, *Don Quixote*, I.26, 296. It should not be forgotten that during the meeting with the priest and the barber, the priest mentions that perhaps Don Quixote could be an archbishop, which affects Sancho's motivation; that, in turn, will dominate the way he remembers and guides his memories towards a personal purpose or motive. Sancho's ability to improvise is the result of his ability to manipulate memory.

76 For more on the concept of "transactive memory" in relationships, see the study by social psychologist Daniel Wegner.

77 Cervantes, *Don Quixote*, I.26, 296.

78 Frenk, *Entre la voz*, 75. As Frenk has explored, the habit of reading letters aloud and memorizing them was quite common at the time, so it should not surprise us that Sancho pounces on such audacity. Thus, for example, Juan Valdés's friends read his letters in his absence because in this way they refreshed their "ánimos la memoria del amigo ausente" (cited in Frenk, *Entre la voz*, 34).

79 Cervantes, *Don Quixote*, I.26, 296.

80 Ong, *Orality and Literacy*, 33.

81 Ong, *Orality and Literacy*, 33.

82 Aurelio González speaks of other characteristic processes of the oral tradition, such as the "tendencia al acortamiento del texto, oscilación en los nombres propios, adaptación al contexto, alternancia de las formas verbales, sustitución de tópicos y expresiones formularias por otras equivalentes" ("Versiones," 119).

83 Rubin, *Memory*, 7.

84 Minchin, *Homer*, 4.

85 Minchin, *Homer*, 29.

86 "[T]hey are remarkable, also, as poems which were composed and performed without the aid of writing" (Minchin, *Homer*, 1).

87 Minchin, *Homer*, 2.

88 Emphasis added, Ong, *Orality and Literacy*, 60.

89 Frenk, *Entre la voz*, 124.

90 Lope de Vega, *Arcadia*, 199.

91 Cervantes, *Don Quixote*, I.26, 296.

92 Emphasis added, Ong, *Orality and Literacy*, 67. In this respect, for example, Francis Peabody observes that "[f]rom all over the world and from all periods of time ... traditional composition has been associated with hand activity" (cited in Ong, *Orality and Literacy*, 67). According to Ong, Marcel Jousse has also indicated the intimate nexus between "rhythmic oral patterns, the breathing process, gesture, and the bilateral symmetry of the human body in ancient Aramaic and Hellenic Targums, and therefore also in the ancient Hebrew" (41).

93 Anonymous, *Tratado*, 56v.
94 "Esta es la primera invención de Sancho respecto a Dulcinea; en la segunda parte de la novela se atreverá a ir más lejos" (Riquer, *Aproximación*, 94).
95 Cervantes, *Don Quixote*, I.30, 357.
96 Cervantes, *Don Quixote*, II.10, 700.
97 "Sepamos ahora, Sancho hermano, adónde va vuesa merced. ¿Va a buscar algún jumento que se le haya perdido? – No, por cierto. – Pues ¿qué va a buscar? – Voy a buscar, como quien no dice nada, a una princesa, y en ella al sol de la hermosura y a todo el cielo junto. – ¿Y adónde pensáis hallar eso que decís, Sancho? – ¿Adónde? En la gran ciudad del Toboso. – Y bien, ¿y de parte de quién la vais a buscar? – De parte del famoso caballero don Quixote de la Mancha, que desface los tuertos y da de comer al que ha sed y de beber al que ha hambre. – Todo eso está muy bien. ¿Y sabéis su casa, Sancho? – Mi amo dice que han de ser unos reales palacios o unos soberbios alcázares. – ¿Y habeisla visto algún día por ventura? – Ni yo ni mi amo la habemos visto jamás. – ¿Y paréceos que fuera acertado y bien hecho que si los del Toboso supiesen que estáis vos aquí con intención de ir a sonsacarles sus princesas y a desasosegarles sus damas, viniesen y os moliesen las costillas a puros palos y no os dejasen hueso sano? – En verdad que tendrían mucha." (Cervantes, *Don Quixote*, II.10, 702).
98 Emphasis added, Cervantes, *Don Quixote*, II.10, 703.
99 Rodríguez-Luis, "Lecturas," 130.
100 Cervantes, *Don Quixote*, II.23, 825.
101 See Kraepelin's "Ueber erinnerungsfälschungen."
102 Cited in Tribble, "The Raven," 106.
103 Cervantes, *Don Quixote*, II.11, 712.
104 Emphasis added, Dantisco, *Galateo*, 160.
105 Cervantes, *Don Quixote*, II.8, 687.
106 De Diego López, *Declaración*, Fol. 41v.
107 Patón, *Elocuencia*, 445. The same idea appears in the *Declaración magistral sobre las emblemas de Andrés Alciato* of Diego López: "Tiene otro gran consuelo la verdad, y es, que alivia al hombre de un gran trabajo, porque de qualquiera suerte que hable, si dize verdad, es fácil, pero el que miente deve tener gran memoria, y acordarse, porque luego es cogido" (Fol. 41v).

Epilogue. Lethe and the Laws of Oblivion: Sites of Forgetting in *Don Quixote*

1 Azevedo, *Fénix*, 125v.
2 Cervantes, *Novelas ejemplares*, II 343.
3 Cervantes, *Don Quixote*, I.15, 165.
4 Predmore, *Cervantes*, 183.
5 Cervantes, *Don Quixote*, I.8, 104.

6 Cervantes, *Don Quixote*, I.30, 347.
7 Cervantes, *Don Quixote*, II.3, 655.
8 Cervantes, *Don Quixote*, II.4, 657–8.
9 Lathrop, "Introduction," xvii. On the problem of omission of the theft, see Daniel Eisenberg's "El rucio de Sancho y la fecha de composición de la Segunda Parte del *Quijote*." On the possible reasons for Cervantes's lapses, see Lathrop's "Por qué Cervantes no incluyó el robo del rucio" and the studies by Alberto Sánchez and Jesús Botello.
10 Cervantes, *Don Quixote*, II.52, 1058.
11 Cervantes, *Don Quixote*, I.7, 93.
12 Cervantes, *Don Quixote*, II.46, 1003.
13 Saint Augustine will reflect on oblivion in several instances in his *Confessions*: "But what is forgetfulness but the privation of memory? How then is it present that I remember it, since when present I cannot remember? But if what we remember we hold it in memory, yet, unless we did remember forgetfulness, we could never at the hearing of the name recognize the thing thereby signified, then forgetfulness is retained by memory. Present then it is, that we forget not, and being so, we forget … Who now shall search out this? Who shall comprehend how it is?" (180).
14 Carruthers, *Book*, x–xi.
15 Engel, "Decay," 22.
16 Covarrubias, *Emblemas*, 568v.
17 Weinrich, *Lethe*, 3. Later on, the deponent verb would be replaced by *oblitare*, derived from *oblitus*, the past participle of *oblivisci*.
18 Azevedo, *Fénix*, 125v.
19 Azevedo, *Fénix*, 125v.
20 Although born just from an anecdote, the art of forgetting would continue under other names, such as "amnestonics" (from amnesia), "lethognomics" or "lethotechnics," from Lethe, the river of forgetting (Weinrich, *Lethe*, 12).
21 See Weinrich. Umberto Eco's "An Ars Oblivionalis? Forget it!" refers to the art of memory as a semiotic system: "to make present something absent" (258).
22 Azevedo, *Fénix*, 125v.
23 Carducho, *Diálogos*, 208.
24 Emphasis added, Cervantes, *Don Quixote*, I.20, 208.
25 Beecher, "Recollection" 384.
26 Cervantes, *Don Quixote*, II.25, 841.
27 Le Goff, *History and Memory*, 63.
28 Cervantes, *Don Quixote*, I. Prólogo, 17.
29 A form of punishment in Rome applied to powerful figures declared enemies of the state. As a consequence of this disciplining, images of them were destroyed and inscriptions with their names were removed.

30 Weinrich, *Lethe*, 33.
31 "La invención de la novela moderna y su fama y memoria imperecederas nacieron curiosamente con voluntad de olvido" (Egido, "Memoria y el *Quijote*," 77).
32 Cervantes, *Don Quixote*, I.34, 400.
33 Oblivion, like memories, acquires materiality and contagiously *stains* everything that comes in contact with it as it spreads through that space. The exception, of course, is Don Quixote's own glories, which he deems as "Nunca sus glorias el olvido mancha" (Cervantes, *Don Quixote*, I.52, 594).
34 Cervantes, *Don Quixote*, II.32, 896.
35 Weinrich, *Lethe*, 4.
36 Chartier, *Inscribir*, 59.
37 Cervantes, *Don Quixote*, II.35, 922.
38 As explained in the *Aeneid*, it was believed that souls were forced to drink the waters of the Lethe before being reincarnated, so they would not remember their earthly past lives. Similar scenes are also found in *The Divine Comedy*, where souls about to enter heaven drink from it in order to forget sins. Being a river between the Earth and Hades, the underworld hell, it symbolizes something negative, a sort of sinful condition. In Virgil's *Aeneid*, Aeneas travels to Lethe to meet his father's ghost: "The souls that throng the flood / Are those to whom, by fate, are other bodies ow'd: / In Lethe's lake they long oblivion taste, / Of future life secure, forgetful of the past" (Dante, *Divine Comedy*, 231).
39 Cervantes, *Don Quixote*, I.13, 144.
40 Erasmus, *Folly*, 18.
41 Cervantes, *Don Quixote*, I. Prólogo, 11.
42 González Echevarría, "Introduction," 3.
43 Weinrich, *Lethe*, 6.
44 Weinrich, *Lethe*, 5.
45 Azevedo, *Fénix*, 35.
46 Ivic and Williams, *Forgetting*, 4.
47 Sullivan, *Memory*, 22.
48 Ivic and Williams, *Forgetting*, 4.
49 Burke, *Varieties*, 54.
50 Burke, *Varieties*, 56–9.
51 Ivic and Williams, *Forgetting*, 5.
52 Sullivan, *Memory*, 27.
53 Sullivan, *Memory*, 27.
54 Sullivan, *Memory*, 2.
55 Sullivan, *Memory*, 13. Sullivan distinguishes between two elements, forgetting and forgetfulness. The first refers to the unavailability of memory traces to recollection. The second, on the other hand, refers to a model of being and a pattern of behaviour.

56 Sullivan, *Memory*, 15.
57 Barish, "Remembering," 218.
58 González Echevarría, "Introduction," 6.
59 González Echevarría, "Introduction," 5.
60 Cervantes, *Don Quixote*, I.1, 37.
61 Johnson, *Quest*, 40.
62 See Wardropper, "Cervantes and Education," 181.
63 Ivic and Williams, *Forgetting*, 6.
64 Anderson, *Imagined Communities*, 208.
65 Ivic and Williams, *Forgetting*, 16.
66 Ivic and Williams, *Forgetting*, 5.
67 González Echevarría, "Introduction," 4.
68 Schacter states that our memories belong to us in that they are solely ours "not quite those of anybody else" (*Searching*, 15).
69 See also Egido, "Memoria y el *Quijote*," 77.
70 See Baras Escolá: "Hemos extraído del CORDE (Corpus Diacrónico del Español) de la Real Academia Española, a título de ejemplo, más de cincuenta citas no cervantinas anteriores al *Quijote* … Siempre está por medio una decisión voluntaria y consciente."

Bibliography

Ágreda, María de Jesús. *Cartas entre Felipe IV y Sor María Jesús de Ágreda*, 1654.

Aguilera, Juan de. *Ars memorativa*, Salamanca, 1536.

Álava de Viamont, Diego. *El perfecto capitán* (1590). Edited by Cristina Blas. Salamanca: CILUS, 2000.

Alcalá-Galán, Mercedes. "La noción de museo en el *Persiles*: las colecciones de arte en la imaginación literaria." *Revista de Occidente* 439 (2017): 61–76.

Alciato, Andrea. *A Book of Emblems: The Emblematum Liber in Latin and English*. Translated and edited by John Moffitt. London: McFarland, 2004.

Álvarez Miraval, Blas. *Libro intitulado la conservación de la salud del cuerpo y del alma ... agora nuevamente impreso con un singular tratado de la firme y tenaz memoria y del bueno y claro entendimiento*, 1599.

Anderson, Benedict. *Imagined Communities: Reflections on the Origin and Spread of Nationalism*. New York: Verso, 1983.

Anonymous. *Rhetorica ad Herennium*. Edited by Harry Caplan. Cambridge, MA: Harvard University Press, 1954.

– *Tratado médico*, 1500.

Arce de Otálora, Juan. *Coloquios de Palatino y Pinciano*. Madrid: Fundación José Antonio De Castro, 1995.

Arellano, Ignacio. "Cultura visual y emblemática en las *Novelas ejemplares* de Cervantes." *Anales Cervantinos* 45 (2013): 93–108.

– "Motivos emblemáticos en el teatro de Cervantes." *Boletín de la Real Academia Española* 77 (1997): 419–43.

Arias Montano, Benito. *Rhetoricum Libri IV*, 1569.

Aristotle. *Aristotle on Memory*. Edited by Richard Sorabji. London: Duckworth, 1972.

Artiga, Francisco José. *Epítome de la elocuencia española*, 1770.

Augustine. *The Confessions of St. Augustine*. Translated by Edward Pusey. New York: Collier, 1909.

Avalle-Arce, Juan Bautista de. *Don Quijote como forma de vida*. Valencia: Fundación Juan March-Castalia, 1976.

– "*Don Quijote* o la vida como obra de arte." In *El Quijote de Cervantes*, edited by G. Haley, 204–34. Madrid: Taurus, 1981.

– "La *Penitencia de Amadís* en la Peña Pobre." In *Josep María Solá-Solé: Homage, homenaje, homenatge: (miscelanea de estudios de amigos y discípulos)*, Vol. 2, edited by Antonio Torres-Alcalá, 159–70. Barcelona: Puvill, 1984.

Avalle-Arce, Juan Bautista, and Edward C. Riley. "Don Quijote." In *Suma cervantina*, edited by J.B. de Avalle-Arce and E.C. Riley, 47–79. London: Tamesis Books, 1973.

Avery, William. "Elementos dantescos del Quijote." *Anales Cervantinos* 9 (1961–2): 1–28.

– "Elementos dantescos del Quijote (Segunda parte)." *Anales Cervantinos* 13–14 (1974–5): 1–28.

Báez Rubí, Linda. "El arte de la memoria y la emblemática." In *Dimensiones del arte emblemático*, edited by Bárbara Skjnfill Nogal and Eloy Gómez Bravo, 327–38. Michoacán: Colegio de Michoacán, 2002.

Bailón Blancas, José Manuel. *La psiquiatría en El Quijote*. Barcelona: Ars XXI, 2006.

Baldo, Jonathan. *Memory in Shakespeare's Histories*. New York: Routledge, 2011.

Bances Candamo, Francisco. *Theatro de los theatros de los passados y presentes siglos*. Edited by Duncan Moir. London: Tamesis, 1970.

Bañeza Román, Celso. "Instituciones y costumbres eclesiásticas en Cervantes." *Anales Cervantinos* 29, no. 1 (1991): 73–91.

Baras Escolá, Alfredo. *De cuyo nombre no quiero acordarme*. Alicante: Biblioteca Virtual Miguel de Cervantes, 2005.

Barbeito Díaz, Pilar. "¿El Brocense o Pedro Juan Núñez? Sobre la introducción en España de la dialéctica ramista." *Humanismo y pervivencia del mundo clásico: Homenaje al Profesor Luis Gil*, Vol. 2, edited by José María Maestre Maestre, Luis Charlo Brea, and Joaquín Pascual Barea, 735–46. Cádiz: Universidad de Cádiz, Servicio de Publicaciones, 1997.

Barish, Jonas. "Remembering and Forgetting in Shakespeare." In *Elizabethan Theater: Essays in Honor of S. Schoenbaum*, edited by B. Parker and S.P. Zitner, 214–21. Newark: University of Delaware Press, 1996.

Barona, Josep Lluís. *Sobre medicina y filosofía natural en el Renacimiento*. Valencia: Universidad de Valencia, 1993.

Barreiro González, Germán, and Serafín de Abajo Olea. *Hipócrates en el Quijote*. León: Universidad de León, 2007.

Barros, Alonso de. *Filosofía cortesana moralizada* (1587). Edited by Enrique Suárez Figaredo. *Lemir* 23 (2019): 203–26.

Bartlett, Frederic Charles. *Remembering: A Study in Experimental and Social Psychology*. Cambridge: Cambridge University Press, 1955.

– "Some Experiments on the Reproduction of Folk-Stories." *Folklore* 31, no. 1 (1920): 30–47.

Bath, Michael. *Emblems in Scotland: Motifs and Meanings*. Leiden: Brill, 2018.

Battista, Eugenio, and Giuseppa Saccaro Battisti. *Le Machine Cifrate di Giovanni Fontana*. Milan: Arcadia, 1984.

Beecher, Donald. "Introduction." In *Ars Reminiscendi. Mind and Memory in Renaissance Culture*, edited by Donald Beecher and Grant Williams, 17–24. Toronto: Centre for Reformation and Renaissance Studies, 2009.

– "Recollection, Cognition, and Culture: An Overview of Renaissance Memory." In *Ars Reminiscendi. Mind and Memory in Renaissance Culture*, edited by Donald Beecher and Grant Williams, 367–426. Toronto: Centre for Reformation and Renaissance Studies, 2009.

Beecher, Donald, and Grant Williams, eds. *Ars Reminiscendi. Mind and Memory in Renaissance Culture*. Toronto: Centre for Reformation and Renaissance Studies, 2009.

Blair, Ann. "Reading Strategies for Coping with Information Overload, ca. 1550–1700. *Journal of History of Ideas* 64, no. 1 (2003): 11–28.

– *Too Much to Know. Managing Scholarly Information before the Modern Age*. New Haven, CT: Yale University Press, 2011.

Blasco, Javier. *Filosofía cortesana moralizada*. ePub, Agilice Digital, 2014.

Bolzoni, Lina. "The Art of Memory and the Erotic Image in 16th and 17th Century Europe: The Example of Giovan Battista Della Porta." In *Eros and Anteros: The Medical Traditions of Love in the Renaissance*, edited by Donald A. Beecher and Massimo Ciavolella, 103–22. Toronto: University of Toronto Press, 1992.

– "El espectáculo de la memoria." In *La idea del teatro. Giulio Camillo*, edited by Lina Bolzoni, 9–36. Madrid: Siruela, 2006.

– *The Gallery of Memory: Literary and Iconographic Models in the Age of Printing Press*. Toronto: University of Toronto Press, 2001.

– "The Play of Images. The Art of Memory from its Origins to the Seventeenth Century." In *The Enchanted Loom. Chapters in the History of Neuroscience*, edited by Pietro Corsi, 16–65. Oxford: Oxford University Press, 1991.

Borges, Jorge Luis. *Ficciones*. Madrid: Alianza, 1971.

Boscán, Juan. *Traducción de El cortesano de Baltasar de Castiglione*. Madrid: Cátedra, 1994.

Botello, Jesús. "Los descuidos cervantinos del *Quijote*: entre la ecdótica y la imitatio paródica de los clásicos." *Anales Cervantinos* 51 (2019): 33–49.

Bouza Álvarez, Fernando. *Communication, Knowledge, and Memory in Early Modern Spain*. Philadelphia: University of Pennsylvania Press, 2004.

– *Corre manuscrito. Una historia cultural del Siglo de Oro*. Madrid: Marcial Pons. Ediciones de Historia, 2002.

– *Del escribano a la biblioteca. La civilización escrita europea en la alta edad moderna*. Madrid: Síntesis, 1992.

Brito Díaz, Carlos. "Cervantes al pie de la letra: Don Quijote a lomos del 'Libro del Mundo.'" *Cervantes* 19, no. 2 (1999): 37–54.

Brunschwig, Hieronymus. *The Noble Experience of the Virtuous Handy Warke of Surgery*, 1525.

Bundy, Murray Wright. *The Theory of Imagination in Classical and Medieval Thought*. Champaign: University of Illinois Press, 1927.

Burke, Peter. *The Renaissance Sense of the Past*. London: Arnold, 1969.

– *Varieties of Cultural History*. Ithaca, NY: Cornell University Press, 1997.

Burton, Robert. *The Anatomy of Melancholy*. Vol. 1. New York: W. J. Widdleton Publisher, 1875.

Byrne, Susan. *Ficino in Spain*. Toronto: University of Toronto Press, 2015.

Carducho, Vicente. *Diálogos de la pintura*, 1633.

Caro Baroja, Julio. "Cervantes y los inventos." In *Los hombres y sus pensamientos*, 9–19. San Sebastián: Txertoa, 1989.

Carpintero, Helio. *La historia de la psicología en España*. Madrid: Eudema, 1994.

Carruthers, Mary. *The Book of Memory*. 2nd ed. Cambridge: Cambridge University Press, 2008.

– *The Craft of Thought: Meditation, Rhetoric. and the Making of Images. 400–1200*. Cambridge: Cambridge University Press, 1998.

Casalduero, Joaquín. "Explicando la primera frase del *Quijote*. (Tres notas sobre Cervantes)." *Bulletin Hispanique* 36, no. 2 (1934): 137–48.

Castiglione, Baldassare. *The Book of the Courtier*. New York: Charles Scribners, 1903.

Castillo Gómez, Antonio. "Hojas embetunadas y libros en papel: escritura y memoria personal en la España moderna." *Horizontes antropológicos* 10, no. 22 (2004): 37–65.

– "La escritura representada: Imágenes de lo escrito en la obra de Cervantes." In *Volver a Cervantes: Actas del IV Congreso Internacional de la Asociación de Cervantistas*, Vol. 1, edited by Antonio Pablo Bernat Vistarini, 311–26. Palma: Universitat de les Illes, 2001.

Castro, Américo. *La Celestina como contienda literaria*. Madrid: Revista de Occidente, 1965.

Cave, Terence. "The Mimesis of Reading in the Renaissance." In *Mimesis from Mirror to Method, Augustine to Descartes*, edited by John D. Lyons and Stephen G. Nichols, Jr., 143–58. Hanover, NH: University Press of New England, 1982.

Cervantes Saavedra, Miguel de. *Comedias y tragedias*. Madrid: Real Academia Española, 2015.

– *Don Quijote de la Mancha*. Barcelona: Crítica, 1998.

– *Entremeses*. Madrid: Cátedra, 1995.

– *La Galatea*. Madrid: Cátedra, 1995.

– *Los trabajos de Persiles y Sigismunda*. Madrid: Cátedra, 2004.

– *Novelas ejemplares*. Vols. 1 and 2. Madrid: Cátedra, 1990.
– *Poesías*. Madrid: Cátedra, 2016.
Cevolini, Alberto, ed, *Forgetting Machines: Knowledge Management Evolution in Early Modern Europe*. Leiden: Brill, 2016.
Chaparro Gómez, César ."La memoria en el Examen de ingenios para las ciencias de Juan Huarte de San Juan." Estudios de humanismo español. Baeza en los siglos XVI–XVII, edited by Águeda Moreno Moreno, 93–104. Baeza: Ayuntamiento de Baeza, 2007.
– "Per locos et imagines." Prologue to *Retórica y artes de memoria en el humanismo renacentista*, 9–11. Cáceres: Universidad de Extremadura, 2007.
– "Retórica y libros de caballerías. La presencia de *exempla* en la *Rhetorica christiana* de Diego Valadés." *Cuaderno de Filología Clásica* 24, no. 2 (2004): 257–92.
Chartier, Roger. *The Author's Hand and the Printer's Mind*. Cambridge: Polity, 2014.
– *Inscribir y borrar. Cultura escrita y literatura (siglos XI-XVIII)*. Buenos Aires: Katz, 2006.
Chartier, Roger, and Antonio Saborit. "Miguel de Cervantes y el librillo de memoria de Cardenio: Un intercambio." *Historias* 60 (2005): 3–10.
Chevalier, Maxime. "Huellas del cuento folklórico en el Quijote." In *Cervantes, su obra y su mundo. Actas del I Congreso Internacional sobre Cervantes*, edited by M. Criado de Val, 881–93. Madrid: EDI-6, 1981.
– *Lectura y lectores en la España del siglo XVI y XVII*. Madrid: Turner, 1976.
– "Un personaje folklórico de la literatura del Siglo de Oro: el estudiante." In *Seis lecciones sobre la España de los siglos de oro*, 39–58. Sevilla: Universidad de Sevilla, 1981.
Chiong Rivero, Horacio. "'A imitación del hilo del laberinto de Perseo': El nexo narrativo de las ficciones laberínticas en Sierra Morena." *Modern Language Notes* 121, no. 2 (2006): 278–98.
Ciavolella, Massimo. "Eros and the Phantasms of *Hereos*." In *Eros and Anteros: The Medical Traditions of Love in the Renaissance*, edited by Donald A. Beecher and Massimo Ciavolella, 75–85. Toronto: University of Toronto Press, 1992.
Ciruelo, Pedro. *De arte memorativa*. Alcalá, 1528.
Close, Anthony. "Sancho Panza: Wise Fool." *Modern Language Review* 68 (1973): 344–57.
Coleman, Janet. *Ancient and Medieval Memories: Studies in the Reconstruction of the Past*. Cambridge: Cambridge University Press, 1992.
CORDE. Corpus Diacrónico del Español. Real Academia Española. http://corpus.rae.es/cordenet.html.
Covarrubias, Sebastián de. *Emblemas morales*. Madrid, 1610.
Daly, Peter M. *The Emblem in Early Modern Europe*. Burlington, VT: Ashgate, 2014.
Danziger, Kurt. *Marking the Mind. A History of Memory*. Cambridge: Cambridge University Press, 2008.
Daza Chacón, Dionisio. *Práctica y teórica de la cirugía en romance y latín*. 1580.

De Armas, Frederick A. "Cervantes and Della Porta: The Art of Memory in *La Numancia, El retablo de las maravillas, El Licenciado Vidriera,* and *Don Quijote.*" *Bulletin of Hispanic Studies* 82, no. 5 (2005): 633–47.

– *Cervantes, Raphael and the Classics*. Cambridge: Cambridge University Press, 1998.

– "Painting Dulcinea: Italian Art and the Art of Memory in Cervantes' *Don Quijote.*" *Yearbook for Comparative and General Literature* 49: 4–19.

– *Quixotic Frescoes. Cervantes and Italian Renaissance Art*. Toronto: University of Toronto Press, 2006.

– "Simple Magic: Ekphrasis from Antiquity to the Age of Cervantes." In *Ekphrasis in the Age of Cervantes,* edited by Frederick de Armas, 13–31. Cranbury: Buknell, 2005.

– *Tesoro de la Lengua Castellana o Española*. Barcelona: Editorial Alta Fulla, 2003.

De la Cruz, San Juan. *Llama de amor viva*. Edited by Luce López-Baralt and Eulogio Pacho. Madrid: Alianza Editorial, 1991.

Deyermond, Alan. "La literatura oral en la transición de la Edad Media al Renacimiento." *Edad de Oro* 7 (1988): 21–32.

Díaz, Francisco. *Tratado de todas las enfermedades de los riñones, vexiga y carnosidades de la verga y orina,* 1588.

Dominguez, Julia. "A Window onto the Heart: Cervantes and the Cardiocentric Self." *Hispanic Review*. Forthcoming.

– "'Básteme tener el Christus en la memoria para ser buen gobernador:' Sancho y las cartillas de instrucción Áurea." *Yo no le trocaría con otro escudero:" Sancho Panza ante la crítica. eHumanista/Cervantes* 7 (2019): 97–114.

– "Cervantes and the Mother of the Muses: Views of Memory in Early Modern Spain." In *Cervantes and the Early Modern Mind,* edited by Julien Simon and Isabel Jaén, 118–37. New York: Routledge, 2021.

– "Imaginar mundos: memoria y ciencia ficción en la obra de Cervantes." *Cervantes: Special Issue: Cervantes and Science Fiction* 40, no. 2 (2020): 33–51.

– "The Internal Senses in *Don Quixote* and the Anatomy of Memory." In *Beyond Sight,* edited by Steven Wagschal and Ryan Giles, 47–65. Toronto: University of Toronto Press, 2018.

– "The 'Janus Hypothesis' in *Don Quixote*: Memory and Imagination in Cervantes." In *Cognitive Approaches to Early Modern Spanish Literature,* edited by Julien Simon and Isabel Jaén, 74–90. Oxford: Oxford University Publishing, 2016.

– "Writing to Rescue from Oblivion: The Phantasms of Captivity in Cervantes's Theater." In *Beyond the Playhouse: Cervantes's Theatrical Revelations,* edited by Adrienne Martin and Esther Fernández. Toronto: University of Toronto Press, 2022.

Dopico Black, Giorgina. "Canons Afire: Libraries, Books, and Bodies." In *Cervantes' Don Quixote: A Casebook,* 95–123. Oxford: Oxford University Press, 2005.

Douclos, Cory. "A Squire's Schooling: The Education of Sancho Panza." *Confluencia* 30, no. 3 (2015): 69–85.

Draaisma, Douwe. *Metaphors of Memory. A History of Ideas about the Mind.* Cambridge: Cambridge University Press, 2001.
Dudai, Yadin, and Mary Carruthers. "The Janus Face of Mnemosyne." *Nature* 434 (March 2005): 567.
Durán, Manuel. "Cervantes' Harassed and Vagabond Life." In *Cervantes' Don Quixote. A Casebook*, 23–34. Oxford: Oxford University Press, 2005.
Eco, Umberto. "An Ars Oblivionalis? Forget It!" *PMLA* 103, no. 3 (1988): 254–61.
Egido Martínez, Aurora. *Cervantes y las puertas del sueño.* Barcelona: PPU, 1994.
– *De la mano de Artemia: Literatura, emblemática, mnemotecnia y arte en el Siglo de Oro*. Barcelona: UIB, 2004.
– "El arte de la memoria y *El Criticón.*" In *Gracián y su Época: actas de la I Reunión de Filólogos Aragoneses*, 25–66. Zaragoza: Institución Fernando el Católico, 1986.
– "La memoria ejemplar y *El coloquio de los perros.*" *Cervantes: Estudios en la víspera de su centenario. Estudios de literatura* 24/25, Vol. 2 (1994): 465–82.
– "La memoria y el arte narrativo del *Persiles.*" *Nueva Revista de Filología Hispánica* 38, no. 2 (1990): 621–41.
– "La memoria y *El Quijote.*" *Cervantes* 11, no. 1 (1991): 3–44.
– "Literatura efímera: oralidad y escritura en los certámenes y academias de los siglos de oro." *Edad de Oro* 7 (1988): 69–88.
Eisenberg, Daniel. "El rucio de Sancho y la fecha de composición de la Segunda Parte del *Quijote.*" *Nueva Revista de Filología Hispánica* 25 (1976): 94–102.
– "La biblioteca de Cervantes. Una reconstrucción." In *Studia in Honorem Prof. Martín de Riquer*, II, 271–328. Barcelona: Quaderns Crema, 1987.
Engel, William. "The Decay of Memory." In *Forgetting in Early Modern English Literature and Culture: Lethe's Legacies*, edited by Christopher Ivic and Grant Williams, 21–40. New York: Routledge, 2004.
– *Mapping Mortality: The Persistence of Memory and Melancholy in Early Modern England*. Amherst: University of Massachusetts Press, 1995.
Engel, William E., Rory Loughnane, and Grant Williams, eds. *The Memory Arts in Renaissance England*. Cambridge: Cambridge University Press, 2016.
Erasmus, Desiderius. *The Aim and Method of Education*. Edited by William Harrison Woodward. Cambridge: Cambridge University Press, 1904.
– *Collected Works of Erasmus*. Edited by Craig R. Thompson. Toronto: University of Toronto Press, 1978.
– *The Praise of Folly*. London: Penguin Books, 1993.
Escribano, F.S. "De un tema ignaciano en el *Quijote* II, v." *Revista de literatura* 10 (1956): 147–8.
Espinel, Vicente. *Vida del escudero Marcos de Obregón*. Madrid: Castalia, 1972.
Estella, Fray Diego de. *Modo de predicar*. Madrid: Instituto Miguel de Cervantes, 1951.

Fentress, James, and Chris Wickham. *Social Memory: New Perspectives on the Past*. Oxford: Oxford University Press, 1992.

Fernández López, Jorge. "Retórica y enciclopedia en el Renacimiento: *Eloquentia* en la *Polyanthea* de Mirabelli-Lang." *Minerva* 22 (2009): 177–204.

Finello, Dominick L. "En la Sierra Morena: Quijote I, 23–26." In *Actas del Sexto Congreso Internacional de Hispanistas*, edited by Alan M. Gordon and Evelyn Rugg, 242–4. Toronto: University of Toronto Press, 1980.

Flórez Miguel, Cirilo. "Pedro Ciruelo y el arte renacentista de la memoria." In *Homenaje a Pedro Sáinz Rodríguez* Vol. 1, 283–94. Madrid: Fundación Universitaria Española, 1986.

Fludd, Robert. *Utriusque cosmi … historia*, 1617.

Foer, Joshua. *Moonwalking with Einstein: The Art and Science of Remembering Everything*. New York: Penguin Books, 2012.

Forster, E.S. *The Works of Aristotle*, vol. 7: *Problemata*. Oxford: Clarendon Press, 1927.

Freedberg, David. *The Power of Images*. Chicago: University of Chicago Press, 1991.

Freeman, Rosemary. *English Emblem Books*. New York: Octagon Books, 1966.

Frenk, Margit. *Entre la voz y el silencio*. Alcalá de Henares: Centro de Estudios Cervantinos, 1997.

Fuentes, Alonso de. *Filosofía Natural* (1547). Edited by Guillermo Herráez Cubino. Salamanca: CILUS, 2000.

Funes, Juan de. *Libro intitulado Arte militar* (1582). Edited by Cristina Blas. Salamanca: CILUS, 2000.

Furió Ceriol, Fadrique. *El concejo y consejero del príncipe*. Madrid: Tecnos, 1993.

Gállego, Julián. *Visión y símbolos en la pintura española del Siglo de Oro*. Madrid: Cátedra, 1996.

García Barreno, Pedro. "La medicina en El Quixote y su entorno." In *La ciencia y* El Quixote, edited by José Manuel Sánchez Ron, 155–80. Barcelona: Crítica, 2005.

García de la Concha, Víctor. "Un arte memorativa castellana." In *Serta Philologica Fernando Lázaro Carreter natalem diem sexagesimum celebranti dicata*, 187–97. Madrid: Castalia, 1983.

García, William. "La educación de Sancho." *Revista de Estudios Hispánicos* 3. no. 2 (1969): 257–63.

Gasta, Chad. "'Señora, donde hay música no puede haber cosa mala: Music, Poetry, and Orality in *Don Quijote*." *Hispania* 93. no. 3 (2010): 357–67.

– "Writing to Be Heard: Performing Music in *Don Quixote*." In *Cervantes in Perspective*, edited by Julia Domínguez, 85–108. Madrid: Iberoamericana Vervuert, 2013.

Geary, Patrick. *Phantoms of Remembrance: Memory and Oblivion at the End of the First Millenium*. Princeton, NJ: Princeton University Press, 1994.

Genovart, Gabriel. "La caballería como una pedagogía superior y Don Quijote de la Mancha." *Revista de Educación* (2004): 165–75.

Gerli, Michael. "El Castillo interior y el 'Arte de la memoria.'" *Bulletin Hispanique* 86, nos. 1–2 (1984): 154–63.

Gesualdo, Filippo. *Plutosofia. Nella quale si spiega l'Arte de la Memoria con altre cosa notabili*. Vicenza, 1600.

Gil Fernández, Luis. *Panorama social del humanismo español (1500–1800)*. Madrid: Alhambra, 1981.

Gilman, Stephen. *The Spain of Fernando de Rojas: The Intellectual and Social Landscape of La Celestina*. Princeton, NJ: Princeton University Press, 1972.

Gómez-Bravo, Ana. *Textual Agency: Writing Culture and Social Networks in Fifteenth-Century Spain*. Toronto: University of Toronto Press, 2013.

Gómez de Liaño, Ignacio. *Giordano Bruno: Mundo, magia, memoria*. Madrid: Taurus, 1973.

González, Aurelio. "¿Existen 'versiones' en el romancero nuevo?" In *Homenaje a Margit Frenk*, 111–20. México: UNAM, 1989.

González Echevarría, Roberto. "Introduction." In *Cervantes' Don Quixote: A Casebook*, 3–22. Oxford: Oxford University Press, 2005.

Gracián, Baltasar. *Agudeza y arte de ingenio*. Edited by E. Correa Calderón. Madrid: Castalia, 1987.

Gracián Dantisco, Lucas. *Galateo español*. 1593.

Granada, Fray Luis de. *Guía de pecadores*. Madrid: Espasa Calpe, 1953.

Granjel, Luis. *La medicina española del siglo XVII*. Salamanca: Universidad de Salamanca, 1978.

Grataroio, Guglielmo. *The Castle of Memory*. 1562.

Green, Otis. *España y tradición occidental*. Madrid: Gredos, 1969.

Greenblatt, Stephen. *Renaissance Self-Fashioning: From More to Shakespeare*. Chicago: University of Chicago Press, 1980.

Gutiérrez de Godoy, Juan. *Disputationes Philosophicae et Medicae super libros Aristotelis 'De memoria et reminiscentia' duobus libri*. Jaén, 1629.

Gutiérrez de los Ríos, Gaspar. *Noticia general para la estimación de las artes*. Edited by Alegría Alonso González. Salamanca: CILUS, 2000.

Halbwachs, Maurice. *On Collective Memory*. Chicago: University of Chicago Press, 1952.

Harvey, E. Ruth. *The Inward Wits: Psychological Theory in the Middle Ages and the Renaissance*. London: Warburg Institute, 1975.

Harvey, Leonard. "Oral Composition and the Performance of Novels of Chivalry in Spain." In *Oral Literature. Seven Essays*, edited by Joseph J. Duggan, 84–100. New York: Harper and Row, 1975.

Heiple, Damiel L. "Renaissance Medical Psychology in *Don Quijote*." *Ideologies and Literature* 2, no. 9 (1979): 65–72.

Helfer, Rebeca. "The State of the Art of Memory and Shakespeare Studies." In *The Routledge Handbook of Shakespeare and Memory*, edited by Andrew Hiscock and Lina Perkins Wilder, 315–28. New York: Routledge, 2018.

Heller-Roazen, Daniel. "Common Senses: Greek, Arabic, Latin." In *Rethinking the Medieval Senses*, edited by Stephen Nichols and Alison Calhoun, 30–50. Baltimore, MD: Johns Hopkins University Press, 2008.

Heninger, S.K. *Touches of Sweet Harmony: Pythagorean Cosmology and Renaissance Poetics.* San Marino, CA: The Hungtinton Library, 1974.

Herrero, Javier. "Sierra Morena as Labyrinth: From Wildness to Christian Knighthood." *Forum for Modern Languages Studies* 17, no. 1 (1981): 55–67.

Hiscock, Andrew. "Debating Early Modern and Modern Memory: Cultural Forms and Effects: A Critical Retrospective." *Memory Studies* 11, no. 1 (2018): 69–84.

– *Reading Memory in Early Modern Literature*. Cambridge: Cambridge University Press, 2011.

Hiscock, Andrew, and Lina Perkins Wilder, eds. *The Routledge Handbook of Shakespeare and Memory.* New York: Routledge, 2018.

Horozco y Covarrubias, Juan de. *Emblemas morales*. Segovia, 1591.

Huarte de San Juan, Juan. *Examen de ingenios para las ciencias*. Madrid: Cátedra, 1989.

Huerta, Jerónimo de. *Historia natural de los animales de Plinio*, 1599.

Huguet-Termes, Teresa, Jon Arrizabalaga, and Harold J. Cook. *Health and Medicine in Hapsburg Spain: Agents, Practices, Representations*. London: Wellcome Trust Centre for the History of Medicine at UCL, 2009.

Hunter, John. "The Well-Stocked Memory and the Well-Tended Self: Erasmus and the Limits of Humanist Education." In *Ars Reminiscendi. Mind and Memory in Renaissance Culture*, edited by Donald Beecher and Grant Williams, 171–86. Toronto: Centre for Reformation and Renaissance Studies, 2009.

Infantes, Víctor. "De Officinas y Polyantheas: los diccionarios secretos del Siglo de Oro." In *Homenaje a Eugenio Asensio*, 243–57. Madrid: Gredos, 1998.

– "Ludo ergo sum. La literatura gráfica del juego áureo." In *Pictavia Aurea. Actas del IX Congreso de la Asociación Internacional del Siglo de Oro*, edited by Alain Bègue and Emma Herrán Alonso, 35–55. Toulouse: Presses Universitaires du Midi, 2013.

Iriarte, Mauricio. *El doctor Huarte de San Juan y su* Examen de ingenios: *Contribución a la historia de la psicología diferencial*. Madrid: Consejo Superior de Investigaciones Científicas, 1948.

Ivic, Christopher, and Grant Williams. *Forgetting in Early Modern English Literature and Culture: Lethe's Legacies*. New York: Routledge, 2004.

Jaén, Isabel. "Cervantes and the Cognitive Ideas of His Time." *Cervantes* 32, no. 1 (2012): 71–98.

Jaén, Isabel, and Julien Simon. *Cognitive Approaches to Early Modern Spanish Literature.* Oxford: Oxford University Press, 2016.

– *Cervantes and the Early Modern Mind.* New York: Routledge, 2021.

Jesús, Santa Teresa. *Obras de Santa Teresa de Jesús*. Barcelona: Librería Religiosa, 1887.
Jiménez Fajardo, Salvador. "The Sierra Morena as Labyrinth in Don Quixote I." *Modern Language Notes* 99, no. 2 (1984): 214–34.
Jiménez Patón, Bartolomé. *Elocuencia española en arte*. Barcelona: Puvill, 1993.
– *Mercurius Trimegistus* ..., 1621.
Johnson, Carroll. *The Quest for Modern Fiction*. Long Grove, IL: Waveland Press, 1990.
Kemp, Simon, and Garth J.O. Fletcher. "The Medieval Theory of the Inner Senses." *The American Journal of Psychology* 106, no. 4 (1993): 559–76.
Klibanskly, R., E. Panofsky, and F. Saxl. *Saturn and Melancholy. Studies in the History of Natural Philosophy, Religion and Art*. London: Nelson, 1964.
Kraepelin, Emil. "Ueber erinnerungsfälschungen." *Archiv für Psychi Nervenkrankheiten* 17 (1886): 830–43.
Laguna, Ana. *Cervantes and the Pictorial Imagination: A Study on the Power of Images and Images of Power in Works by Cervantes*. Lewisburg, PA: Bucknell University Press, 2009.
Laguna, Andrés. *Annotationes in Dioscoridem Anazarbeum*. 1554.
Laín Entralgo, Pedro. *La medicina hipocrática*. Madrid: Alianza, 2007.
Lathrop, Thomas. "Introduction." In *Don Quijote*, edited by Thomas Lathrop. Newark, NJ: Cervantes and Co. European Masterpieces, 2005.
– "Por qué Cervantes no incluyó el robo del rucio" *Anales Cervantinos* 22 (1984): 207–12.
Lausberg, Heinrich. *Manual de retórica española*. Madrid: Gredos, 1968.
Lechuga, Cristóbal. *Discurso en que trata de la artillería con un tratado de fortificación*, 1611.
Ledda, Giuseppina. *Contributo allo studio della letteratura emblematica in Spagna (1549–1613)*. Pisa: Universita di Pisa, 1970.
– "Los jeroglíficos en los sermones barrocos. Desde la palabra a la imagen, desde la imagen a la palabra." In *Literatura emblemática hispánica: actas del I Simposio Internacional*, edited by Sagrario López Poza, 111–28. A Coruña: Universidade de Coruña, 1996.
Le Goff, Jacques. *History and Memory*. New York: Columbia University Press, 1992.
Leporeus, Gulielmus. *Ars Memorativa*. 1520.
Lerner, Isaías. "Misceláneas y polianteas del Siglo de Oro español." *Congreso Internacional sobre Humanismo y Renacimiento* II (1998): 71–82.
Lida de Malkiel, María Rosa. *El cuento popular y otros ensayos*. Buenos Aires: Losada, 1976.
Lobera de Ávila, Luis. *Libro de las cuatro enfermedades cortesanas*. 1544.
– *Libro del régimen de la salud*. 1551.
Loftus, Elizabeth, and Katherine Ketcham. *Witness for the Defense: The Accused, the Eyewitness, and the Expert Who Puts Memory on Trial*. New York: Martin Press, 1991.

Lope de Vega, Félix. *El cuerdo loco: Teatro antiguo español: Textos y estudios IV.* Madrid: Sucesores de Hernando Quintana, 1922.
– *La Arcadia: comedia famosa*. Madrid: Librerías del Castillo, 1804.
– *La prueba de los ingenios. Obras de Lope de Vega. Tomo XIV: Comedias novelescas.* Madrid: Real Academia, 1913.
– *Novelas a Marcia Leonarda*. Edited by Francisco Rico. Madrid: Alianza Editorial, 1968.
– *Trecena parte de las comedias de Lope de Vega Carpio*. Madrid: Viuda de Alonso Martín, 1620.
López, Diego. *Declaración magistral sobre las emblemas de Andrés Alciato*. 1615.
López de Montoya, Pedro. *Libro de la buena educación y enseñanza de los nobles* … Salamanca, 1595. Edited by E. Hernández Rodríguez. *Las Ideas pedagógicas del Doctor Pedro López de Montoya*. Madrid: CSIC, 1947.
López Díez, Patricia. *El Ars Memorativa de Juan de Aguilera*. Tesis Universidad de Extremadura, 2019.
López Martínez, Isabel. *La llave de escribir: Teoría y creación en los siglos de oro.* Sevilla: Renacimiento, 2014.
López Méndez, H. *La medicina en* El Quijote. Madrid: Quevedo, 1969.
López-Muñoz, F., C. Alamo, and P. García-García. "Locos y dementes en la literatura cervantina: a propósito de las fuentes médicas de Cervantes en materia neuropsiquiátrica." *Revista de neurología* 46, no. 8 (2008): 16–30.
López Pinciano, Alonso. *Filosofía antigua poética*. Valladolid: Libreros de la Universidad, 1894.
– *Hippocratis prognosticum* …, 1596.
López Piñero, José María. *Medicina e historia natural en la sociedad española de los siglos XVI y XVII*. Valencia: Publicacións de la Universitat de Valencia, 2007.
López Poza, Sagrario. "Florilogios, polyantheas, repertorios de sentencias y lugares comunes. Aproximación bibliográfica." *Criticón* 49 (1990): 61–76.
– "Los libros de emblemas como tesoros de erudición auxiliares de la inventio." In *Emblemata Aurea: La emblemática en el Arte y la Literatura del Siglo de Oro*, edited by Rafael Zafra and José Javier Azanza, 263–79. Madrid: Akal, 2000.
– "Polianteas y otros repertorios de utilidad para la edición de textos del Siglo de Oro." *La Perinola* 4 (2000): 191–214.
Luria, Alexander. *The Mind of a Mnemonist: A Little Book about a Vast Memory*. Cambridge, MA: Harvard University Press, 1968.
Lyne, Raphael. *Memory and Intertextuality in Renaissance Literature*. Cambridge: Cambridge University Press, 2016.
Madariaga, Salvador de. *Guía del lector del Quijote: ensayo psicológico sobre el Quijote*. Madrid: Espasa Calpe, 1926.
Magnus, Albertus. *De bono: Opera omnia*. Edited by H. Kühle, C. Feckes, B. Geyer, and W. Kübel. Monasterii Westfalorum in Aedibus Aschendorff, XXVIII (1951).

– *De memoria et reminiscentia, Opera omnia*. Edited by August Borgnet. Paris: Vivés, 1890.

Mancing, Howard. "Sancho Panza's Theory of Mind." In *Theory of Mind and Literature*, edited by Paula Leverage, Howard Mancing, Jennifer Marston William, and Richard Schweickert, 123–32. West Lafayette, LA: Purdue University Press, 2010.

Mandigorra Lavata, Maria Luz. "La configuración de la identidad privada: diarios y libros de memoria en la baja edad media." *Historia, instituciones y documentos* 29 (2002): 217–35.

Manning, John. *The Emblem*. London: Reaktion Books, 2002.

Maravall, José Antonio. *Antiguos y modernos*. Madrid: Sociedad de Publicaciones, 1966.

– *La cultura del Barroco*. Barcelona: Ariel, 1998.

Márquez, Antonio. *Los alumbrados: Orígenes y filosofía (1525–59)*. Madrid: Taurus, 1980.

McLuhan, Marshall. *The Gutenberg Galaxy*. Toronto: University of Toronto Press, 1962.

Mejía, Pedro. *Silva de varia lección*, vols. 1–2. Madrid: Cátedra, 1989.

Méndez, Cristóbal. *Libro del ejercicio corporal y de sus provechos …*, 1553.

Menéndez y Pelayo, Marcelino. *Estudios Cervantinos*. Buenos Aires: Editora y Distribuidora del Plata, 1947.

Menéndez Pidal, Ramón. "The Genesis of Don Quixote." In *Cervantes' Don Quixote. A Casebook*, 63–94. Oxford: Oxford University Press, 2005.

Merino Jerez, Luis. *Artificiosa Memoria*. http://www.artificiosamemoria.es/index.php.

– "La memoria en el *Mercurius Trimegistus* de Bartolomé Jiménez Patón." In *Estudios de humanismo español: Baeza en los siglos XVI-XVII*, edited by Águeda Moreno Moreno, 411–26. Baeza: Ayuntamiento de Baeza, 2007.

– "La memoria en la retórica de Arias Montano." In *Benito Arias Montano y los humanistas de su tiempo*, edited by José María Maestre Maestre, Eustaquio Sánchez Salor, Manuel Antonio Díaz Gito, Luis Charlo Brea, and Pedro Juan Galán Sánchez, 327–34. Mérida: Editorial Regional de Extremadura, 2006.

– "Memoria y Retórica en El Brocense." In *El Brocense y las humanidades en el siglo XVI*, edited by Carmen Codoñer Merino, Jesús Ureña Bracero, and Santiago López Moreda, 211–30. Salamanca: Universidad de Salamanca, 2003.

– "La retórica de la imagen en Arias Montano." In *Legado clássico no Renascimento e sua receção*, edited by Nair de Nazaré Castro Soares and Cláudia Teixeira, 213–24. Coimbra: Coimbra University Press, 2017.

– *Retórica y artes de memoria en el humanismo renacentista*. Cáceres: Universidad de Extremadura, 2007.

Minchin, Elizabeth. *Homer and the Resources of Memory*. Oxford: Oxford University Press, 2001.

Molho, Maurice. *Cervantes: Raíces folklóricas*. Madrid: Gredos, 1976.

Molina, Tirso de. *Comedias de Tirso de Molina*: Tomo 1. Edited by Emilio Cotarelo y Mori. Madrid: Bailly Bailliére e Hijos, 1906.

Moner, Michel. "Técnicas del arte verbal y oralidad residual en los textos cervantinos." *Edad de Oro* 7 (1988): 119–27.

Montaigne, Michel Eyquem de. *The Education of Children*. New York: Appleton and Co., 1899.

Montero Reguera, José. "Humanismo, erudición y parodia en Cervantes: del *Quijote* al *Persiles*." *Edad de Oro* XV (1996): 87–109.

Morcillo Romero, Juan José. *El ars memorativa de G. Leporeo*. Tesis doctoral. Departamento de Ciencias de la Antigüedad, 2015.

Morreale, Margherita. "Luciano y las invectivas 'antiescoláticas' en *El Scholástico* y en *El Crotalón*." *Bulletin Hispanique* 54, no. 34 (1952): 370–85.

Muñoz Delgado, Vicente. "Juan de Aguilera y su *Ars memorativa* (1536)." *Cuadernos de historia de la medicina española* 15 (1975): 175–89.

Nebrija, Elio Antonio de. *Retórica*. Edited by Juan Lorenzo. Salamanca: Ediciones Universidad de Salamanca, 2006.

Neisser, Ulrich. "Memory with a Grain of Salt." In *Memory. An Anthology*, edited by Harriet Harvey Wood and A.S. Byatt, 80–8. London: Chatto & Windus, 2008.

Nikulin, Dmitri. "Introduction: Memory in Recollection of Itself." In *Memory. A History*, edited by Dmitri Nikulin, 3–34. Oxford: Oxford University Press, 2015.

–, ed. *Memory. A History*. Oxford: Oxford University Press, 2015.

– "Memory in Ancient Philosophy." In *Memory. A History*, edited by Dmitri Nikulin, 35–84. Oxford: Oxford University Press, 2015.

Oelschläger, Víctor. "Quixotessence." *Quaderni Ibero-Americani* 4, no. 27 (1961): 143–57.

Olivares Zorrilla, Rocío. "Historia crítica sobre los emblemas en el Quijote." *Espéculo* 30 (2005). http://www.ucm.es/info/especulo/numero30/emblquij.html.

Ong, Walter. *Orality and Literacy: The Technologizing of the Word*. London: Rutledge, 1982.

Orozco, Emilio. *Mística, plástica y Barroco*. Madrid: Cupsa, 1977.

Ortiz, Lorenzo. *Memoria, entendimiento y voluntad*. Sevilla, 1677.

– *Ver, oir, oler, gustar, tocar* … Lyon, 1687.

Pacheco, Francisco. *Arte de la pintura*. Sevilla, 1649.

Pagán, Flor María. "Geografía, ansiedad e 'imitatio' en la penitencia de Sierra Morena." *Neophilologus* 81, no. 4 (1997): 551–62.

Palma, Jose-Alberto, and Fermín Palma. "Neurology and *Don Quixote*." *European Neurology* 68, no. 4 (2012): 247–57.

Percas de Ponseti, Helena. *Cervantes y su concepto del arte*. Vols. 1 and 2. Madrid: Gredos, 1975.

Peset, José Luis. "Melancólicos e inocentes: la enfermedad mental entre el Renacimiento y el Barroco." In *La ciencia y* El Quixote, edited by José Manuel Sánchez Ron, 181–8. Barcelona: Crítica, 2005.

Pfandl, Ludwig. *Cultura y costumbres del pueblo español en los siglos XVI y XVII.* Madrid: Araluce, 1942.

Pinillos, Carmen. "Emblemas en el *Quijote*: El episodio de las bodas de Camacho." *Criticón* 71 (1997): 93–104.

Plato. *Complete Works*. Edited by John Cooper and D.S. Hutchinson. Cambridge, MA: Hackett Publishing, 1997.

– *The Dialogues of Plato*, Vols. 1–4. Edited by B. Jowett. Oxford: Clarendon Press, 1871.

Pliny the Elder. *Historia natural de Cayo Plinio Segundo*. Translated by Geronimo de Huerta. Madrid, 1624.

Pollmann, Judith. *Early Modern Memory in Europe, 1500–1800*. Oxford: Oxford University Press, 2017.

Pollmann, Judith, and Erika Kuijpers. "Introduction: On the Early Modernity of Memory." In *Memory before Modernity*, 1–24. Leiden: Brill, 2013.

Praz, Mario. *Mnemosyne: El paralelismo entre las literatura y las artes visuales.* Madrid: Taurus, 1979.

Predmore, Richard. *Cervantes*. New York: Dodd, Mead, 1973.

Quevedo, Francisco de. *La cuna y la sepultura*. 1634.

Ramée, Pierre de la. *Dialecticae Partitiones*. 1543.

Redondo, Augustin. *Otra manera de leer el Quijote: Historia, tradiciones culturales y literatura*. Madrid: Editorial Castilla. 1997.

Reina, Francisco de. *Libro de albeitería*. 1564.

Reisch, Gregor. *Margarita Philosophica*. 1503.

Resina, Joan Ramón. "Medusa en el laberinto: locura y teatralidad en el *Quijote*." *Modern Language Notes* 104, no. 2 (1989): 286–303.

Ricard, Robert. "Los vestigios de la predicación contemporánea en *El Quijote*." In *Estudios de literatura religiosa española*, 254–78. Madrid: Grados, 1964.

Richardson, Alan. "Defaulting to Fiction: Neuroscience Rediscovers the Romantic Imagination." *Poetics Today* 32, no. 4 (2011): 663–92.

Rico, Francisco. *El pequeño mundo del hombre*. Madrid: Castalia, 1970.

Ricoeur, Paul. *Memory, History and Forgetting*. Chicago: University of Chicago Press, 2004.

Riley, Edward C. *Cervantes's Theory of the Novel.* Newark, NJ: Juan de la Cuesta, 1992.

– "Don Quixote from Text to Icon." *Cervantes*. Special Issue (1988): 103–15.

– *Introducción al Quijote*. Barcelona: Crítica, 1990.

Ripa, Cesare. *Iconologia del Cavaliere Cesare Ripa*. Perugia, 1764.

Riquer, Martín de. *Aproximación al Quijote*. Navarra: Teide, 1969.

– "El *Quijote* y los libros." *Papeles de Son Armadans* XIV (1969): 9–24.

Rodrigues Vianna Peres, Lygia. "*El Quijote* y el teatro de la memoria de Giulio Camilo." In *Cervantes y su mundo*, Vol. 3, edited by Kurt Reichenberger and Darío Fernández-Morera, 519–42. Kassel: Reichenberger, 2005.

Rodríguez de la Flor, Fernando. "*Ars oblivionis* (Arte del olvido)." *Cuadernos Hispanoamericanos* 527 (1994): 45–56.

– "El Palacio de la memoria: *las Confesiones* agustinianas y la tradición retórica española." *Cuadernos salmantinos de filosofía* 13 (1986): 113–22.

– *Emblemas: lecturas de la imagen simbólica*. Madrid: Alianza, 1995.

– "Estudio introductorio." In *Fénix de Minerva o Arte de memoria*, vii–lii. Valencia: Tératos, 2002.

– "La compañía de Jesús: imágenes y memoria." *Hiperión* 3 (1979): 62–72.

– "La imagen leída: retórica, Arte de la Memoria y sistema de representación." *Ephialte* II (1990): 102–15.

– "La literatura espiritual del Siglo de Oro y la organización retórica de la memoria." *Revista de Literatura* 45, no. 90 (1983): 39–86.

– *Teatro de la memoria. Siete ensayos sobre mnemotecnia española de los siglos XVI y XVII*. Junta de Castilla y León: Consejería de Educación y Cultura, 1996.

– "*Tecnologías de la imagen* en el Siglo de Oro: del arte de la memoria a la emblemática (pasando por la 'composición de lugar' ignaciana)." *Cuadernos de Arte e Iconografía* (1992): 180–6.

– "Un arte de memoria rimado en el *Epítome de la Elocuencia Española*, de Francisco Antonio de Artiga." *Anales de literatura española* 4 (1985): 115–29.

Rodríguez-Luis, Julio. "Lecturas complementarias. Capítulo X." In *Don Quijote de la Mancha*, Volumen complementario, 130–2. Barcelona: Crítica, 1998.

Rodríguez Marín, Francisco. "Función y pertinencia del folklore en el *Quijote*." *Anales Cervantinos* XVII (1978): 41–51.

Romberch, Johannes. *Congestorium artificiose memoriae*, 1520.

Rothstein, Marian. *Reading in the Renaissance: Amadis de Gaule and the Lessons of Memory*. Newark: University of Delaware Press, 1999.

Rosselli, Cosimo. *Thesaurus artificiosae memoriae* …, 1578. Hathitrust Digital Library.

Rossi, Paolo. *Logic and the Art of Memory*. London: Continuum, 2006.

Rubin, David C. *Memory in Oral Traditions: The Cognitive Psychology of Epic, Ballads, and Counting-out Rhymes*. Oxford: Oxford University Press, 1995.

Saavedra Fajardo, Diego de. *Idea de un príncipe político cristiano*. Milán, 1642.

– *República Literaria*. Edited by Francisco Javier Díez de Revenga. Murcia: Real Academia Alfonso X el Sabio, 2008.

Sabuco, Olivia. *Nueva filosofía de la naturaleza del hombre, no conocida ni alcanzada de los grandes filósofos antiguos, la qual mejora la vida, y la salud humana* (1587). Madrid, 1728.

Sacks, Oliver. *The Man Who Mistook His Wife for a Hat*. New York: Touchstone, 1998.

– *The River of Consciousness*. Toronto: Knopf, 2017.

Salillas y Panzano, Rafael. *Un gran inspirador de Cervantes: El doctor Juan Huarte de San Juan y su Examen de Ingenios*. Madrid: Eduardo Arias, 1905.

Salinas, Miguel de. *Rhetorica en lengua castellana*, Alcalá, 1541.

Sánchez, Alberto. "Dos notas para el *Quijote*." *Anales Cervantinos* 30 (1992): 177–82.

Sánchez de las Brozas, Francisco. *Artificiosa memoriae ars*. Amberes, 1582.

–, ed. *Emblemas de Alciato*. 1573.

Santa Cruz, Alonso de. *Sobre la melancolía: Diagnóstico y curación de los afectos melancólicos*. Pamplona: Universidad de Navarra, 2005.

Schacter, Daniel. *Searching for Memory*. New York: Basic Books, 1996.

Sebastián, Santiago. *Emblemática e historia del arte*. Madrid: Cátedra, 1995.

Selig, Karl Ludwig. "Cervantes and the Jesuits." *Modern Language Notes* 73. no. 7 (1958): 514–15.

Serés, Guillermo. "Introducción." In *Examen de ingenios*, 11–134. Madrid: Cátedra, 1989.

Shakespeare, William. *Hamlet*. Toronto: Dover, 1992.

Simon, Julien, Barbara Simerka, and Howard Mancing. *Cognitive Cervantes*. *Cervantes* 32, no. 1 (2012).

Slater, John, Maríaluz López-Terrada, and José Pardo-Tomás. *Medical Cultures of the Early Modern Spanish Empire*. New York: Routledge, 2014.

Solórzano Pereira, Juan. *Emblemata centum regio-politica*. 1653.

Sorabji, Richard. *Aristotle on Memory*, 2nd ed. Chicago: University of Chicago Press, 2004.

Soufas, Teresa S. *Melancholy and the Secular Mind in Spanish Golden Age Literature*. Columbia: University of Missouri Press, 1990.

Spitzer, Leo. *Estilo y estructura en la literatura española*. Madrid: Crítica, 1980.

Stallybrass, P., R. Chartier, J.F. Mowery, and H. Wolfe. "Hamlet's Tables and the Technologies of Writing in Renaissance England." *Shakespeare Quarterly* 55, no. 4 (2004): 379–419.

Stephanus, Carolus. *Dictionarium historicum, geographicum, poeticum*, 1603.

Suárez de Figueroa, Cristóbal. *Plaza universal de todas ciencias y artes*. Edited by Enrique Suárez Figaredo. Barcelona, 2004. https://users.pfw.edu/jehle/CERVANTE/othertxts/Suarez_Figaredo_PlazaUniversal.pdf.

Sullivan, Garrett. *Memory and Forgetting in English Renaissance Drama*. Cambridge: Cambridge University Press, 2005.

Sutton, John. "Spongy Brains and Material Memories." In *Embodiment and Environment*, edited by Mary Floyd-Wilson and Garrett Sullivan, 14–34. New York: Palgrave, 2007.

Sutton, John, Celia Harris, Paul G. Kiel, and Amanda J. Barnier. "The Psychology of Memory, Extended Cognition, and Socially Distributed Remembering." *Phenomenology and the Cognitive Sciences* 9, no. 4 (2010): 521–60.

Taylor, René. *Arquitectura y magia*. Madrid: Siruela, 1992.
– *El arte de la memoria en el Nuevo Mundo*. Madrid: Swan, 1987.
Torquemada, Antonio de. *Jardín de flores curiosas*. Madrid: Castalia, 1983.
Tribble, Evelyn. *Cognition in the Globe: Attention and Memory in Shakespeare's Theatre*. New York: Palgrave, 2011.
– "'The Raven o'er the Infectious House.' Contagious Memory in *Romeo and Juliet* and *Othello*." In *The Routledge Handbook of Shakespeare and Memory*, edited by Andrew Hiscock and Lina Perkins, 105–15. New York: Routledge, 2018.
Tribble, Evelyn, and Nicholas Keene. *Cognitive Ecologies and the History of Remembering: Religion, Education, and Memory in Early Modern England*. New York: Palgrave, 2011.
Tribble, Evelyn, and John Sutton. "Cognitive Ecology as a Framework for Shakespearean Studies." *Shakespeare Studies* 39 (2011): 94–103.
Urbina, Eduardo. *El sin par Sancho Panza: parodia y creación*. Barcelona: Anthropos, 1991.
Vargas, Miguel de. *Tesoro de la memoria y del entendimiento y arte fácil y breve para toda sabiduría*. Madrid, 1658.
Vegas, Damián de. *Coloquio entre un alma y sus tres potencias, donde se introduce irse dellas, amotinada por el mal servicio que le hacen*. In *Romancero y cancionero sagrados*, edited by J. De Sancha. Biblioteca de Autores Españoles, vol. 35. Madrid: Atlas, 1950.
Velázquez de Azevedo, Juan. *El Fénix de Minerva y arte de memoria*. Madrid: Gonçalez, 1626.
Viardot, Louis. *L´ingénieux hidalgo Don Quichotte de la Manche*. Paris: Hachette and Co., 1863.
Vigo, Giovanni de. *Practica in Arte Chirurgica Copiosa*. 1514.
Vilanova, Antonio. *Erasmo y Cervantes*. Barcelona: Lumen, 1989.
Virgil. *Aeneid*. Translated by John Dryden. New York: P.F. Collier and Son Corporation, 1960.
Vistarini, Bernat. "Algunos motivos emblemáticos en la poesía de Cervantes." In *Actas del II Congreso de la Asociación Internacional de Cervantistas*, edited by Giuseppe Grilli, 83–95. Napoli, 1995.
Vives, Juan Luis. *Obras completas*, 2 vols. Edited by Loorenç Riber. Madrid: Aguilar, 1947.
Wardropper, Bruce W. "Cervantes and Education." In *Cervantes and the Renaissance*, edited by M.D. McGaha, 178–93. Newark, DE: Juan de la Cuesta, 1980.
Wegner, Daniel M., Ralph Erber, and Paula Raymond. "Transactive Memory in Close Relationships." *Journal of Personality and Social Psychology* 61, no. 6 (1991): 923–9.
Weiger, John. *The Substance of Cervantes*. Cambridge: Cambridge University Press, 2010.

Weinrich, Harald. *Lethe: The Art and Critique of Forgetting*. Ithaca, NY: Cornell University Press, 2004.

Williamson, Edwin. "Lecturas complementaria:. Capítulo XX." In *Don Quijote de la Mancha*, 58–60. Volumen complementario. Barcelona: Crítica, 1998.

Wolfson, Harry Austryn. "The Internal Senses in Latin, Arabic, and Hebrew Philosophic Texts." *Harvard Theological Review* 28, no. 2 (1935): 69–133.

Yates, Frances A. *The Art of Memory*. Chicago: University of Chicago Press, 1966.

Yciar, Juan de. *Arte breve y provechoso de cuenta castellana y arithmetica donde se muestran las cinco reglas de guarismo por la cuenta castellana y reglas de memoria* (1559).

Index

TORONTO IBERIC

1 Anthony J. Cascardi, *Cervantes, Literature, and the Discourse of Politics*
2 Jessica A. Boon, *The Mystical Science of the Soul: Medieval Cognition in Bernardino de Laredo's Recollection Method*
3 Susan Byrne, *Law and History in Cervantes'* Don Quixote
4 Mary E. Barnard and Frederick A. de Armas (eds), *Objects of Culture in the Literature of Imperial Spain*
5 Nil Santiáñez, *Topographies of Fascism: Habitus, Space, and Writing in Twentieth-Century Spain*
6 Nelson Orringer, *Lorca in Tune with Falla: Literary and Musical Interludes*
7 Ana M. Gómez-Bravo, *Textual Agency: Writing Culture and Social Networks in Fifteenth-Century Spain*
8 Javier Irigoyen-García, *The Spanish Arcadia: Sheep Herding, Pastoral Discourse, and Ethnicity in Early Modern Spain*
9 Stephanie Sieburth, *Survival Songs: Conchita Piquer's* Coplas *and Franco's Regime of Terror*
10 Christine Arkinstall, *Spanish Female Writers and the Freethinking Press, 1879–1926*
11 Margaret Boyle, *Unruly Women: Performance, Penitence, and Punishment in Early Modern Spain*

12 Evelina Gužauskytė, *Christopher Columbus's Naming in the* diarios *of the Four Voyages (1492–1504): A Discourse of Negotiation*
13 Mary E. Barnard, *Garcilaso de la Vega and the Material Culture of Renaissance Europe*
14 William Viestenz, *By the Grace of God: Francoist Spain and the Sacred Roots of Political Imagination*
15 Michael Scham, Lector Ludens*: The Representation of Games and Play in Cervantes*
16 Stephen Rupp, *Heroic Forms: Cervantes and the Literature of War*
17 Enrique Fernandez, *Anxieties of Interiority and Dissection in Early Modern Spain*
18 Susan Byrne, *Ficino in Spain*
19 Patricia M. Keller, *Ghostly Landscapes: Film, Photography, and the Aesthetics of Haunting in Contemporary Spanish Culture*
20 Carolyn A. Nadeau, *Food Matters: Alonso Quijano's Diet and the Discourse of Food in Early Modern Spain*
21 Cristian Berco, *From Body to Community: Venereal Disease and Society in Baroque Spain*
22 Elizabeth R. Wright, *The Epic of Juan Latino: Dilemmas of Race and Religion in Renaissance Spain*
23 Ryan D. Giles, *Inscribed Power: Amulets and Magic in Early Spanish Literature*
24 Jorge Pérez, *Confessional Cinema: Religion, Film, and Modernity in Spain's Development Years, 1960–1975*
25 Joan Ramon Resina, *Josep Pla: Seeing the World in the Form of Articles*
26 Javier Irigoyen-García, *"Moors Dressed as Moors": Clothing, Social Distinction, and Ethnicity in Early Modern Iberia*
27 Jean Dangler, *Edging toward Iberia*
28 Ryan D. Giles and Steven Wagschal (eds), *Beyond Sight: Engaging the Senses in Iberian Literatures and Cultures, 1200–1750*
29 Silvia Bermúdez, *Rocking the Boat: Migration and Race in Contemporary Spanish Music*
30 Hilaire Kallendorf, *Ambiguous Antidotes: Virtue as Vaccine for Vice in Early Modern Spain*
31 Leslie Harkema, *Spanish Modernism and the Poetics of Youth: From Miguel de Unamuno to* La Joven Literatura
32 Benjamin Fraser, *Cognitive Disability Aesthetics: Visual Culture, Disability Representations, and the (In)Visibility of Cognitive Difference*
33 Robert Patrick Newcomb, *Iberianism and Crisis: Spain and Portugal at the Turn of the Twentieth Century*
34 Sara J. Brenneis, *Spaniards in Mauthausen: Representations of a Nazi Concentration Camp, 1940–2015*

35 Silvia Bermúdez and Roberta Johnson (eds), *A New History of Iberian Feminisms*
36 Steven Wagschal, *Minding Animals In the Old and New Worlds: A Cognitive Historical Analysis*
37 Heather Bamford, *Cultures of the Fragment: Uses of the Iberian Manuscript, 1100–1600*
38 Enrique García Santo-Tomás (ed), *Science on Stage in Early Modern Spain*
39 Marina Brownlee (ed), *Cervantes'* Persiles *and the Travails of Romance*
40 Sarah Thomas, *Inhabiting the In-Between: Childhood and Cinema in Spain's Long Transition*
41 David A. Wacks, *Medieval Iberian Crusade Fiction and the Mediterranean World*
42 Rosilie Hernández, *Immaculate Conceptions: The Power of the Religious Imagination in Early Modern Spain*
43 Mary Coffey and Margot Versteeg (eds), *Imagined Truths: Realism in Modern Spanish Literature and Culture*
44 Diana Aramburu, *Resisting Invisibility: Detecting the Female Body in Spanish Crime Fiction*
45 Samuel Amago and Matthew J. Marr (eds), *Consequential Art: Comics Culture in Contemporary Spain*
46 Richard P. Kinkade, *Dawn of a Dynasty: The Life and Times of Infante Manuel of Castile*
47 Jill Robbins, *Poetry and Crisis: Cultural Politics and Citizenship in the Wake of the Madrid Bombings*
48 Ana María Laguna and John Beusterien (eds), *Goodbye Eros: Recasting Forms and Norms of Love in the Age of Cervantes*
49 Sara J. Brenneis and Gina Herrmann (eds), *Spain, World War II, and the Holocaust: History and Representation*
50 Francisco Fernández de Alba, *Sex, Drugs, and Fashion in 1970s Madrid*
51 Daniel Aguirre-Oteiza, *This Ghostly Poetry: Reading Spanish Republican Exiles between Literary History and Poetic Memory*
52 Lara Anderson, *Control and Resistance: Food Discourse in Franco Spain*
53 Faith Harden, *Arms and Letters: Military Life Writing in Early Modern Spain*
54 Erin Alice Cowling, Tania de Miguel Magro, Mina García Jordán, and Glenda Y. Nieto-Cuebas (eds), *Social Justice in Spanish Golden Age Theatre*
55 Paul Michael Johnson, *Affective Geographies: Cervantes, Emotion, and the Literary Mediterranean*
56 Justin Crumbaugh and Nil Santiáñez (eds), *Spanish Fascist Writing: An Anthology*

57 Margaret E. Boyle and Sarah E. Owens (eds), *Health and Healing in the Early Modern Iberian World: A Gendered Perspective*
58 Leticia Álvarez-Recio (ed), *Iberian Chivalric Romance: Translations and Cultural Transmission in Early Modern England*
59 Henry Berlin, *Alone Together: Poetics of the Passions in Late Medieval Iberia*
60 Adrian Shubert, *The Sword of Luchana: Baldomero Espartero and the Making of Modern Spain, 1793–1879*
61 Jorge Pérez, *Fashioning Spanish Cinema: Costume, Identity, and Stardom*
62 Enriqueta Zafra, *Lazarillo de Tormes: A Graphic Novel*
63 Erin Alice Cowling, *Chocolate: How a New World Commodity Conquered Spanish Literature*
64 Mary E. Barnard, *A Poetry of Things: The Material Lyric in Habsburg Spain*
65 Frederick A. de Armas and James Mandrell (eds), *The Gastronomical Arts in Spain: Food and Etiquette*
66 Catherine Infante, *The Arts of Encounter: Christians, Muslims, and the Power of Images in Early Modern Spain*
67 Robert Richmond Ellis, *Bibliophiles, Murderous Bookmen, and Mad Librarians: The Story of Books in Modern Spain*
68 Beatriz de Alba-Koch (ed), *The Ibero-American Baroque*
69 Deborah R. Forteza, *The English Reformation in the Spanish Imagination: Rewriting Nero, Jezebel, and the Dragon*
70 Olga Sendra Ferrer, *Barcelona, City of Margins*
71 Dale Shuger, *God Made Word: An Archaeology of Mystic Discourse in Early Modern Spain*
72 Xosé M. Núñez Seixas, *The Spanish Blue Division on the Eastern Front, 1941–45: War Experience, Occupation, Memory*
73 Julia Domínguez, *Quixotic Memories: Cervantes and Memory in Early Modern Spain*